Texture

Texture

A Cognitive Aesthetics of Reading

PETER STOCKWELL

EDINBURGH UNIVERSITY PRESS

Edinburgh University Press Ltd
22 George Square, Edinburgh

www.euppublishing.com

Typeset in 10/12 Times New Roman
by Servis Filmsetting Ltd, Stockport, Cheshire, and
printed and bound in Great Britain by
CPI Antony Rowe, Chippenham and Eastbourne

A CIP record for this book is available from the British Library

ISBN 978 0 7486 2581 9 (hardback)

Contents

Acknowledgements

This book has been a long time coming, and so I have accumulated even more debts than usual. I would firstly like to thank all those people who took an interest in my work beyond the limits of mere politeness. Several people suggested things for me to read: thanks to Guy Cook for lament texts back to ancient Rome, John McRae for 'his' Daffodils, Sarah Grandage for pointing me to Shakespeare's *King John*, Jane Hodson for that other *Bleak House* passage, and Lykara Ryder for giving me the Rumer Godden. My friends and colleagues have read drafts and made kindly observations, allowing me to remove some of the worst excesses and generally improving the texture: many thanks to the incomparable Ron Carter, and to Joanna Gavins, Alison Gibbons, Dan McIntyre, Andi Macrae, David Peplow, Chantelle Warner and Sara Whiteley. These and other members of the cognitive poetics research group between Sheffield and Nottingham have been a constant source of energy and ideas: thanks and acknowledgement to Alice Bell, Joe Bray, Julie Millward, Mel Evans, Katie Wales and honorary guest the late Mary Ellen Ryder. I am grateful to Richard Gerrig and Kathy Conklin for sound advice from a psycholinguistic perspective, and Mark Robson, Julie Sanders, Dominic Head and Philip Essler for sensible literary criticism. Marcelo Dascal, Michael Toolan and Vyv Evans have commented wisely and separately on work that has found its way into this book.

It will be evident from my discussions that I have been fortunate in being able to present some of this work at various invited events around the world, too numerous to mention all of them here. However, I would particularly like to thank Nick Davis and Michaela Mahlberg and the audience at the University of Liverpool; Monika Fludernik and Greta Olson at the University of Freiburg; Joan Swann and Rob Pope for the Open University creativity seminars; Astrid Hjorth Balle, Torben Jelsbak, Frederik Stjernfelt and Nikolaj Zeuthen for the Carlsberg Academy symposium in Copenhagen; Harri Veivo, Bo Pettersson and Merja Polvinen at Helsinki University; Miquel Berga at the University Pompeu Fabra in Barcelona; Masanori Toyota of the University of Kansai Gaidai and the audience at his former University of Kyoto; and the students at the University of Nottingham, Ningbo campus in China. My own cognitive poetics and literary linguistics students over the years at the University of Nottingham have shaped my thinking and been the first audience and critics of many of the ideas contained here.

I have had many conversations that have influenced this book with Peer Bundgaard, Michael Burke, Wallace Chafe, Peter Crisp, Cathy Emmott, Ray Gibbs, Frans Gregersen, Craig Hamilton, David Herman, Laura Hidalgo-Downing, Lesley Jeffries, Henrik Jørgensen, Frank Kyørup, Ernestine Lahey, Marina Lambrou, Carmen Llamas, John McKenny, Dominique Maingueneau, Uri Margolin, David Miall, Chris Montgomery, Roshni Mooneeram, Emma Moore, Eva Müller-Zettelmann, Ansgar Nünning, Kieran O'Halloran, Alan Palmer, Brian Richardson, Elena Semino, Mick Short, Paul Simpson, Gerard Steen, Reuven Tsur, Willie van Peer, Peter Verdonk, Jean Jacques Weber and Werner Wolf. This stellar cast should have ensured a better book than I could have hoped for. My colleagues at Nottingham in Modern English Language continue to provide a supportive and energetic atmosphere, one of the best places to study and research in the world: aside from those mentioned above, thanks to Svenja Adolphs, Zoltán Dörnyei, Val Durow, Kevin Harvey, Louise Mullany, Norbert Schmitt and Violeta Sotirova. I have been fortunate in my current and recent research students, who have often guided my ideas as much as the other way round: thanks to Dany Badran, Emma Dawson, Christiana Gregoriou, Mimi Huang, Eirini Panagiotidou, Nicola Snarey, Odette Vassallo, Sunanta Wannasin and Maha Zaghloul. I outlasted two editors at EUP, and thanks must go to Sarah Edwards and her successor Esmé Watson for persistence, good humour and vision throughout.

In spite of this supporting cast of thousands and their best efforts to improve this book, any faults are my responsibility for disregarding or misunderstanding their good advice.

Finally, every page owes as much to Joanna Gavins as to my own thinking. This book is for her, and Ada and Edith, my three girls who have given me its texture.

PJS
Nottingham

The author and publishers extend their grateful thanks to the following for permission to reprint copyright material:

Tony Harrison and his literary agent Gordon Dickerson for the extract 'Long Distance II', originally in *From 'The School of Eloquence' and Other Poems*, published by Rex Collings (London, 1978), reprinted in *Selected Poems* and *Collected Poems* (Penguin, 1987, 2007).

The executors of the literary estate of Jon Silkin for 'Death of a Son' from *The Peaceable Kingdom*, originally published by Chatto and Windus (London, 1954). Please subscribe to *Stand* magazine <www.standmagazine.org>

1 Text, Textuality and Texture

This is a work of literary criticism, and literature is defined by its texture.

The proper business of literary criticism is the description of readings. Readings consist of the interaction of texts and humans. Humans are comprised of minds, bodies and shared experiences. Texts are the objects produced by people drawing on these resources. Textuality is the outcome of the workings of shared cognitive mechanics, evident in texts and readings. Texture is the experienced quality of textuality.

Literary criticism has settled recently into a paradigm which is improper and marginalising. Across most of the higher education institutions of the world, and in the pages of the scholarly and quality press, literary scholarship has become an arid landscape of cultural history. Contexts and biographies, influences and allusions, multiple edited textual variants of literary works and their place in social history have become the focus of concern. Interpretation is offered to illuminate critical theory, or to validate a historiography. Aside from a few oases of enlightenment, engagement with text, textuality and texture has largely disappeared from the profession. There are those who call themselves literary scholars who have lost the skills of textual analysis, and who know little or nothing of their basic crafts: linguistics, psychology, sociology, and their inter-disciplines. While cultural and social and political history has its place in literary criticism, the mass migration of thinkers away from the heart of their discipline has rendered the field vacuous. Rational thought, discipline, systematicity, clarity of expression, transparency of argument, evidentiality and analytical knowledge have become the preserve of the few. Meanwhile, discussions of literature become ever more abstruse, further distant from the works themselves, divorced from the concerns of natural readers outside the academy, self-aggrandising, pretentious, ill-disciplined and, in the precise sense, illiterate.

There is of course another way, with origins in the practices of ancient rhetoric – a tradition that has never abandoned the core concern with texts and textuality. Under evolving names and projects, there has always been a thread of literary scholarship which has tried to understand systematically and in principle how language – the essence of literary art – works. Over time, insights and innovations in philosophy and science have fed into this tradition, allowing thinkers to adjust and improve their ideas about literature in general and literary works in particular. The revolution of linguistics in the last century offered a series of insights into literary texts and literary readings. The most recent advances in human knowledge about ourselves are currently in the process of revivifying the discipline once again. The application of progress in cognitive science to questions in literary reading has produced a cognitive poetics that stands intellectually at the heart of literary scholarship. This book is a modest contribution to that enterprise.

Principles of cognitive poetics

Cognitive poetics takes many of its models, methods, assumptions and validity from the various branches of cognitive science, but it is important to realise that the application to literary reading changes the status of several aspects of the source disciplines in the transplanted context. Certain assumptions need to be recast, and certain conclusions need to be hedged and complicated under literary analysis. This makes cognitive poetics a discipline in its own right, as well as an applied form of cognitive science. Furthermore, cognitive science – and cognitivism – are not single projects but encompass a range of activities and approaches that share some general principles and interests. Cognitive science is usually taken to comprise cognitive linguistics, cognitive psychology, the philosophy of mind, and some aspects of neurology. Other disciplines with a current or historical attachment to the field include artificial intelligence research, computer modelling, evolutionary biology, and medical research on the brain-body relationship.

Experientialism

Though there are significant theoretical variations in the assumptions on which all these disciplines are based, to qualify as cognitivist approaches they all fundamentally share a commitment to *experiential realism*. This is the view that there is a world outside the body that exists objectively (realism), but our only access to it is through our perceptual and cognitive experience of it. Cognitivists thus do not deny that there are objects and relationships in the world that are available to be discovered and understood, but those phenomena can only be accessed, conceptualised and discussed within the constraints that our human condition has bequeathed to us.

Generalisation

This leads to perhaps the most important principle in cognitive science which is that there are common aspects of humanity so that claims made about one group of people and their cognitive capacities must also be true of all people. Of course, this is not to deny cultural, ethnic, racial, gendered, geographical, historical, ideological or other myriad differences across humanity, but the broad window of human possibilities is constrained by the common way in which our minds work and our bodies interact with reality. This generalisation arguing for a single view of human capability (though not a monolithic view of human performance) corresponds with a view of language that is also holistic and unified. Cognitivists regard language as a key manifestation of the mechanics of the mind, with the same principles operating throughout the system. There are continuities, for example, between how you understand phonemes and how you understand syntax, between the way you learn to manipulate physical objects in spaces and the way you learn to use language to have effects on other people, between finding your way around a room and finding your way round a text, between how you imagine a friend of a friend and how you imagine a character, and so on. In other words, language is not modular, language and cognition are not separate, literature and natural conversation are on a continuum with each other.

Stylistics

This generalisation commitment (Lakoff 1990) in cognitive science sometimes looks like a search for idealised universals – and it is true that some work in cognition is primarily concerned with mind rather than with the singularities of the example in hand. This idealisation is a particular problem in literary applications, since the danger in some unthinking deployment of cognitive science to reading is that all literary texts are reduced to a processing mechanism, and the singularities (Attridge 2004) that make literature literary are downgraded. It seems to me that this particular risk is greatest in those studies that make the most direct link between brain activity and literary effect. Though there are doubtless valuable insights for neurology and psychology in mapping MRI scans and literary forms, it seems to me that the value for literary criticism is relatively small. The necessary antidote to this reductionism, in my view, is to insist on the detailed attention to textuality and its textural effects in the reader. Cognitive poetics, for me, is best when it is in the stylistic tradition, rather than being treated as another critical theory (see Stockwell 2008b).

Continuity

Another principle of cognitive poetics, mentioned above, is the continuity between the language of literature and natural language. There is no special literariness module in the brain or as a phenomenon of mind that is activated when we 'do' literature. Instead, our natural language capacities are exploited by writers and activated in literary reading. Certainly there are peculiar and amazing things that literature can do, but none of it is transcendent of our human capacity – it is just that our human potential is extraordinarily adaptable. The strong sense, however, that literature is special (Miall 2005) does not contradict this principle. The feeling that literature is the highest form of language art to the extent that it appears disjunctive with everyday talk is a matter of the value with which it is framed, the intensity with which it is read, and the disposition to find and accept aspects in a literary work that would not even be sought out in ordinary language. This framing renders literariness as a powerful felt effect, but the framing capacity itself is an aspect easily accountable within cognitive poetics.

Miall (2005) also points out that most early work in cognitive poetics has concerned itself with meaningfulness and informativity. This is a proper criticism, and Miall's work over recent years serves as the best example that aims to remedy it. My *Cognitive Poetics* introduction (Stockwell 2002a) is almost entirely concerned with meaning and significance, and the same is generally true of the two key collections of work that appeared around that time (Semino and Culpeper 2002; Gavins and Steen 2003). The importance and excitement of being able to discuss interpretation systematically was a large part of the attraction of the cognitive turn in literary studies, but with hindsight it is surprising that emotion, feeling and aesthetics were not so prominent despite the discipline drawing on detailed stylistic analysis and cognitive psychology. This book is my attempt to contribute some redress.

However, it is important not to fall victim to the sort of extremist swings of mood that characterise the faddism of literary theory. A cognitive poetic concern for aesthetics does not entail an abandonment of informativity; feeling does not appear at the expense of interpretation. This is not simply a progressive desire to escape a pendulum effect in the evolution of the discipline, but is a core principled consequence of accepting the cognitive basis of both feeling and meaning, and the continuities between them.

Embodiment

The mind, in cognitive science, is an embodied mind (Johnson 1987, 2007; Turner 1991, 1996). We are products of our evolution, and our human size, shape and configuration, in relation to the world, provides the framework within which our brains understand the world, and ourselves. The mind is not limited to the brain, in this conceptualisation, but is a combined notion made up of what brains and bodies together do in the world (see Lakoff and Johnson 1999). There are two important consequences of this principle. Firstly, the physical material and sensible world and the abstract idealised and conceptual world are intimately bound together: mind/body dualism is rejected, and along with it, other false discontinuities such as rationalism and emotion, form and function, literal and metaphorical, real and fictional, and so on. Where these divisions seem to have any everyday value, the motivation

to make the distinctions must be accountable according to cognitive principles. Secondly, the distinction between nature and artifice is not tenable.
Humans are natural beings, and the things we do, even in the name of high
art, are natural things that all cultures do. Creating literature is natural;
reading is a natural process – both draw on our natural cognitive capacities
even as they create a sense of transcendence. This is a holistic and ecological
view of human activity that does not place humans in opposition to other
species or even other parts of our environment. In a world that has recently
come to realise how closely human activity is bound up with the nature of the
planet, an ecology of language is a necessary principle and one which cognitive poetics shares.

Ecology

Again, the connection between the physical and the conceptual does not
reduce intellect to a simply material correlate. As thinking beings we are not
bound by our immediate environment or the physical objects we can move in
it. Fundamental to our extraordinary adaptability as a species and feats of
soaring creativity, imagination and invention is the capacity for metaphorical
projection that allows immediate objects to become transformed into ideas,
speculations, rationalisations, hypotheses, and rich imaginary worlds. The
business of cognitive poetics is not to reduce any of this to structural types or
labels, but to understand its intricate workings and marvel at the new adaptations that our capacities continue to allow. This leads me to a consequence of
cognitive poetics in the stylistic tradition that sounds very old-fashioned for
literary criticism: it is *appreciation*. One of the beauties of detailed and principled cognitive poetic exploration is the extent to which it enables you to
appreciate the writerly skill or the readerly sensitivity, or simply the brilliance
of the literary work itself as an object of art in the world.

All of these principles of connection and continuity, a holistic and ecological sense of our place in the world and our literary articulations, entail a key
new form of analysis. It is not possible to talk about a literary text as if it were
a thing, other than in very elementary and uninteresting terms as paper or
screen and print. It is equally not possible to talk about a reader in isolation,
without a sense of the whole person and viewpoint of which that reader is a
partial avatar. Crucially, we must get used to talking about literary works
that are the combined products of texts and readers in particular configurations (texts are autonomous objects, but literature is a heteronomous object,
in Ingarden's 1973a, 1973b terms). It is not a question of focusing on either
texts or readers, but recognising that the object of analysis is *texture* – the
sense of textuality. This requires a new form of calibration and explanation,
which draws on both traditional linguistic description and cognitive scientific
accounts, and tries to combine them. In this book, it may look from time to
time as if I am switching eclectically between textual description and readerly

sense, but the aim, if you step back from this close grain and view the book as a whole, is to offer an integration of what literary reading is.

Models and methods

In the course of this book, I draw on a large body of work across most of the cognitive science disciplines, as well as on other related fields such as sociology, anthropology and philosophy, wherever the local requirement of the discussion leads. I thought it more readable if I delineated the analytical models as I use them, rather than having a separate preliminary chapter that sets out the complete toolkit. This is largely how the book is arranged. However, there are certain key models and methods that have become paradigmatic in cognitive poetics and which feature prominently in this book, and so a quick sketch in this section will be useful.

When I look back at the areas I chose to explain in *Cognitive Poetics* (Stockwell 2002a), especially with a view to adapting my teaching from that book, it became apparent that applications in the field fall into two broad areas: close cognitive stylistic analysis, and more general schematic or world-level analysis. Approaches that have proven very fruitful in cognitive poetics include applications of the notions of frames, schemas, scenarios, domains, possible worlds, and text worlds. These are all different theoretical frameworks for accounting for more or less the same phenomenon: that is, how general knowledge and experience are deployed as a central factor in the particularities of a literary reading. The differences between each of these approaches (see Stockwell 2002a for detailed references to the history of this work) lie mainly in how they account for the fact that not all of a reader's knowledge is brought to bear in any one reading. The nature and outcome of the selection of knowledge as appropriate to the literary work in hand is the focus of each model. In schema theory, for example, context-dependent headers instantiate a certain schema, so certain keywords or apposite register cue up an area of familiar knowledge that is then ready to contextualise the text in hand and bring rich meaning to it. Text world theory relies on the notion of text-drivenness to specify which parts of readers' experiential knowledge are most likely required in any given situation.

Text worlds

I make quite extensive use of text world theory in this book (Werth 1999, Gavins 2007). One reason for this is that, of all the world-type models available, it seems to me that it best accounts for the connections between areas of knowledge and stylistic specification. It should be obvious how this is crucial for an account of texture. The detail of the text world approach is provided where it is used in the book, but a very brief preparatory sketch here is in order.

Text world theory is a cognitive discourse grammar which regards inter-locutors as occupying a discourse world. Together, utterers and receivers (writers and readers, in literary terms here) create a text world on the basis of perceived common ground knowledge that they seem to share. The text world is a readerly mental representation of the alternate world – disjunctive from their own – in which there might be other characters, objects, history or loca-tion. Readers' text worlds are rich worlds, filled in from their own past experi-ences. The status of the text world shifts as new elements are added to it (as world-builders) or as events move on within it (as function-advancers). Certain further disjunctions create further sub-worlds that are switched from the text world, embedded in them. World-switch triggers include flashbacks, flashforwards, hypotheticals and speculation, representation of beliefs, wishes, or obligations though modalisation, metaphors, negations, and direct speech. These switched worlds have the same structure as the text world (world-builders and function-advancers), and multiple worlds can be embed-ded within worlds. The verifiability of aspects of each world level is an onto-logical matter either of character accessibility or participant accessibility.

Louwerse and van Peer (2009) observe the surprising fact that cognitive poetics, in spite of its ancestry in stylistics, has tended to draw its models more from cognitive psychology than cognitive linguistics. In an effort to redress this imbalance, I have adapted cognitive psychological work always with a focus on stylistic texture, even where I use world-level models. I have also consciously drawn more heavily on cognitive linguistic frameworks than either I or most other writers in cognitive poetics have done in the past (for an exception, see Hamilton 2003, 2007). This deliberate cognitive linguistic focus has enabled me to engage more precisely with the stylistic side of texture, while not losing the connections with psychological plausibility overall.

I draw on text world theory particularly towards the end of Chapter 3 where I discuss the worlds that are generated in empathetic readings of lam-entation poems, and also in Chapters 4 and 5 in developing a cognitive poetic approach to characterisation and viewpoint. Text worlds are an especially useful way of understanding ethical positioning, which is explored at the end of Chapter 5.

Prototypicality

A key concept which appears several times in this book is the cognitive lin-guistic notion of prototypicality (Lakoff 1987; Evans and Green 2006: 248–83). This formed the basis of cognitive linguistics and is an insight into language patterning that informs several aspects of cognitive science in general. Human categorisation, which is key to our conceptual system, does not in fact seem to operate on the basis of discrete membership classes, as has traditionally been imagined. Instead, there is a great deal of evidence to suggest that categorisation is very much more fluid, provisional, adaptable and contingent than this. To give the most simple example, here is a set of concepts referred to by 'grass, trees, herb bed, bench, barbecue grill, children's slide, railwayman's lamp, gas cooker, scaffolding poles, industrial guttering'. Given the category of 'things in a garden', I imagine most people would include the first five or six objects, would exclude the final three, and there would be some disagreement about the railwayman's lamp. In fact, these are all objects I can see in my garden right now out of the window; they have a variety of uses in my garden, including waiting to be recycled.

This illustrates several aspects of how categorisation works. There are central, best examples of the category, more peripheral examples, and very poor examples. From central examples of prototypicality, the less and less good examples can be regarded as being placed outwards on a radial structure. The most decentred examples are in fact better examples of other categories whose radial structures might be seen as impinging on the category in hand. We can even say that there is no such thing as an out-of-category item, just items that are very very bad examples of the category. For example, a Challenger tank, the remnants of a Blue Streak rocket, llamas, clothes mannequins set in threatening poses, over 100 rotting VW camper vans, and a linguistics study centre are all unlikely garden features but are in fact in gardens that I know (not all in the same garden, though!). The category of 'garden' itself displays prototype effects, and each person's arrangement of these is dependent on experience: the garden behind my house here is very different from the Duke of Devonshire's estate over the hills, and these are very different from a tea garden in Kyoto, a roof garden in Athens, the botanical garden in Helsinki, and the beer-garden behind the pub down the road. Category membership alters depending on the situation (my car-keys are not usually tools but they become a type of screwdriver when they are the only thing to hand that will do the job).

In cognitive linguistics, prototypicality is a key pervasive notion, operating at all levels. The examples given above have implications for how we understand lexical semantics and meaning relationships. The sense that there is a socially-shared and embodied normative pattern in a typical set of circumstances allows us to understand why variations from that pattern generate certain effects. In this book, the notion of prototypicality appears throughout much of the discussion, but it proves particularly useful in exploring types of character relationships in chapter 4.

Projection

Alongside prototypicality is the importance of how figure and ground relationships are conceptualised in cognitive linguistics (see Ungerer and Schmid 2003). On the principle of continuity from physical to embodied to conceptual space, the visual field is partitioned as it is perceived into foregrounded and backgrounded features, with the former in focus and the latter in secondary focus or regarded as an undifferentiated non-focused setting. (Clearly protoypicality gradation applies to this scale as well.) Figure and ground cognition is the key to attention, whether the object being attended to is a moving physical object or a virtual fictional one.

Complex advanced abstract thinking rests ultimately on extensions of the basic sense we have of figural objects, grounded objects and backgrounded spaces, which we begin to develop even before birth. These physical experiences are generalised as schematised knowledge, and the abstraction is then easy to apply in later life to many other examples, both concrete and also abstract. These abstractions are known as image-schemas, and they form the basis of prepositional positioning, our understanding of physical and conceptual relationships, and syntactic ordering in the clause.

The importance of figure and ground and image-schemas relies on the human capacity for projection: taking one domain and mapping it onto another in order to gain access of understanding of the new domain. This is fundamentally a metaphorical process, and research into conceptual metaphor has been one of the most longstanding threads within cognitive linguistics. Our capacity for projection is what enables our intellectual life to be developed on the basis of our physical bodies and environment. We can abstract general principles and reapply them in different circumstances (the basis of prototypicality). We can imagine alternative scenarios, recall past events and call up future events, cast ourselves into the imagined minds of others, sympathise, empathise, perceive differences and resist them (the basis of world theories). We can understand that one phenomenon can be symbolic, emblematic or iconic of another, and we can build abstract relationships between idealised objects.

The complex consequence of the cognitive linguistic understanding of figure and ground forms the basis of the discussion of resonance and intensity in Chapter 2. It also appears as a key notion in Chapter 4, and it underlies the discussion of image schemas. Image schemas are drawn on throughout the early chapters of the book, but are particularly useful in the discussion of motion and vectors in Chapter 4, and as part of the application of cognitive grammar in Chapter 6. Conceptual metaphor underlies the discussions of models of reading in Chapter 3.

Cognitive grammar

As part of my focus on the detailed workings of literary works and their texture, a close stylistic analysis forms the main method of this book. Though the models of analysis that I use draw on various linguistic traditions, the main source in this book is cognitive grammar, developed mainly by Langacker (1987, 1991, 2008). As this is the main grammatical approach within cognitive linguistics, there are obvious reasons for drawing on this model. Cognitive grammar builds on the notions set out above of prototypicality, figure/ground relations, image-schemas and metaphorical projection, in order to offer a linguistic description that is psychologically founded. There are, of course, other models of language that fall broadly within the cognitivist field – they are mostly classified as construction grammars – but the features of Langacker's cognitive grammar suitable for our purposes in this book are roughly common to all of them.

Very briefly, cognitive grammar explains how clauses are construed on the basis of a windowing of attention of different parts of the clause, a process called profiling. Langacker draws continuities between grammatical realisations and visualisation in terms of focus, focal adjustment, viewing position, and so on. The clause is conceived of as an action chain, with an energetic force transmitted along it from agent to patient. This approach rests on a basic force-dynamic image-schema. Different construal effects are generated as different parts of the action chain are profiled, and the reader is encouraged to profile certain parts rather than others by the stylistic realisation (the grammaticalisation) of the event or state being presented.

I rely on cognitive grammatical terms throughout the book, but especially in Chapter 6, where I develop the literary analysis across stretches of extended discourse.

The value of cognitive poetics

In arranging the discussions in this book, I have organised them by the effects of literary reading rather than by cognitive linguistic models. So instead of chapters called 'deixis', or 'grammar', or 'attention', and so on, I am more concerned to deploy insights from cognitive science to illuminate phenomena such as literary resonance, intensity, sensation, empathy, voice, resistance, and so on. Notions like these are difficult to specify, though they are experientially real and, it seems to me they form the core of what literature is as a feature of our lives.

It is easy to anticipate negative criticisms of the sort of procedure I adopt here. The most simple to reject are those based on conservatism and tradition. Readerly matters of feeling, taste, preference, relationships with characters, sense of action, and so on, have not generally been regarded as part of the remit of serious scholarship. There are two explanations for this. Firstly, as literary criticism has emerged as a university and college discipline over the last century, it has embraced complexity and abstraction as the trappings of seriousness; difficulty and abstruseness have been elevated into a virtue. Secondly, it has not until recently been apparent how these vague readerly senses could be explored systematically or in a principled way. The consequence of these two factors has been that academic literary discourse has diverged from the discourse of natural readers to an untraversible extent.

In response to my argument that cognitive poetics in a stylistic tradition offers a bridge across this divide, an obvious criticism would be that natural readers without a linguistic or cognitivist training are unlikely to find this book very accessible, with its heavy technical terminology and sometimes dense arguments. Though I have tried to write readably, this is a reasonable argument about the discourse of cognitive poetics. However, it is important to remember that this is a discipline, with disciplinary standards and principles. Though the object of analysis is often natural reading, the analytical discourse itself is necessarily technical in order to avoid constant lengthy explanations. There is no denying the fact that multidisciplinary work involves adapting terms and concepts from different traditions, and assimilating a range of different methodological practices and ways of thinking. There is a danger in literary criticism, including cognitive poetics, of misunderstanding or misusing the insights of other disciplines when they are applied or adapted to the literary domain. The challenge is to ensure the multidisciplinarity is genuine and rigorous.

Literary scholarship has neglected textual engagement for so long that detailed and systematic analysis of textuality in itself is sometimes regarded with suspicion. The argument goes that you can analyse too closely, identifying textual patterns that no natural reader could possibly notice; the only readings that cognitive poetics produces are those of cognitivist readers. This is a poor argument that would abandon all attempts at rigour and precision. A major insight from cognitive science is that much of our mental capacity occurs below the level of conscious awareness. There is even evidence to show that the unconscious mind (in the scientific rather than psychoanalytical sense) is primary. We tend to think that we decide to do something (move a finger, watch a person walking, form an argument) and then we do it, but it seems increasingly clear that in fact our embodied unconscious mind does these things and then rationalises them very quickly after the fact. Most things we do, most perceptions and cognitive processing are aspects of the unconscious mind, below the level of conscious awareness. The careful and detailed analyses I present in this book are not online conscious streaming of reading awareness (unless you are a very self-conscious unnatural academic reader), but are attempts to account systematically for the unconscious processes that result in observable and experiential effects.

My argument here has another difficult consequence, which is known in social science generally as the observer's paradox. In sociolinguistics, for example, it is well-known that when a researcher enters a speech community with a view to observing its language, the very presence of this observer will alter the speech patterns of that community, rendering any findings invalid. The problem of this for literary reading is exponentially greater, and potentially devastating, since the object of analysis (literary reading) is itself a form of consciousness. As soon as you raise any aspect of this object to analytical and conscious awareness, you alter its state irreparably. Whatever it is you are investigating, then, it is not natural literary reading.

Those studies which rely solely on single-method empirical testing are most prone to the distorting effects of the observer's paradox. Psychologically-based studies and informant-based investigations of literary reading tend to use literary excerpts rather than full texts, so the contextual and even the natural co-textual experience is compromised. Such studies have also tended to use students and semi-professional readers as informants rather than 'civilians': as a result we know an awful lot about the reading responses of young middle-class educated people in college under test situations, but not so much about everyone else. Running an empirical test under laboratory conditions involves the analyst, the setting and the test situation distorting the results.

In other social sciences, this observer's paradox can be minimised by various ingenious methods: for example, self-awareness of accent features can be minimised by an informal setting, or by a peer-group interviewer, or by misinforming the subject about the purpose of the study. These mitigations are possible because the object of study is a tangible phenomenon. However, in research on literary reading, the object of study is a form of self-consciousness in itself, and it is extremely difficult to mitigate the observer's paradox in these circumstances.

This is not to say that the enterprise is hopeless. The sociolinguistic solution of co-ordinating several approaches to the same problem can be used to 'triangulate' the literary reading. However, the only way to ensure that the object of analysis is absolutely unaffected by the investigation is to examine pre-existing data that were not generated in a test situation. Traditional open-ended seminar discussions of literature (not on cognitive poetics courses) are a good example. Another obvious source of such data on the reading experience is the huge number of online reading group discussions. For example, there are an estimated 50,000 people in reading groups in the UK, many of which have online blogs which offer a wealth of unmediated data. I refer to this sort of reader-evidence across this book. A second solution, which might be regarded here as valid given the nature of reading as self-consciousness, is to allow the theoretical model to emerge from the data – much as Richard Gerrig (1993) did in his 'literature as transportation' work or Ray Gibbs (2002) in his 'emotion as movement' work; I follow a similar procedure in Chapters 2 and 3. A third form of validation is to deflect the observer's paradox effects by applying an analytical model that has some empirical validity in another domain, as I do in drawing on the well-established consensus of research in attention (Chapter 2) or in cognitive grammar (Chapter 6). A final form of validation lies in the openness and transparency in which cognitive poetic arguments are articulated. There is an implicit invitation, in all this work, to compare your own intuitions of well-formedness and well-arguedness with my own claims; I present them in the hope that they are made as clearly as possible and with an openness to falsifiability.

The cognitive poetics practised in this book does not encompass all forms of the discipline. I have not found it particularly necessary, for example, to include extended use of computational methods and corpus stylistic techniques, other than some rather simple examples. This is not an omission that should be interpreted as antagonistic; it is simply a matter of space and the particular requirements of what I am trying to do. I am sure that several of my arguments could be further illuminated by corpus stylistic elaboration. Similarly, I have not framed many of my arguments in any sophisticated statistical analysis. Again, this is not because I feel antipathetic to such practice; it is just that I do not think my arguments would be much enhanced or clarified by its inclusion. Furthermore, I do think that there are some dangers in a high level of statistical manipulation. Firstly, statistical values can be overlaid onto assumptions that are rather vague or uncritical, and they thus serve to reify questionable methods and findings. Secondly, there can occasionally be a tendency to fetishise statistics as imparting a patina of scientism where this is unnecessary. For example, in Chapter 2 I observe that around two-thirds of my audiences on various occasions were visibly moved by a particular literary text. I could have counted these informants quite precisely, but in fact nothing much would have been gained by knowing that the proportion was 60 per cent or 68 percent or whatever – in this case, the rough reckoning is perfectly good enough (and easier data to collect, of course). There is also often a confusion made in statistically-rich analyses between the formulaic significance within the parameters of a test and the intuitive significance felt by readers. The latter might be highly eccentric and idiosyncratic, and might fall below the threshold of significance in the other sense, but felt significance also needs to be accounted for in cognitive poetics.

The triangulation principle means that I am happy to set my work in this book against these and other, necessary traditions. In isolation, none of them can be as successful as their combined deployment in constituting the discipline as a whole.

Cognitive poetics, as I suggest above, has been particularly successful in accounting for meaningfulness and information-monitoring in literary reading, especially when it is built on a stylistic sensibility. It can always account for readings in a principled way, and can explain how interpretations of significance can be held by particular readers. Its combination of general cognitive mechanics and subjective experientiality allows it to account for variant readings across individuals and cultures and across time. This also means that it describes constraints on possible interpretations, not so much in terms of demonstrating that some readings are allowed and some are not, but in prototypical terms. Some readings are better than others, relative to their social circumstances. Some eccentric academic readings are poor examples of interpretations, judged within the radial structure of natural readings. This means that cognitive poetics is not simply a descriptive enterprise but is one with an evaluative component too. It must be added that some of the joy of cognitive poetics and stylistics – and this is in large part responsible for my enjoyment of writing this book – lies in the surprising and brilliant things that detailed and principled analyses can demonstrate. In this last sense, cognitive poetics is productive and enriching as well as descriptive and explanatory.

Texture

In addition to its achievements in accounting for information-processing, I offer this book as a contribution to similar success in framing aesthetics. The focus is on texture – the experiential quality of textuality – but the discussion ranges into the aesthetic senses of value, attractiveness, utility and their opposites as well. These are all part of the textural experience of reading literature. Indeed, I argue that in most cases the aesthetic motivation for reading is stronger than the desire for informational patterning and completion. If the book encourages more research in cognitive poetics in aesthetics, it will have served its purpose. It will also open up another front into the territory now occupied by cultural historians, with a view to returning literary criticism to something richer, more diverse and more worthwhile.

The book overall moves from feeling to meaning. Chapter 2 explores resonance as a sense of powerful literary impact and its ability to linger in the mind after the reading is completed. Resonance is closely linked to the sense of intensity in reading, which is determined by readerly disposition. I propose a model of resonance and intensity based on the cognitive psychology of attention, adapted for stylistic texture in the literary context. In Chapter 3 I extend this discussion of intensity into a sense of textual richness, and connect this virtual sense with physical sensations. The power of literary texts to move us, and return more emotion than we invest in effort, is explored through several lamentation poems that I have collected, as the discussion turns to empathy. These two chapters constitute just under half of the book.

Extending the natural face-to-face primary situation of language and cognition to literary fiction, where authors, characters and readers are displaced from each other, is the ground of Chapter 4. I offer a new, cognitively informed model of viewpoint, especially directed at the relationship of readers and characters. I use the discussion to try to find a way between regarding characters as entirely real people and regarding them as merely marks on a page. The importance of deixis as a central rather than peculiar and marginal aspect of language is asserted, in order to return to an earlier discussion of the precise nature of the edges of conceptual worlds.

Implicit in the arguments of this chapter is a model of personality that is explored in more detail in Chapter 5. Up until this point in the book, the notion of the reader has been largely taken as unproblematic, so here I elaborate it in relation to the prior discussion of voice in literary reading. I adapt the use of psychological projection to account for the mind-modelling of other characters, and use this to discuss readerly identification and resistance.

The ethical dimension of these aesthetic manoeuvres is also discussed, in terms of choices between parallel worlds. Throughout, I attempt to balance the psychology of reading and its social status by drawing on the sociological notion of the nexus.

The final chapter draws closely on cognitive grammar to show the aesthetic dimension in meaning-making, through a consideration of construal. Where cognitive grammar largely rests at clause-level, I extend its principles to be able to account for cohesion and coherence in literary texture. I also suggest ways in which a cognitive discourse grammar might be used for extended literary discussion.

Across all of the chapters, literary texts appear not simply as examples to demonstrate a cognitive poetic feature but in their own right as examples of literary critical practice. For this reason, I have deliberately chosen literary texts that are popular or canonical or both. I want to show that there are innovative things that can be said about even the most well-worked texts, and I want to demonstrate cognitive poetics working on those literary works that people evidently find valuable, powerful and affecting. This unfortunately means that the selection of literary texts is not particularly adventurous, and it is representative of traditional canonising forces (white western men, for the most part). Ideally I would have wanted to do all this and have a more richly diverse representation, but then the book would have to be three times as long, and I could not justify my own indulgence. So I apologise and invite the reader to continue this work.

Literary reading is a heteronomous object, and texture too is a heteronomous phenomenon. It can be accounted for precisely neither by purely textual description nor by purely psychological modelling, but by a properly holistic blending of both aspects into a unitary analysis. It is very difficult, in linear discussion and the two dimensions of paper, to capture consistently and equally these two interanimating facets of texture. I have no doubt that at different moments of the book I have leaned too heavily one way or the other. However, in the spirit of the interanimation itself, I rely on the reader to remember that texture is always the experienced quality of textuality, and even if the text itself does not always exactly embody it, this book should be read with that always in mind.

Reading

Throughout the book I have attempted to restrict the density of referencing, so as to allow the book to be more accessible and readable than a scholarly paper or standard research monograph. Where necessary, references are given within the body of my text, but each chapter will also end with a short 'Reading' section of the key material which either informs the chapter or is the essential next step.

Tsur (1987, 1992) coined the term *cognitive poetics* and has produced some of the best work over the past couple of decades. His current position (Tsur 2008a) is more precisely focused than others in the field: see Tsur (2008b), and my response (Stockwell 2008a). On cognitive poetics in relation to critical theory, see Stockwell (2008b), the response by Kelleter (2008), and reply by Fricke (2008).

The only introduction to cognitive poetics remains my own textbook (Stockwell 2002a), to which this present volume can be regarded as a more advanced sequel. Cognitive approaches have found their way into recent mainstream stylistics textbooks (Simpson 2004; Gregoriou 2009). Some excellent collections of cognitive poetics work include Gavins and Steen (2003), Semino and Culpeper (2002), and Brône and Vandaele (2009). Statements of cognitive poetics and the literary application of cognitivism in general include Anderson (1996), Currie (1995, 2004), Currie and Ravenscroft (2002), Hogan (2003a, 2003b), and Turner (1991, 1996, 2006).

On the principles of cognitive linguistics, see Croft and Cruse (2004), Dirven (2000), Dirven and Verspoor (2004), Evans (2007), Evans and Green (2006), Geeraerts (2007), Lakoff and Johnson (1999), and Ungerer and Schmid (2003). Specifically on text worlds, see Werth (1999) and Gavins (2007), and for proto-typicality and image schemas, see Lakoff (1987) and Brugman (1989).

2 Resonance and Intensity

One of the most difficult aspects of literary experience to describe rigorously is the way in which reading a literary work can create a tone, an atmosphere in the mind that seems to persist long after the pages have been put down. Literature is valued because of this *resonance* which is difficult to articulate or define. The difficulty is twofold, firstly in the graded and variable sense of the phenomenon itself: resonance is not an object but a textured prolonged feeling that can be revivified periodically after the initial experience. A sense of significance and personal salience can strike the reader on a first reading, or may emerge only later on, and then several times in ongoing life with different intensities and depths. Secondly, the difficulty in pinning down resonance also lies in the poverty of our analytical apparatus for describing it, in literary criticism. Typically, where the feeling is ever discussed, it is described in impressionistic terms. The vagueness of the discourse reflects and perpetuates the sense of vagueness of the concept. Much of this discussion aims not so much at capturing the notion of resonance descriptively as re-enacting it in the rhetorical texture of the critic's own language.

However, impressionism is a good place to start a more analytical journey, in order here to try to explain the subjective experience that I am talking about, and to generate some key terms. Here is a definition of resonance from a writing-aids website (Kathy Krajco's *Lighthouse Writing Tips*, posted 20 January 2008):

Literary Resonance in the Art of Writing

To 'resonate' literally means to bounce back and forth between two states or places. Resonate comes from the Latin word for 'resound'. In sound, resonance is a prolonged response to something that caused things to vibrate. When sound reverberates, it's resonating within a bounded space, like the body of a guitar. Thunder often resonates/reverberates across an uneven landscape.

Resonance in writing is something that affects us the same way. It's an aura of significance, significance beyond the otherwise insignificant event taking place. It's caused by a kind of psychic reverberation between two times, places, states, or spheres – one common and the other extraordinary. So, for example a Biblical epigraph for a poem about an empty school bus in a snowstorm resonates between the temporal and eternal, lending the bus an aura of cosmic significance.

[. . .]

The end of Graham Greene's *The Power and the Glory* is a [. . .] study in resonance prolonged to wring the last bit of emotion from you. It resonates like thunder, except that the reverberations get louder and more intense. Subtle, relentless references to the weather establish the main character as a Christ figure going to his death. Similarly, in Shakespeare's King Lear, the climactic moment brings on a violent thunderstorm, as though this betrayal of a king and father has cosmic implications.

(Krajco 2008)

Resonance in literary reading here focuses on the dual properties of a *prolonged response* and an *aura of significance*. The term clearly draws on its primary usage in mechanics and music. In mechanics, resonance is a feature of oscillating or vibrating objects, where two bodies share a similar or sympathetic structure so that oscillation in one at a particular frequency will cause the other object to vibrate at the same frequency. The way that a tuning fork causes a string on a musical instrument to play the same natural note when held in close proximity is an example. Some instruments – especially Indian stringed instruments like the sitar – have resonant strings which are not plucked or struck directly but sound out in sympathy when a string with the right frequency is played. Different strings will sound not only when the frequency matches but also when a multiple of their shared frequencies matches: these resonances are called *overtones*.

In mechanics, resonance has a measurement of *intensity*, which refers to the size of the variation of the oscillation from a central, normal resting position. Resonance is reduced by *damping*, typically where a separate object with a different structural resonance interferes in the oscillating system, and the speed of the damping effect is measured by the *decay* in the resonance. For example, a musical string struck forcefully can be said to have a higher intensity than one struck gently; a bridge, capo or palming of the instrument will damp down the sound; and a large echoing cavity, such as in a grand piano or acoustic guitar, will reduce or stall the decay in the sound, increasing the *echo* or *persistence*.

When people speak of resonance in texts, it is clear that they are using the term as a metaphorical extension of the mechanical-musical sense, and for most people this will not be a discourse informed by physics or music theory. In fact, the vagueness of most people's understanding of resonance verges on magical ineffability, which is probably what makes it attractive as an impressionistic term to use for the vague ineffability of the experience. (Notice how Krajco's account above slips easily from acoustic resonance to 'psychic reverberation'.) However, the precise formulations of the mechanics of resonance can be useful here. If people have a sense that literary resonance involves a prolonged response, generating an aura of significance, with sympathetic overtones, from an initially intense moment followed by interference, damping, and decay or persistence, then those are the terms that need to be fixed at the heart of our account.

In this chapter, I suggest an analytical means of discussing the concept of literary resonance, drawing on cognitive scientific principles. The aim is not to recapture or re-enact the feeling of the literary experience but to offer an analytical framework within which this feeling can be discussed. Perhaps surprisingly, my starting point is work on *attention*. Traditionally in cognitive poetics, theories of attention have been deployed in order to account for meaningfulness rather than textural experience. However, I think the mechanisms for describing the semantic significance of attention are the same for experiential texture.

According to a founding principle of cognitive science, higher-level functions (such as literary resonance) are augmentations and adaptations of more basic existing cognitive mechanisms. Readerly attention is evidently at base a matter of visual perception (and there is more research work on visual than auditory perception: see Styles 2006). Therefore textual analogues of aspects of the extensive cognitive science work on visual perception and recognition can be made with some confidence.

The human visual field beyond a few metres' distance is essentially two-dimensional: the stereoscopic effect of our two eyes can make objects jump left or right against the background when they are fairly close, so that one eye effectively sees behind what is blocked from the other eye, but this effect diminishes greatly with distance. The moon follows your car as if fixed to it while driving on a clear night. The trees at the bottom of the garden seem pinned to the sky beyond. The view of a valley from the top of a mountain can seem like a flattened painting, a patchwork or jigsaw of intricate but seamed shapes. The perceptual field arrives in the eye, lensed upside-down, as a flat mosaic of shapes, coloured at the centre, monochrome at the edge, undifferentiated at the levels of significance or meaning. Everything beyond this basic input of tone, colour and shape is given to the view by the cognitive processes of the brain, which delineates objects from the background and from each other, and denotes what is seen with qualitative information. The visual field is rendered as a conceptual space, populated by discrete objects in a constructed foreground and background. The viewer's attention acts either like a spotlight or zoom lens, focusing in turn on one object or another, and the viewer can be distracted by new, odd or more interesting objects that were either already in the field of view but unregarded, or that come into the attentional space by some means.

There are five key research questions for cognitive psychologists in this area (following Logan 1996). How is space represented? What is an object? What determines the shape of the 'spotlight' of attention? How does selection occur within the focus of attention? How does selection between objects occur? There are several issues that have analogues in the literary space that concerns us here, as follows, and these will be addressed in the course of this chapter:

- What is the experiential nature of literary space?
- What are literary objects in this space and what are their properties and edges?
- How is the reader engaged by some features, and then distracted by other features, and what is the effect of the disengagement?
- How does selection for attention account for feelings of alertness, literary intensity and wilful disposition?
- How does a rich field of objects generate a sense of richness in depth in a literary work?

A model of resonant space

The conceptual space generated by reading a literary work, whether a naturalistic description of a scene (most fictional narratives) or a stylised set of propositions (a lyric), is, like most visual encounters, a 'cluttered array' (Spelke 1990) in cognitive perceptual terms. That is, it consists of a number of colours, edges, forms and surface textures that are available for processing into recognisable and attended objects: more objects vying for attention than can be assimilated in totality, so that one interpretative configuration or another must be imposed to make sense of what is being experienced. The configuration that is actually chosen will be the product of a moment-by-moment adjustment in which certain elements in the space distract the attention of the reader and others are relatively neglected. (See Figure 2a for a schematic summary, which will be explored with examples throughout this chapter).

Elements that take the viewer's attention can be termed *attractors*: in the literary sphere, these can be specified stylistically, as set out in the next subsection. An attractor can come to attention by being newly introduced into the literary space, or it can be an existing element that is revivified in attentive working memory, again by various stylistic means. Once invoked, attractors can be maintained in focus either positively by certain sustaining techniques, or negatively by the absence of any shift devices. Incidentally, there is some research that suggests that the left hemisphere of the brain dominates

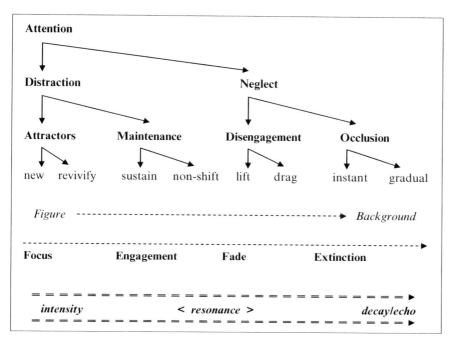

Figure 2a An attention-resonance model

attractor-invocation while sustaining attention is largely the business of the right hemisphere (see Robertson and Manly 1999; Styles 2006: 67–8). The left hemisphere tends to control local and specific interpretations, while the right controls global configurations. Furthermore, the right hemisphere seems to be the dominant one for the entire process of attention: attentional disabilities are more likely to result from right parietal injuries or lesions than left hemisphere ones (Posner 1993; Corbetta et al. 1993). Given the usual specialisation of (crudely) the linguistic left and the emotional right (see Purves et al. 2008), this suggests to me that attention is the right place to look not just for matters of informativity but also and perhaps primarily for emotional experiential matters of literary resonance.

Alternatively to attractors, elements which are either no longer the focus of attention, were never prominent features, or have been deliberately backgrounded can be said to be relatively *neglected*. Neglect can be a matter primarily of readerly disengagement, and this can take the form of a reader consciously *lifting* the element out of the focused domain of awareness: there is a sense that the element is still 'there' but is on its way out of focus. Alternatively, the readerly disengagement can be more a matter of attentional *drag*, with a sense that the element is now part of the background but there is still a whiff of it in the air. Lastly, the neglect can seem to be more a matter of textual patterning, such that another focused element comes to *occlude* the previously focused figure. This occlusion can be instant for an element that is linguistically removed from the scene (for example, by negation or a verb of disappearance, death or removal), or it can be gradual, where the element simply fades away by not being mentioned for a duration of several clauses.

The felt effects of these elements in textual attention are focus, engagement, fading and extinction, which in turn represent a scale of figure and background. Figure/ground in cognitive linguistics and in cognitive poetics tends to be regarded as a polar category, whereas from the perspective of scaled readerly attention, it is a cline of prominence, ranging through degrees of foregrounding into vague, undifferentiated but rich background. Altogether, the scale briefly sketched out above represents a cline of resonance, with striking literary intensity at one end, and decay or echo tailing off into a rich sense of textual resonance towards the other.

Note that, for any practical analysis such as those that follow in this chapter, the attention-resonance model will require the exploration both of linguistic features in the text as well as readerly disposition. The degree of resonance in any given literary reading is not simply a matter of the stylistic power of the text but is also a matter of the reader's intensity of alertness, degree of resistance, or willingness to invest themselves emotionally in the experience. These factors will be also taken up in later chapters in this book.

Literary objects in resonant spaces

In 1929, the Belgian surrealist painter René Magritte (1979) produced a visual essay, 'La poésie est une pipe' (Poetry is a pipe), in which he described the nature of the relationships between drawn objects (such as sketches of a leaf, a boat, a cloud, a tree, and so on), drawn words (such as 'ciel' sky, 'soleil' sun, 'brouillard' fog, and so on), the concepts of those objects in the mind, and the concepts in the mind of the words outside the drawings denoting the objects. This complex of relationships forms the basis of the textural experience of looking at his famous paintings featuring a drawing of a pipe with 'Ceci n'est pas une pipe' (This is not a pipe), a painting entitled *La Trahison des Images* (The Treason of Images) 1928, or later an apple above the words 'Ceci n'est pas un pomme' (This is not an apple) 1964, or a whole series of similar word-image canvases in the early 1930s collectively known as *La Clef des Songes* (The Key to Dreams). Magritte was tapping into the early insights of *gestalt* ('shape' or 'form' in German) *psychology*, being developed in the 1920s and 1930s by Max Wertheimer (1958), Wolfgang Köhler (1947, 1959), Kurt Koffka (1935) and others. Much of this work consisted of developing experimental techniques with ordinary informants to discover how objects were recognised and conceptualised, based on the principle of Prägnanz ('conciseness', 'succinctness', 'precision' or generally 'regularity'). Gestalt psychology still forms the basis of the description of the foregrounding of objects from the perceptual field, though later neuroscience turns this description into an explanation of perceptual processing.

An object is perceived as a figure, out of the mosaic of shapes in the visual field, if it can be resolved along one or more of the following principles (these vary according to author and translation, but they are more or less consistent):

The principle of closure. If an object appears to have a complete and continuous outer circumference, then it is likely to make a good figure. This principle is so strong that perceivers will often mentally complete the circumference of an incomplete shape in order to see it as a closed entity (for example if it is broken, fragmented, or partially hidden from view).

The principle of continuity. This derives from the last observation, in that objects are assumed to continue behind other objects with the same colours, pattern, texture or other properties that can actually be seen. The effect is particularly strong if the blocked object protrudes from both sides of the blocking object, so that the hidden shape behind the blocking object can be guessed.

The principle of proximity. Objects that are grouped together are likely to be perceived as sharing properties, or even as sharing a unified identity.

The principle of similarity. Additionally, objects that look similar to each other will be assumed to be related. Similarity can be perceived on the basis of similarity of shape, colour, size, or function.

The principle of symmetry. Regular, stable or predictable shapes are more easily perceived as figures than irregular, amorphous or protean shapes. This principle underlies the fact that familiarity with a shape will quickly render that shape as a figure, whereas a newly encountered entity might need to be studied before it can be resolved into a perceivable object.

The principle of common fate or function. If two features in the perceptual field change at the same time, are pushed at the same time by something else, are squashed or destroyed simultaneously, change colour or brightness at the same time, or are otherwise apparently connected by the same event, then those features are likely be treated as parts of the same single object.

Magritte's sketches in the essay illustrate many of these principles in action. Above a drawing of an isometric, three-dimensional view of a brick wall, he asserts that 'Un objet fait supposer qu'il y en a d'autres derrière lui' (An object makes you think that there are other objects behind it). And, 'Or, les contours visibles des objets, dans la réalité, se touchent s'ils formaient une mosaïque' (It seems that the visible edges of objects, in reality, touch each other as if they formed a mosaic), above a sketch of clouds whose edges have been interrupted by a brick wall and a tree. In each of these cases, what we do not see is a mosaic, but different focused elements with a foreground and background. In each, it is easy to see that the furry little outline is a cloud, the regular tiled edge is part of a wall, and the three bare lines are a tree trunk, even though each of these objects is incomplete. However, Magritte also draws the side-profile of a human face, with the jawline edge also serving as the edge of a cloud. Given the objectively equal choice between a cloud and a face, it is much easier to see a face with an odd-shaped elongated beard, rather than a cloud with a facial expression – indicating that there is some-thing more figural in the human shape than the amorphous shape.

In terms of literary discourse, we need to establish what are the features by which we might recognise objects that constitute good figures. In other words, drawing on what we know about the perceptual field, what are likely to be the characteristics of features in a literary text that attract the reader's attention? In line with the principles set out above, good attractors in texts will be referred objects that are presented as having a unified and coherent structure and identity: these are likely to be textualised as noun phrases. Because of a perceptual phenomenon known as the *inhibition of return*, by which the eye gets bored by static unchanging objects and is attracted by vari-ation and newness, current or new objects are likely to make good attractors. Good attractors are also likely to exhibit a textual persistence that is strong enough to overcome the repetitious cause of inhibition of return: that is, they will be maintained in co-reference, perhaps by repeated naming or pronomi-nalisation, by elegant synonym variation, or by verb-chaining. Referred objects are also likely to be good attractors if the verbs to which they are attached are active, positive (in the ordinary sense of the meanings of those verbs rather than in the grammatical senses of these terms) and energetic.

Noun phrases and verbs which describe and imply closeness (literal fore-groundedness) are likely to form good attractors. Closeness can be perceived in terms of large volume (near objects are perceptually bigger than distant ones), high volume in terms of noisiness, high volume in terms of brightness and heat. Familiar objects in the visual field are more readily resolved as figures, since a conceptual template is already available, so humans are readily attractive figures in this sense. Furthermore, human speakers (because of their activeness) are better attractors than a description of a hearer; but humans, whether speaking or listening, tend to be more figural than animals; animals are more figural than objects; and objects are more figural than abstractions, in general. This empathy scale demonstrates that referents are often characterised by more than one feature of attraction. Lastly, motion and spatial relationships are also matters of attentional change. Carstensen (2007: 8) describes attentional change as being a *shift* (which has the effect for the viewer of apparent motion), or a *zoom* (which renders apparent change in size), or a *state change* (in which sudden appearance or newness is the major feature).

Gathering these points together, we can produce a list of the typical features of good textual attractors:

- *newness*
  (currency: the present moment of reading is more attractive than the previous moment)
- *agency*
  (noun phrases in active position are better attractors than in passive position)
- *topicality*
  (subject position confers attraction over object position)
- *empathetic recognisability*
  (human speaker > human hearer > animal > object > abstraction)
- *definiteness*
  (definite ('the man') > specific indefinite ('a certain man') > non-specific indefinite ('any man'))
- *activeness*
  (verbs denoting action, violence, passion, wilfulness, motivation or strength)
- *brightness*
  (lightness or vivid colours being denoted over dimness or drabness)
- *fullness*
  (richness, density, intensity or nutrition being denoted)
- *largeness*
  (large objects being denoted, or a very long elaborated noun phrase used to denote)
- *height*
  (objects that are above others, are higher than the perceiver, or which dominate)
- *noisiness*
  (denoted phenomena which are audibly voluminous)
- *aesthetic distance from the norm*
  (beautiful or ugly referents, dangerous referents, alien objects denoted, dissonance).

This inventory gives us a checklist of parameters to trace through a literary text. Note that the categories cut across traditional linguistic matters, with grammatical notions at the top and experiential notions towards the end. A consequence of adopting a cognitive linguistic perspective is that grammar and experience are not separate categories. Another oddity about the list is that the degree of attraction is affected both by the nature of the object and by the relationship of that object to other elements in the field of attention. The relative status of non-figured objects as they are placed or fade into the background is relevant: for example, a moment of brightness in a text can be enhanced by a description of dimness in the co-text.

These features can be used to observe the techniques in the following examples.

When You Are Old

When you are old and grey and full of sleep,
And nodding by the fire, take down this book,
And slowly read, and dream of the soft look
Your eyes had once, and of their shadows deep.

How many loved your moments of glad grace,
And loved your beauty with love false or true;
But one man loved the pilgrim soul in you,
And loved the sorrows of your changing face;

And bending down beside the glowing bars,
Murmur, a little sadly, how Love fled
And paced upon the mountains overhead
And hid his face amid a crowd of stars.

William Butler Yeats (1893)

The intuitive resonance of this poem for many readers lies in the subdued, melancholy and nostalgic tone set up in the first half, to be followed then by a more poignant and startling sense of sadness and loss towards the end. The poem works mainly by exploiting specific attractors along several dimensions, some simultaneously and others sequentially. On the dimension of brightness, the poem begins by dimming down the background ('grey', 'soft', 'shadows'), and it draws in parallel on the backgrounding potential of the scale of height (here, dimness is echoed by down-ness in 'nodding', 'take down', 'deep'), and the contrary, inactive end of the scale of activeness ('old', 'sleep', 'slowly'). The other terms here are affected by their proximity to these general qualities: 'old' here is construed as slow, sad and weak rather than experienced, contented and wise; the invocation of books and reading is rendered passive and patient; and readers with whom I have informally discussed the poem report a mental picture of the fire as a grate of glowing embers rather than a blazing hearth, which confirms the same resonant effect. (Incidentally, a reading of 'glowing bars' as an electric bar heater on low power works as well but is historically inaccurate, these fireplaces only being invented in 1892, the same year that the poem was composed.) By contrast, the human speaker of the first stanza is figured strongly, relatively defined by the backgrounded, inactive, listening 'you'. The implicit speaking 'I' of the poem is made somewhat more explicit in the deictic (and close) reference to 'this book'.

The second stanza continues to set up a subdued background, with non-specific 'How many' and abstractions 'glad grace' and 'beauty'. The agency of the verb *love* is pluralised and made indefinite by these first two lines, only for the strong figural attractor of 'one man' in the third line to enter very forcefully. This force is enhanced by the fact that the active human and specific agent of 'one man' occurs after a series of abstractions ('grace', 'beauty', 'love', and falsity and truth – the latter reversed from its usual idiomatic sequence ('true or false') so that 'true' is linked proximally with 'one man'). The figuration is signalled by 'But', and this pivotal attentional moment occurs exactly in the middle of the poem. The 'you' character is relatively backgrounded by all this patterning, such that even the suggestion that the 'you' is in motion on a journey is carried not by a verb-element but by the meaning of the modifier in 'pilgrim soul', which is statically located 'in' you, and then by the modifier in 'changing face'. In the final stanza, though the 'you' is the actor in bending down and murmuring, this actor is profiled passively: the grammar of the first two lines here picks up the agency structure of the first stanza, where 'bending down' and 'murmur' are positioned at the same deictic level as 'nodding', and 'take down . . ., . . . read, and dream'.

The brightness and activity contrast is worth tracing here. The poem dims down the future moment of old age in the first stanza, in order to enhance the memory of a past love in the second; then at the beginning of the third stanza it dims down the old-age future again using the same elements as previously (down-ness and dimness in 'bending down' and 'glowing bars'), and it simultaneously makes the poem quiet ('Murmur') and diminishes the intensity and specificity of feeling ('a little sadly'). The quiet, dim, small and sad scene is thus reset after the brief contrastive figuration of 'one man's' love, in order to explode in a flurry of volume, action and light over the final three lines of the poem. An abstraction ('Love') is pulled leftwards on the empathy scale by personification, becoming a rich attractor especially conjoined with the most active verbs yet, 'fled And paced'. The down-ness and dimness is replaced by height and brightness 'upon the mountains', which are even explicitly related to the human scale 'overhead', underlining the personification of 'Love' and reinvoking the human attractor end of the empathy scale. The third verb 'hid' and 'his face' enhance all of this again, and the noise, brightness, height and dissonance of the final metaphor are all simultaneously fired by 'amid a crowd of stars'.

The poem thus finishes with a startling and striking metaphorical image that many readers find resonant, its force intensified by the relative calming of the attentional background (and the power of newness always remains on final lines for longer than any preceding lines because nothing appears next to distract attention). Of course, the grammatical anomalies across the stanza boundaries point to the poignancy of the situation being invoked by the poem. In spite of the full-stop at the end of the first stanza, the next line, 'How many. . .', could easily follow grammatically on from the first sentence (and indeed sounds exactly as if it did on a spoken reading). Similarly, there is a grammatical disjunction at the start of the third stanza, where 'bending' picks up the addressed 'you' of the first stanza, interrupted by the memory of the past. That apparent past (when 'one man loved the pilgrim soul in you') is actually in the present moment of utterance of the poem, in which the speaker (in most readings strongly identified with that 'one man') imagines a distant future of lonely old age for you, because you did not grasp the opportunity now in your near-future for loving him back. You could forestall the most attentionally-arresting image of desperate loss in the final two lines, if you heed the implicit plea of the poem as a whole. The quiet, indirect speaker (both the unarticulated 'I' and the strongly suggested 'one man') and the addressee 'you' imagined in your old age, are swept from the scene in the third person personification and dissonant final image. The poem leaves you there – it does not return you temporally either to the present moment nor to the imagined distant future – in the suspended, awful, striking and emotionally intense possible time which is the immediate consequence of the opportunity you now, back in your current life after the poem, have to grasp.

The striking and resonant phrases in this poem, when readers are asked what springs to mind, tend to come from the following set: 'dream of the soft look your eyes had once', 'moment of glad grace', 'the pilgrim soul in you', 'how Love fled', 'And paced upon the mountain overhead', and 'hid his face amid a crowd of stars'. The relative prominence or focus, the strength of these attractors, in different permutations, account for most readings of the poem. For example, another reading of the poem profiles the dimness, age and down-ness in the first stanza as evocative of a moment of extreme old age near death. The religious connotations of several phrases ('glad grace', 'love false or true', 'pilgrim soul') suggest a speaker who is the dead partner of the addressee (referring back to his younger, living self as the 'one man' who grew old with you). In this reading, the personification of 'Love' combines the abstraction as a blend with the actual younger living man; in contrast with the dim interior fireside scene, the speaker refers to himself in an exterior and infinite space, between mountains and stars amongst crowds, where he has passed into heaven. This reading is less nostalgic and more anticipatory, but it remains within the profiling possibilities of the attentional patterning scheme outlined above.

Once this sort of analysis is undertaken, certain patterns emerge in literary texts that are surprising. For example, it is interesting how many literary texts owe their cognitive mechanics to the manipulation of light and shade. The

fact that so many writers intuitively dim down the background in order to
enhance the figural attractors in their texts suggests that this sort of visual
contrast is deep-seated in perceptual consciousness. For example, here is
Milton describing a dream of his dead wife:

Sonnet XXIV

Methought I saw my late espoused Saint
  Brought to me like *Alcestis* from the grave,
  Whom *Joves* great Son to her glad Husband gave,
  Rescu'd from death by force though pale and faint.
Mine as whom washt from spot of child-bed taint
  Purification in the old Law did save,
  And such as yet once more I trust to have
  Full sight of her in Heav'n without restraint,
Came vested all in white, pure as her mind:
  Her face was veild, yet to my fancied sight
  Love, sweetness, goodness in her person shin'd
So clear, as in no face with more delight.
  But O as to embrace me she enclin'd
  I wak'd, she fled, and day brought back my night.

John Milton (1658)

Dimness and paleness dominate the first half of the poem, in explicit denota-
tions such as 'pale and faint', by reference to dirt and stains, and by conventional association with graves and death. The brightness is suddenly turned
up at the beginning of the second half of the poem:

  Full sight of her in Heav'n without restraint,
  Came vested all in white, pure as her mind: . . .

Denotational brightness ('white') is matched with associated brightness and
whiteness ('pure'), accompanied by a cue to the full visual perspective
('sight'), together with high-volume ('without restraint') fullness ('full', and
'all in'). These all appear as elements around the active verb 'came vested'.
The next few lines maintain and increase the light: 'shin'd', 'clear', '(de)light'.
The contrastive lighting is paralleled by a series of three metaphorical comparisons ('like *Alcestis*', 'as . . . the old Law', 'as yet . . . in Heaven'), which
evoke pagan pre-history, the Old Testament, and the heavenly promise of
salvation in the New Testament. The comparison phrase ('as') continues to
evoke his wife's 'mind' and 'face', but the final occurrence ('as to embrace me
. . .') denotes an intention (the metaphorical meaning of 'enclin'd') that is
never realised. The reversals of the dream vision are captured in the sudden
shift to active verbs ('enclin'd' as material action, 'wak'd', and 'fled'), and the

dissonant paradox, 'day brought back my night'. This, of course, draws on a metaphor of the darkness of night as emotional darkness, but biographically also refers to Milton's blindness where his days were also literally dark. (See Stockwell 2002b for further analysis.)

Engagement, depth and distraction

In the two analyses above of Yeats and Milton, I have indicated the common phenomenon whereby one dimension of resonant force (brightness, in both cases) is paralleled by other dimensions operating to the same polarity. So an increase in brightness is often co-located with large volume, noisiness, activity, involved agency, empathetic identification, and so on. Even where the accompanying elements in the close co-text are not in themselves aligned with these scales, the force of the attractor phrases is often so deeply intense that other parts of the text become coloured by the same perceptual quality. This is analagous to the halo effect that a bright white object confers on other light objects nearby, in visual terms. For example, in the Yeats poem, 'old' is lined up as a feature of slowness and sadness, rather than any of the other, more positive possible connotations of the term in general: the grounded elements in the text are given overtones by the presence of strong resonant attractors. This can be seen in the following famous sonnet by Shakespeare

Sonnet 18

Shall I compare thee to a summer's day?
Thou art more lovely and more temperate.
Rough winds do shake the darling buds of May,
And summer's lease hath all too short a date.
Sometime too hot the eye of heaven shines,
And often is his gold complexion dimmed,
And every fair from fair sometimes declines,
By chance or nature's changing course untrimmed;
But thy eternal summer shall not fade,
Nor lose possession of that fair thou ow'st,
Nor shall Death brag thou wander'st in his shade,
When in eternal lines to time thou grow'st.
   So long as men can breathe or eyes can see,
   So long lives this, and this gives life to thee.

William Shakespeare (published 1609)

A hugely popular poem generally read as a straightforward declaration of love, this is also one of those several sonnets by Shakespeare that are as much, if not more, focused on the talent of the writer and the memorial power of writing as on the object of affection addressed in the sonnet. The main feature of attraction is, again, light and brightness, but this is aligned and polarised with other dimensions, including volume as a means of delineating time, action as a means of distinguishing passing and eternal events, empathy in the form of personifications, and the nature of topicality and agency throughout. Because these dimensions are lined up throughout the sonnet, other elements are also placed in balance, and balance as an organising principle is established in the explicit comparison that is signalled in the first line.

Furthermore, since several attractor features are aligned, the sonnet has freedom to exploit both main forms of ongoing attentional change: shift and zoom. According to Carstensen (2007: 8), attention is caught most obviously by a 'state change': that is, the appearance of a new attractor in the perceptual field (*newness*, in my feature list above). Once the field is established, however, attention is moved around either by being shifted – this involves distraction from one figural attractor to another – or zoomed – that is, focused inward with a greater granularity or intensity. In the sonnet above, the initial attractor effecting the state change from the reader's pre-textual activity is the explicitly named and speaking/writing 'I'; this figure is quickly occluded by a distraction to two other perceptual objects: 'thee' and 'a summer's day'. This is a shift of attention, which involves temporarily backgrounding the 'I' (in fact, the 'I' remains backgrounded until right at the end of the poem). The two newly established attractors remain alternately in focus for most of the rest of the sonnet, as a consequence of the comparison being made between them. As I will show in detail below, the 'thee' figure tends to be associated with shifts of attention, while the 'summer's day' figure is characterised more by a zooming in and out of attention.

Lacuna effects

Developing gestalt principles, Carstensen (2007) formulates an approach to attention that focuses on the ontological status of perceived objects. He identifies gestalt shapes as *blobs* (if perceived singularly) or *groups of blobs* if perceived as a connected or continuous collection. A group of blobs can be attentionally zoomed to the granularity of an individual blob, of course. Thus, a person (such as the addressee 'thee' of the sonnet) is in abstract terms a unitary blob, while 'a summer's day' is in the first line a single blob, but is then delineated down to its several aspects as a group of blobs in the rest of the poem (a summer's day consists of the other elements mentioned in the text, which are zoomed in on as the reader progresses through the sonnet). Further in Carstensen's scheme, blobs can be positive (figures like 'thee' or 'day') or negative (part of the bounded background like 'I' through most of the poem). In natural everyday terms, concepts like 'dent', 'hole', 'fissure' or 'valley' are negative blobs, since they can be the focus of attention but they are defined by being *not* something which is in their immediate vicinity. The final key element in Carstensen's scheme is an emphasis on edges and bound-edness, as a means of defining attentional relationships between blobs. Positive blobs have edges by definition; negative blobs *only* have edges (that is, there is nothing in the middle of them). A hollow, a shadow, a large crack in the wall might all be perceived as negative blobs (let's call this phenomenon a figural *lacuna* in literary reading). Blobs are defined by their edges, and it is important to note that the edge itself belongs to the blob: Peterson and Enns (2005) offer evidence to show that the ground side of an edge is not processed, whereas the figure side is processed with the figure itself. Furthermore, figures and the nature of their edges (defined, or irregular, bright, or soft, and so on) are more likely to be recalled from memory on subsequent encounters than grounds: in other words, they have resonance. These insights correspond with the intuitive sketches of Magritte as outlined above.

In the Shakespeare sonnet, the addressee 'thee' figure is sustained as the primary focus of attention in the second line ('Thou art more lovely and more temperate') by being placed initially in topic position, where it also governs the voluminous pair 'more lovely' and 'more temperate'. The 'summer's day' at this point is relatively backgrounded, implicit as the second part of the *more / less* comparison. The next six lines ('Rough winds . . . course untrimmed') shift attention to different aspects of the 'summer's day', with the addressee 'thee' temporarily neglected by non-mention: this is a gradual occlusion. The attractor feature of comparable volume in terms of physical size and length, brightness and heat is prominent in these lines: 'all too short a date' (here volume as an analogue of time), 'too hot', 'shines' / 'dimmed', 'declines', 'changing course', 'untrimmed'. The binary comparisons between the current figure 'summer' and the backgrounded blob 'thee' are obvious throughout these phrases, but volume as an attractor feature is also deployed less obviously in the acquisitional verb 'hath', in the conventional dead meta-phor that volumises time 'sometime' and 'sometimes', and even through the additive concept central to the three line-initial occurrences of 'And'. The final word of these six lines that focus on 'summer's day' – 'untrimmed' – contains the figural relationship in itself as a complex, self-referential lacuna (a negative blob).

These six lines represent an attentional zoom into the 'summer's day'. The succession of aspects for attention are attractive because of volume, as out-lined above, but this is reinforced by a simultaneous and rich attraction real-ised in parallel terms too. Firstly, empathetic familiarity is deployed through a series of personifications: rather conventionally, the winds are described with a human trait 'rough' and are given an agency that can be read as wilful 'do shake'; less conventionally, the buds are humanised as 'darling' (the seasons are polarised here into a *winter / summer* binary, with summer from mid-May to the end of August, according to popular Renaissance perception rather than astronomical accuracy); there is an implicit personification of summer as the holder of a 'lease', and an even more implicit and grounded personified Time or Nature as landlord; the metaphor 'eye of heaven' for the sun involves an embedded personification of a face, which is what makes 'his gold complexion' a sustaining attractor; and 'chance' or 'nature' are personified as being on a journey and being capable of undoing the trim of summer's natural order. Secondly, action and agency are placed in parallel with the dimensions of volume and empathy: the verbs of summer all occur at the ends of lines ('shines', 'dimmed', 'declines', 'untrimmed') where they are placed in such a way that the subject position appears as a complex phrase. Adjuncts that would normally occur later or would follow the verb ('too hot', 'often is', 'from fair', 'by chance or nature's changing course') are brought forward to precede the verb and sit within the subject phrase. This complexity (also a matter of the physical volume of words on the page) further zooms attention to the different aspects of the summer's day. Lastly, again, there is an evident parallelism in the dimensions of brightness and heat, which are raised up and down to create a rich texture: 'hot . . . shines', 'gold . . . dimmed', 'fair from fair . . . declines'.

All of these different types of attractor are lined up in parallel while the summer's day is prominent. By contrast with the repetition of 'And', the next line starts with 'But' to signal the shift of attention as a distraction revivifying the addressee: 'But thy eternal summer shall not fade'. The distraction to 'thy' involves the relatively disengaged neglect (backgrounding) of the summer's day, but there is attentional drag apparent here. This line is cognitively complex in its attentional dynamics. The word 'summer' is repeated here, but attention has shifted to 'thy' and this is not a non-shift repetition that would keep the summer's day in focus: in fact, it is a transference of a different sort of summer attributed to the addressee – an 'eternal' one to contrast with the 'changing course' of the shining and dimming summer of the previous six lines. The summer remains in secondary focus as richly resonant background.

The addressee is maintained across the next four lines ('But thy . . . thou grow'st') by non-shift devices such as the continuous syntax linked not by 'And' but by 'Nor' and 'When', and by a sustained pronominal reference ('thy' or 'thou' in every line). The addressee is thus attentionally figured as consistent and continuous, by contrast with the recent memory of the variable and fluctuating summer. However, the stability of the 'thou' figure is simultaneously undermined by the profusion of negative expressions around this point in the sonnet. Though the focus remains on the 'thou' and the negational verbs and particles belong to this addressee figure, the shift from summer to 'thou' is a shift from a positive blob to a negative lacuna. The apparent object of the sonnet – who was focused positively in the first two lines – is by the end being disengaged from. At the same time, other disengagement features are piling up to diminish further the intensity of attention on the 'thou'. It is 'thy eternal summer' not 'thou' which is the subject of the verb 'fade'. Mentioning fading, even while negating it, creates a figural lacuna where 'thou' is faded from attention to a greater degree than if such a verb had not been used at all. The mention of 'lose possession', even though preceded by 'Nor', has exactly the same effect. There is a strong personification attractor in 'Death', who is not only named and pronominalised but also speaks. Lastly, there is an aspect shift that distracts attention from the supposed addressee. Through almost all of the poem, the present tense has been used ('art', 'hath', 'shines', 'declines'), and is even cleverly arranged where it would have been syntactically easier to use a different tense or aspect ('do shake', 'is dimmed'). With the shift of attention to 'thou', however, the aspectual 'shall' is used. By this stage in the poem, the reader might recall the 'Shall' of the first line: there, it creates a question to which the sonnet is the enacted answer. In the later lines, though, 'shall' is used as an assertion that directs attention to the eternal future. All of these parallel dimensions serve to empty the apparent addressee of density, forcing the reader to notice only its defining edges, and thereby maintaining the resonance of the richer summer now in the textual past. The effect is so strong, I think, that even when 'thou' is made the active subject of a volume verb ('thou grow'st'), attention is attracted rather to the 'eternal lines' that are placed prominently earlier in this line, and of course the growing is encompassed 'in' those lines.

The stage is set with a decaying but richly resonant summer and an addressee that is also fading in intensity, and then the final couplet delivers the final attraction. The last focus is on the sonnet itself, and the proximal deictic 'this' is a very powerful attractor for its closeness, newness, currency and by the fact that the referent is an object physically in the reader's hands or the listener's ears. Physical presence is reinforced by 'breathe' and 'eyes [that] can see'; a strong empathy feature is asserted by the concrete 'men', and volume as length is again deployed ('So long') and maintained by repetition. The agency of the final clause, with 'this' sonnet in active subject position and 'thee' in recipient position, sums up the relative attentional status of the foregrounded text and the now secondary addressee. The richly textured summer, and life by extension, and the object of love are both encompassed by an even richer and intense sense of the force and immutability of writing.

The nature of attentional neglect has been prominent in this discussion. Clearly there are several key aspects to the workings of graded backgrounds when new or revivified attractors displace previously focused elements. No previously focused element instantly disappears from consciousness in a reading: even outright predicate removal (such as 'The king died' or 'The shape disappeared') leaves a negative lacuna where a positive blob was perceived, and the trace of its recent existence persists in the memory. Similarly, defeasing or negational expressions only occlude previous figures to a certain degree. We can arrange the three examples 'The ghost never existed', and 'The ghost faded from view' and a text in which a ghost ceases to be mentioned along a cline from instant occlusion to gradual occlusion (see Figure 2a above), but 'instant' occlusion is a relative rather than absolute term: the resonance has a decay that is damped down in different ways. Different forms of negation are clearly important here, including predicate negation (*not* + *verb*), qualitatively negative predicates ('died', 'disappeared', 'untrimmed'), negative particles ('nor', 'never'), negative conjunctions ('but', 'or', 'except'), negatively-oriented lexis ('poor', 'sad'), negative prefixes ('unloved', 'disjointed'), and negative exclamations ('no'). In short texts, such as fourteen-line sonnets, most occlusion is towards the instant end of the scale, since there is not enough textual space simply to allow a previous figure to fade away by a form of gradual occlusion such as non-mention.

Resisting occlusion

Several other of Shakespeare's sonnets feature even more negative expressions than are included in Sonnet 18 above. Perhaps the most popular of all is the following.

Sonnet 116

Let me not to the marriage of true minds
Admit impediments; love is not love
Which alters when it alteration finds,
Or bends with the remover to remove:
O no, it is an ever-fixèd mark,
That looks on tempests and is never shaken;
It is the star to every wand'ring bark,
Whose worth's unknown, although his height be taken.
Love's not Time's fool, though rosy lips and cheeks
Within his bending sickle's compass come;
Love alters not with his brief hours and weeks,
But bears it out even to the edge of doom.
   If this be error and upon me proved,
    I never writ, nor no man ever loved.

William Shakespeare (published 1609)

Here, unlike Sonnet 18, the focus of attention is maintained almost consistently on *love* from the second line to the end. This is surprising given the huge amount and different types of negation in the text, which you might think would successfully distract attention away from the first attractor. Each of the following could potentially disengage the reader from a focus on *love* and occlude this figure with another attractor.

predicate negation	Let me not admit love is not love is never shaken Love's not Time's fool Love alters not I never writ
qualitatively negative predicates	alters bends remove shaken bears
negative particles	not x 4 never x 2 nor no
negative conjunctions	or although though
negatively oriented lexis	impediments alteration remover tempests wand'ring fool bending brief edge of doom error
negative prefixes	remover remove unknown
negative exclamation	O no

The reason why *love* retains its intensity throughout is because of the maintenance features that sustain it and resist the threat from all these negatives to shift attention onto anything else. The concept of *love* persists and in fact increases in intensity as a consequence of coming under repeated threat and yet being sustained. In spite of the mind-warping logical twists of the final couplet, this sonnet remains enormously popular and is a staple reading at wedding ceremonies (of course reinforced by the phrase 'marriage of true minds').

The poem creates a strong attractor, firstly by negatively defining its edges: the impediments (distracting impurities) that are not admitted beyond the boundaries of the marriage (gestalt unity) of true (closely aligned as well as honest) minds. This negative lacuna is then named and rendered attentionally positive: 'love is . . .'. *Love* maintains focus by pronominal co-reference, elision and lexical repetition: 'it alteration finds', '[it] bends', 'it is a mark', 'it is a star', 'Love [i]s not Time's fool', 'Love alters not', '[love] bears it', spread across the middle of the poem. Even in the adjuncts and sub-clauses where love is metaphorically replaced by a counterpart element (an ever-fixèd mark, the star to every wand'ring bark, Time's fool), the brief digression into the metaphorical domain merely reaffirms the focus of attention on *love*, since the counterpart identification is strong and only intervenes for a line or so.

Another major threat of neglect lies in the activeness of potentially distracting elements. The verbs directly associated with *love* are relational or static in nature: 'love is not love', 'it is an ever-fixèd mark', 'It is the star', 'Love's not Time's fool', 'Love alters not'. However, the verbs associated with potentially threatening occluding elements are much more active and material: 'Let me Admit' (meaning both *allow in* and *confess*), '[non-love] alters', [non-love] finds', '[non-love] bends . . . to remove', '[the] mark . . . looks on tempests . . . is never shaken', 'every bark's [boat's] height be taken [measured to ascertain its value in the water]', 'rosy lips and cheeks . . . come within the compass of the sickle'. The most active words are associated with other elements – 'alteration', 'remove', 'tempests', 'shaken', 'wand'ring' – and yet *love* still sustains its focus of attention. This is achieved mainly syntactically. The relational and existential verbs with 'love' as subject tend to be in main clause position. All of the active verbs and potentially occluding figures are relegated to subordinate clauses. So finding alteration is subordinated to 'Which', and bending is placed in parallel at that same subordinate level by 'Or', with 'to remove' as a further subordination later on. Again, looking on tempests is subordinate to 'That', with being shaken co-ordinated with 'and' at the same level. Taking the height of the boat is two levels down as a result of 'Whose' and 'although'. Coming within the range of the sickle is subordinate to 'though', and bearing out time is subordinated with 'But'. These potential distractions fail because as subordinations they remain grounded relative to the figural *love*, and *love* increases in apparent power and intensity as a consequence of resisting occlusion. Furthermore, each metaphorical challenge only attacks for a line or two before the poem switches to another different metaphor, or another aspect of the same nautical metaphor (with even the sickle's 'reach' metaphorised as 'compass'). Metaphor itself can be regarded as a form of negation of the literal, and so the comments above about the sustaining power of negation-resistance might apply in this respect too.

Sonnet 116 has sentences that run across line boundaries, since the subordinate patterning I describe could not fit into one line each. This necessary consequence of the cognitive mechanism contributes to the feeling many readers have of the poem that it runs forward seamlessly with a sense of balance and even-handed reason. This last impression is of course affirmed by the explicit logical reasoning in the final couplet: 'If this be error and upon me proved, I never writ, nor no man ever loved'. However, where 'this' in the final line of Sonnet 18 is most likely to refer to the writing itself, 'this' in Sonnet 116 is more ambiguous. It could refer in general to the whole preceding argument about the affirmation of love (1); it could refer only to the immediately prior point about love outlasting time (2); it could refer alternatively to the strong figural attractor of love itself in general (3); or it could refer restrictively to the initial permissible action, 'Let me not admit impediments' (4). All of these are within the cognitive poetic constraints of the poem.

Of course, there are further permutations to consider. The ambiguous 'this' is embedded between a conditional 'If' and a subjunctive 'be', in a non-literal domain where it could be an 'error'. I suggest that this is too complex a logical relationship for most readers to resolve without a great deal of extended thought. Just in case anyone reaches for an understanding, the speculation is complicated by a further condition, 'and upon me proved'. Even if this line is regarded clearly by a particularly perspicacious reader, the complete couplet is very complex: *if x and y, then* 'I never writ, nor no man ever loved'. The first phrase here, 'I never writ', is oddly intransitive: you would expect a direct object such as 'it' or 'the sonnet' or 'anything'. It feels logically incomplete, even though it is strictly grammatically well-formed. The final phrase, 'nor no man ever loved', combines bewildering negations such that 'never' and 'ever' are rendered the same by different sequential means.

There are, then, many consequences of matching the figure to which 'this' refers and the logical positioning of the final couplet.

(1)   Where 'this' refers to the whole love-affirming argument in the text, then the final line means something like: if my argument is wrong, then I did not write, but since you the reader have the evidence of my writing in your hand, then my argument must be right, and furthermore since you know that people have loved, my argument is also confirmed. This is a reading which regards the poem as a rhetorical defence of love's constancy.

(2)   Where 'this' refers only to the last point about love outlasting time, then the final line means: if love cannot outlast time, then I will never again write and it is not worth anyone being in love again. This is a reading of abject surrender and disillusionment.

(3)   Where 'this' refers to love itself in general, then the final line reads as something like: if love is not as constant and eternal as I say it is,

then I might as well never have written about it. This is a reading of resigned sarcasm.

(4) Where 'this' points back to the initial permit, then the ending means something like: if I admit impediments, then everything is worthless. This reading carries the consequential but implicit moral that impurities and impediments to truth and love should not be contemplated, lest they become self-fulfilling.

These readings are allowable and consistent with my analysis above. However, reading (4) is only found in academic contexts. Readings (2) and (3) tend only to be found in flippant commentaries in online contexts. Reading (1) is by far the most widely held, even though it contains errors of logical connection: there is no reason why the possibility that the argument is wrong should be conditional on having written anything. This is a mere unmotivated assertion. The rhetorical defence of love's constancy is based on a false premise in the final couplet, but this fact is irrelevant to most readers. There are two reasons for this. Firstly, the logical argument is so convoluted by the deictic ambiguity of 'this' and by the negations that most readers simply read the poem as the affirmation that they would like it to be – in other words, they allow the rhetoric to persuade them because accepting it is easier than resisting it by engaging with the logic. Secondly, and connected to this, of course, is the fact that this strategy is exactly the pattern that the poem has set up. The figural attractor, *love*, resists attacks from logical negations, reasonable metaphorical comparisons and analogies, and any attempts to shift it. The most popular, optimistic and love-affirming reading is the most consistent with the most natural patterning of attention. This is why the poem has such intense resonance for so many people. And in this most popular reading, the rhetorical and aesthetic texture over-rides the logical form.

Moving edges

Understanding the cognitive mechanics of figural edges is crucial for my account of attentional engagement and disengagement within a literary reading. In visual cognition, as outlined above, edges belong to figures and are processed with them; even where an object is minimally defined or defined only by *not* being something else (as a lacuna), it is the edges and edge-processing that is crucial. As an object moves across the visual field, its advancing edge occludes the static background: at the visual interface between the two, the latter has no edge, since only figures have edges. At the rear edge of a transiting object, the figural edge allows the redefined background to emerge again. The background does not normally change as it passes behind the figure. In fact, if a differently textured ground appears from an occlusion, it is likely in itself to be distracting and be attentionally regarded as a new figure. It is easy to picture this in the activity of mime-artists who pass a fan across a smiling face to reveal a switched sad face emerging from the other side. The disorientation of a non-static ground is evident when you are looking out through the window while sitting on a train in a station, and you feel your own train carriage moving off as you pass by a parallel train, only for the other train to pass by completely, leaving your eyes looking at the unmoving opposite platform and you realise that it was the other train moving and not yours.

In the list of good textual attractors earlier in this chapter, several aspects are correlates of motion: active verb forms, topical and subjective action, wilful action in a scene, and even fullness, proximity and noisiness are often consequences of the relative motion of the observer and the figure against a ground. Spatial relations are a matter of attentional change, whether zoom or shift between figural objects, because seeing one object in relation to another involves looking first at one *and then* at the other. Since attentional change necessarily involves this sequentiality and thus a time-dimension, even stationary described objects have an apparent attentional motion in the reading process. In other words, reading involves the dynamic apparent or actual motion of figures across a ground. This can be regarded as a psychological basis for the common description of reading as a journey and the perception that texts are dynamic and motive, when in fact it is the reading that gives it this apparent relative motion. Furthermore, in visual perception, figural objects that are in motion are stronger attractors: think of how camouflaged objects like lizards in grass or a person in a crowd of waxwork figurines leap out for attention as soon as they move. Irregular or ill-defined objects (that is, those whose edges are indeterminate because they are irregular, unfamiliar or in the process of alteration) are rendered easier to delineate by their motion across an occluded background (Smith, Johnson and Spelke 2003). Motion also contributes strongly towards depth perception and the richness of a visual field.

These correlations in the literary domain can be illustrated by considering a reading of the following text.

Nantucket

Flowers through the window
lavender and yellow

changed by white curtains –
Smell of cleanliness –

Sunshine of late afternoon –
On the glass tray

a glass pitcher, the tumbler
turned down, by which

a key is lying – And the
immaculate white bed

William Carlos Williams (published 1934)

Most academic readings of this place it in literary history as a modernist or imagist position against the logical syntax of nineteenth-century verse (Hillis Miller 1965; Moore 1986), and almost all readings observe that it is like a verbal still-life painting. Readers comment that it captures exactly the feeling of being on Nantucket island in the north Atlantic on a summer's day. In spite of the phrase 'still-life', which recurs often in readers' comments, and which clearly results from the lack of any main verb, there is a strong sense that the poem is not in fact 'still' but 'moves'. Readers speak of being 'drawn in' by the poem: one of my own student readers described it as 'cinematic', likening the apparent movement of the poem to a zooming or tracking camera shot starting outside and moving slowly through the open window to focus closely at last on the key and the bed.

In 'Nantucket', the strong visual resonance of the poem is generated by the emphasis on very precise figure-ground elements (named by noun phrases) and the precise relations between them. These spatial relationships are established not by verbs but by the deictic positioning of prepositions: 'through', 'by', 'on', 'down', and 'by which'. The first attractor of the poem – 'flowers' – is positioned 'through the window'. In image-schematic terms, 'through' carries a basic semantic profiling of the later point in a trajectory of a figure moving towards and *through* a landmark: there is an inherent motive element in this preposition (see the next section and Chapter 6 for a more detailed explication and application of the notion of action chains and image-schemas). Readers can read this first line either as their own viewpoint moving in through the window, or as the flowers moving virtually towards them. The effect in both cases is that the flowers appear to increase in size as attention zooms in on them, framed by the grounding window. This framing effect at the beginning of the poem, of course, is also likely to be an early cue for an analogy with painting. The emphasis on the core essence of the flowers is carried by the fact that the attributes of 'lavender and yellow', which you might ordinarily expect as distracting pre-modifiers ('the lavender and yellow flowers'), have been moved back syntactically into a post-modification, and even interrupted by the grounding 'through the window'. Since these two modifiers clearly attach to the flowers, rather than the window, the strong figural attractor is sustained across these two lines.

The poem continues by introducing potentially distracting elements, which however turn out instead to be part of a sustained focus on the existing attractor of the flowers. The effect is of an increased intensity of attention. For example, the verb participle 'changed' is potentially a distracting device, especially followed with 'by', suggesting that this is about to be a passive human agent taking readerly attention from the flowers. However, instead of a person we get 'white curtains', and the post-modificatory direction of 'lavender and yellow' has already cued us up to read 'changed by white curtains' as a further post-modification of the flowers. So intensely are the flowers being focused that hardly any readers with whom I have discussed this poem read 'Smell' in the next line as a main verb with 'flowers' as the subject, though of course this is allowable in the syntax and the apt semantic colligation of 'flowers smell'. Instead – and assisted by the capitalisation of 'Smell' – this line tends to be read as a further parallel noun-phrase, and so is the following line, 'Sunshine of late afternoon'. These two attractors take the reader's attention, for these syntactic reasons as well as their position as capitalised line-initial /s/-alliterations; they also have fullness and brightness. However, I would argue that, although they occlude the flowers to a certain extent, they are an example of attentional drag (see Figure 2a earlier in this chapter), by which the resonance of the flowers persists and resists decay. This is because of the semantic sustainability for the flowers provided by 'smell' and 'sunshine'. I would argue, therefore, that the poem falls into an exact first half up to this line, where the strong figural attractor of the flowers is first sustained and then not neglected by occlusion but by an intensifying attentional zoom; the effect of this is to drag out the echo of the flowers and keep their essence in resonant memory.

The rest of the poem effects a further closing-in zoom of attention. The lines following 'On the glass tray' represent the neglect of the flowers by attentional lift, replacing this original figure by a carefully outlined edge (a lacuna) in 'On the glass tray'. Of course, the transparency of this negative attractor is semantically and iconically echoed by the 'glass', repeated too in the occluding attractor of the 'glass pitcher' of the next line. Indeed, the indefinite article ('a glass pitcher') here further establishes the transparency of negativity. (Perhaps the phonetic similarities of 'pitcher' and 'picture' here also suggest an analogy of the poem as a painting, for any reader who notices this.) Phrase by phrase the new attractor becomes more substantial, from its outlined edge ('On the glass tray') to its solid but transparent infill ('a glass pitcher'), to a definite positive figural object ('the tumbler'). However, even this last figural attractor is syntactically presented appositionally as an attribute of 'a glass pitcher'; it is itself semantically downward within the morphology of 'tumbler', and it is further associated with down-ness, both in the word itself in 'turned down' and in the idiomatic meaning of that complete phrase itself (where 'turned down' means 'rejected'). This closeness of reading can even be phonetically justified by the accompanying alliterative distraction of 'tumbler turned'. The glass tray, pitcher and tumbler inside the room have occluded the initial flowers seen through the window, but are being rendered relatively insubstantial in anticipation of the 'key' figural attractor in the next line. Though the clause 'a key is lying' is syntactically embedded in the verbless noun-phrase preceding it, the key itself is a very strong new figural attractor since it is in new-line initial position, it is a familiar and tangible object, and it appears at least locally to be the only predication in the poem. The key suggests a hotel room, which makes the attentional movement and transience of the poem even more apt. Semantically, of course, 'key' is also suggestive of an answer or solution to the meaning of the poem, and so the figure has emblematic value as well as being the most substantial attractor so far.

In spite of the strength of attraction of 'key', it nevertheless remains the darkest object in the poem, and this last diminution serves to prepare the reader's attention for the final bright, striking definite and most closely human attractor in the whole poem, 'And the immaculate white bed', with its implicit semantic connotations of literal, religious and metaphorical virginity as purity and cleanness. This is a last, powerful distraction, which pushes the previous attractors back into the richly resonant background. This ground remains as a strongly persisting echo, however, partly as a result of the new attractor being introduced by 'And', which stands here as a device for only the partial disengagement of the previous set of elements in the poem. The sense of motion, brilliantly enacted by mostly verbless phrases, is entirely a consequence of attentional drag and zoom, and the persisting effect of the poem by the end is of a rich depth of field, with an intensity of focus and a resonance of texture remaining.

Alertness, intensity and disposition

I have been discussing the readerly effects of textual organisation so far as if writers and texts simply had to manipulate readers for exactly the desired effects to fall out. Of course, reading is more active and engaged than this, and whether particular readers align with my sketches above or not will depend not only on the accuracy of my account but mainly on the degree of disposition of those readers. There is a complex mutual feedback loop at the centre of the notion of texture between textual organisation and readerliness, which I have been trying to account for in this chapter. A traditional stylistic analysis can point, with evidence, to features that are undeniably present in a text, but the level of alertness in a reader during a reading determines whether those features make it to the level of effectiveness. Clearly a text can play its role in the prominence of certain features: shocking, jarring, deviant or just unusual textual choices can jolt a reader into attentiveness. But more subtle features can easily be overlooked by a less attentive reader.

It is important at this stage to note that I am not edging towards a claim that inattentive readings are defective, judged against any sort of objective stylistic analysis. All readings are readings, whether minutely attended and sensitive, or skimmed or untrained, or first readings compared with second or group readings, and so on. To a certain extent, the process of systematic stylistic analysis involves altering readings by bringing certain features *that are available in the text* to awareness; the addition of a cognitive turn to the stylistic account entails a responsibility for recognising that reading itself is variable and textured too.

Literary alertness in a reader can be affected by a wide range of factors: motivation for reading or study, tiredness and diet, training and practice, attachment and familiarity with the genre in hand, pressures of time or leisure, and so on. The specificities of these can clearly have a significant effect on the evaluation and experience of reading a literary text. For the most part, though, these specificities are not of interest to the general theoretical account of literary reading, unless they become a theme in group discussions or the socialisation of reading. The use of Shakespeare's 'marriage of true minds' sonnet 116 above as a popular reading at wedding services is an example of the appropriation of the text for a specific local purpose. Similar real, local textures might include reading 'Nantucket' while on holiday on Nantucket; or the full quotation of Yeats' 'When you are old and grey' by Kathleen Turner in the film *Peggy Sue Got Married* (Coppola 1986) with the dramatic irony that the character she plays has time-travelled back to high school in 1960; or the effect when Shakespeare's 'summer's day' sonnet 18 is read by Taiwanese students with a very different experiential schema for a summer's day (see Yang 2005), and so on. These effects are real, and should not be discounted as a personal part of literary criticism, but they represent the particular end of a cline of experiential effects. Most such effects are too finely grained and beyond the scope of a theoretical account.

Depth of processing

In general, we can say that the sort of intensity of poetic reading outlined in the analysis of 'Nantucket' and the other poems above concerns the depth of processing involved. In Todd Oakley's (2004) scheme (see Figure 2b), the depth of readerly processing (that is, the intensity) is consequent upon *alertness, orientation* and a *sharing of attention*. These governing factors usefully blend the dimensions of subjectivity (reader), object (text) and interpersonal socialisation in a model of attention, which I can easily adapt specifically for the literary experience as follows. For example, a reader's *alertness* is a crucial matter of disposition and readiness. A reluctant, bored, unmotivated or disinterested reader is likely to engage with a literary text only shallowly. Such a reader will miss most of the subtleties in the text, and any aesthetic pleasure is likely to be missed or minimal. Most tutors of seminars in literary studies have observed students who have skim-read a text purely for the motivational purpose of the seminar, and the readings such students bring to the seminar are usually characterised by information-content rather than anything more subtle in terms of tone, atmosphere or resonance.

Orienting refers to the reader's desire to select certain elements in the literary array rather than others. Orientation is a good term as it captures the

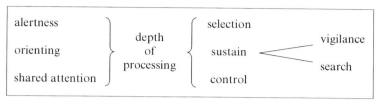

Figure 2b A schematisation of intensity, adapted from Oakley (2004: ch.1)

sense that objects in a literary landscape (fictional people and places, typically) are focused upon on the basis that they both determine and are determined by readerly identity at that moment. So I might have a disposition to read Thomas Hardy's *The Return of the Native*, for example, attracted to it by friends' recommendation, by its status as a great novel in the literary canon, by the current fashion for televisual and cinematic dramatisation of Hardy, and by other more personal factors too. I might be reading it on holiday where I have time to savour the text, rather than reading it fast. These dispositions make me alert to a high degree. Out of the landscape of the opening few pages of the novel, I can orient myself with the English moorland setting ('Egdon Heath'), and with the main characters, Clym Yeobright, Eustacia Vye, Damon Wildeve, and others. These orientations are partly acts of identity, drawing on landscapes and characteristics that interest me, and they are also part of the process of identifying a particular readerly disposition that seems most suitable for the reading in hand. As a certain sort of reader, I am disposed to take up the novel and read it in a certain way; when reading a certain sort of novel, with textual patterns that encourage a certain orientation, I develop a reading personality that can read the text. Identification from orientation is thus both a validating and productive process. (There is more on identification in Chapter 5.)

Thirdly, the intensity and configuration of reading (the depth of processing) are implicated too in a recognition of *shared attention*. Reading can be literally shared, in the form of conversation, discussion, written literary criticism, and so on. But more fundamentally the expectation of social interaction influences the devotion of mental resources to attention: there is a prior 'censoring' of interpretation which excludes configurations that might be thought to be absurd. For example, there are many minor characters in the rest of Hardy's novel that seem two-dimensional, merely part of the background environment. Their names (which I had to look up rather than having readily in my memory) include Humphrey the furze-cutter, Sam, the Cantles, or simply 'the young men', 'fair ones with long curls', 'one happy man', 'elderly dames' (Hardy 1878: IV.iii), and so on. Focusing on these is possible with a great act of attentive will, but neither the textual organisation nor (I would argue) most readerly disposition would permit much development along these lines. The minor characters are literally and metaphorically part of the landscape. Of course, it is possible as the reading progresses to take a reflexive view of this attentional configuration in order to perceive the relative naturalness of these characters compared with the non-natural activities of the main characters – and a moral cline of consequences can emerge from such a reading. Crudely, Damon and Eustacia, identified with artifice, travel and the trappings of civilisation, are destroyed by their non-natural aspirations; the minor characters, steeped in tradition and at ease in the landscape, survive unscathed; Clym, the 'native' who 'returns', merely suffers blindness and loss for his earlier life, but adapts to his native land-scape and survives.

Together, the threefold effects of disposition determine the intensity of the reading experience. It is important to emphasise again that disposition, regarded as a product of alertness, orientation and shared attention, is a blended phenomenon of readerliness, textuality and social situation: these are inextricably compounded and mutually influential in actual life, though they can be analytically separated in this way for convenience. In turn, drawing further on Oakley's framework, the intensity of reading entails different strengths for *selection, sustainability* and *control* of attention during the reading itself. The selection of features for attention in a literary work is partly due to readerly disposition and partly due to the strength of good textual attractors as outlined earlier in this chapter. At any moment in a reading, attention is *clamped* to a particular feature (Oakley 2004, drawing on Glenberg 1997), and this *sustained* fixity of attention represents the mainte-nance of the attractor (refer back to Figure 2a above); it also implicitly entails the resistance to distracting features. Resistance to distraction, again, is partly a matter of readerly disposition and partly a matter of the weakness of potential textual attractors. Those distractions which are resisted by a con-tinuing sustained focus on the existing feature can be regarded as failed attractors.

Sustained vigilance

Oakley (2004: ch.1) describes selection for attention as a 'bottom-up' process driven by local (textual) features, while sustaining attention is more of a 'top-down' process informed by more general and global concerns.

> While selection and sustained attention can function as mutually rein-forcing processes, they can also oppose one another, most notably in rich sensory environments where the alerting and orienting mechanisms are prone to respond to any sensory cue from above and below, front and back, and to the left and to the right. In this respect, it is perhaps best to think of selection and sustain as opposing processes that ensure attentional balance. That is, a high rate of stimulus presentation induces iterations of selective attention, thence decreasing sustained attention.

A sudden sound of an explosion will force me to reckon a different attentional budget to deal with a possible threat. The stimulus and its aftermath may be so intense or consequential as to supplant my original plan and becomes the new focus of attention.

(Oakley 2004: ch.1)

The quick succession of attractors in 'Nantucket' above represents an example in which succeeding selectivity shifts attention from one element to another, without any single element sustaining attention for very long. By contrast, a longer piece of lyrical prose fiction might retain focus on a particular feature, weighing sustained attention over the distraction of selectivity. The opening of Hardy's (1878) *The Return of the Native* has often been regarded (in spite of the early date of writing) as cinematic in its sweeping point of view, but it is specifically more like a long tracking and slow zooming shot rather than a fast edit.

1 A Face on Which Time Makes but Little Impression

A Saturday afternoon in November was approaching the time of twilight, and the vast tract of unenclosed wild known as Egdon Heath embrowned itself moment by moment. Overhead the hollow stretch of whitish cloud shutting out the sky was as a tent which had the whole heath for its floor.

The heaven being spread with this pallid screen and the earth with the darkest vegetation, their meeting-line at the horizon was clearly marked. In such contrast the heath wore the appearance of an instalment of night which had taken up its place before its astronomical hour was come: darkness had to a great extent arrived hereon, while day stood distinct in the sky. Looking upwards, a furze-cutter would have been inclined to continue work; looking down, he would have decided to finish his faggot and go home. The distant rims of the world and of the firmament seemed to be a division in time no less than a division in matter. The face of the heath by its mere complexion added half an hour to evening; it could in like manner retard the dawn, sadden noon, anticipate the frowning of storms scarcely generated, and intensify the opacity of a moonless midnight to a cause of shaking and dread.

In fact, precisely at this transitional point of its nightly roll into darkness the great and particular glory of the Egdon waste began, and nobody could be said to understand the heath who had not been there at such a time. It could best be felt when it could not clearly be seen, its complete effect and explanation lying in this and the succeeding hours before the next dawn; then, and only then, did it tell its true tale. The spot was, indeed, a near relation of night, and when night showed itself an apparent tendency to gravitate together could be perceived in its shades and the scene. The sombre stretch of rounds and hollows seemed to rise and meet the evening gloom in pure sympathy, the heath exhaling darkness as rapidly as the heavens precipitated it. And so the obscurity in the air and the obscurity in the land closed together in a black fraternization towards which each advanced halfway.

The place became full of a watchful intentness now; for when other things sank brooding to sleep the heath appeared slowly to awake and listen. Every night its Titanic form seemed to await something; but it had waited thus, unmoved, during so many centuries, through the crises of so many things, that it could only be imagined to await one last crisis – the final overthrow.

It was a spot which returned upon the memory of those who loved it with an aspect of peculiar and kindly congruity. Smiling champaigns of flowers and fruit hardly do this, for they are permanently harmonious only with an existence of better reputation as to its issues than the present. Twilight combined with the scenery of Egdon Heath to evolve a thing majestic without severity, impressive without showiness, emphatic in its admonitions, grand in its simplicity. The qualifications which frequently invest the facade of a prison with far more dignity than is found in the facade of a palace double its size lent to this heath a sublimity in which spots renowned for beauty of the accepted kind are utterly wanting. Fair prospects wed happily with fair times; but alas, if times be not fair! Men have oftener suffered from the mockery of a place too smiling for their reason than from the oppression of surroundings oversadly tinged. Haggard Egdon appealed to a subtler and scarcer instinct, to a more recently learnt emotion, than that which responds to the sort of beauty called charming and fair.

[. . .]

The most thoroughgoing ascetic could feel that he had a natural right to wander on Egdon – he was keeping within the line of legitimate indulgence when he laid himself open to influences such as these. Colours and beauties so far subdued were, at least, the birthright of all. Only in summer days of highest feather did its mood touch the level of gaiety. Intensity was more usually reached by way of the solemn than by way of the brilliant, and such a sort of intensity was often arrived at during winter darkness, tempests, and mists. Then Egdon was aroused to reciprocity; for the storm was its lover, and the wind its friend. Then it became the home of strange phantoms; and it was found to be the hitherto unrecognized original of those wild regions of obscurity which are vaguely felt to be compassing us about in midnight dreams of flight and disaster, and are never thought of after the dream till revived by scenes like this.

It was at present a place perfectly accordant with man's nature –
neither ghastly, hateful, nor ugly; neither commonplace, unmeaning,
nor tame; but, like man, slighted and enduring; and withal singularly
colossal and mysterious in its swarthy monotony. As with some persons
who have long lived apart, solitude seemed to look out of its counte-
nance. It had a lonely face, suggesting tragical possibilities.

(Thomas Hardy 1878: I.i)

I have quoted this opening necessarily at length, omitting only a paragraph in
which Hardy demonstrates his (self-taught) classical learning with some comparisons of ancient and modern European landscape, and the four paragraphs to the end of the opening chapter. Many readers in discussion report
being able to recall this opening, not in specific detail but in the lasting
impression of tone and the forceful impact of this setting for the novel that
follows.

A reader coming to the novel initially is likely to be at a heightened state of
awareness, and openings of long prose texts are likely to be read with an initially enthusiastic concentration of intensity. It would not be thought
unusual, I think, for a reader to expect a long, nineteenth-century novel to
begin with a description of the setting for the fictional world; however, the
opening to this novel dwells on the scene at some length. It also confounds
expectations and cognitive defaults in several other ways, in the form of
various cognitive disjunctions, and it seems to me that it is because of the
textural quality of this effect that the impact of the passage is significant.

The pathetic fallacy – the perceived human significance of natural scenes
and events – common in nineteenth-century novels is transformed in Hardy
to an ideological commitment. The readerly sense that Egdon Heath is a
character and that, by extension, nature is wilful and forceful is set up very
plainly in the opening to the novel. The landscape is clearly an extremely
strong attractor, presented in the chapter title and very first sentence. The
(conceptual) ground is laid out first with a specific indefinite ('A Saturday
afternoon in November') and a small sense of motion ('was approaching the
time of twilight'). This proves to be a weak attractor as it is almost immediately rendered into the background by the emphatic, definite, large, active,
named and fully pre- and post-modified figure of 'the vast tract of unenclosed
wild known as Egdon Heath' – an attractor which even reflexively controls its
own actions ('embrowned itself'), and includes an anomalous unusual verb
('embrowned') used only in poetic diction by Milton, Pope and others following. Thereafter, the attractor of the landscape is maintained principally by
sustained topicality: synonym variants of the scene occupy the subject position in almost every sentence of the first five paragraphs. These synonym
variants include 'Egdon Heath', 'the whole heath', 'the distant rims of the
world and of the firmament', 'the great and particular glory of the Egdon
waste', 'the spot', 'the sombre stretch of rounds and hollows', 'the place',

'Haggard Egdon', and so on. This elegant stylistic variation in itself serves as a maintenance device, working against the natural inhibition of return whereby attention is lost to an unchanging feature. The effect is the solid persistence of the landscape in the attentional field, while richly different aspects are laid out.

The anthropomorphisation of the landscape is strongly asserted in the attachment to the heath of lexical choices such as 'a face', 'wore', 'the face of the heath', 'tell its true tale', 'a near relation', 'sombre', 'pure sympathy', 'the heath exhaling', 'a black fraternization', 'watchful intentness', 'awake and listen', 'to await', 'waited', 'unmoved', and the entire final paragraph of the passage quoted above. There are also a great number of abstract lexical choices associated with the landscape, such as 'darkness', 'obscurity', 'congruity', 'indulgence', 'solemn', and others. On the scale of empathetic recognition (from the list of good attractors earlier in this chapter), the landscape object and its abstract features are being pulled strongly leftwards towards human consciousness, another example of deviation from the cognitive norm, captured in phrases such as 'swarthy monotony' that again seem to go beyond simple personification and into a thematic commitment.

The fullness of the heath attractor gains exponentially as the passage progresses, and it becomes apparent that the entire first chapter is being filled up by the landscape alone. Within each sentence, there is a preponderance of compound syntax, exaggerated even by the norms of Hardy's prose style in the rest of the novel. However – here is another cognitive disjunction from the norm – even though the syntactic complexity and fullness is apparently made up of progressions, in the form of verbs of motion, verbs of transformation, 'when-then' and other temporal shift clauses, and shifts for comparisons and unrealised possibilities, each time the focus is maintained on the heath itself by lexical repetition and the continuing chain of reference. For example, there are very few plain, unmodalised simple verbs. Instead, we have forms of varying complexity, embeddedness and distancing such as 'was marked', 'would have been inclined', 'could be said to understand', 'appeared slowly to awake and listen', 'combined . . . to evolve', 'it was found to be', 'solitude seemed to look out', and so on. Simple verbs tend to be transformative 'become' or 'reached', and there is a great deal of reflexivity, either in the verb meaning ('returned upon', 'retard the dawn', 'that which responds', 'to reciprocity') or in reflexive particles ('embrowned itself', 'closed together', 'towards which each advanced', 'laid himself'). Even apparently simple assertions, marked strongly by 'in fact' or 'indeed', turn out to be particularly poetically subjective ('in fact, precisely at this transitional point of its nightly roll into darkness the great and particular glory of the Egdon waste began') or metaphorical ('the spot was, indeed, a near relation of night'). So local apparent movement and variability appears merely as surface turmoil that does not distract the focus from the landscape. Indeed, the landscape only becomes richer in the process.

The richness of the landscape increases with the intensity of readerly attention: the harder you look, the more you see. Reflexivity is maintained in
syntactic and lexical balances throughout the text: 'looking upwards . . .,
looking down', 'the world and the firmament', 'division in time . . . division in
matter', 'dawn . . . noon . . . midnight', 'shaking and dread', 'obscurity in the
air and the obscurity in the land', 'awake and listen', and several in the final
paragraph. Many of these phrases appear in pairs, often alliterative and
repetitive: 'moment by moment', 'finish his faggot', 'moonless midnight',
'great . . . glory of. . . Egdon', 'effect and explanation', 'did it tell its true tale',
'sombre stretch . . . rounds and hollows . . . rise and meet', 'smiling champaigns of flowers and fruit'. These small shifts of attention are felt as apparent motion, but the focus throughout is maintained on the landscape, so the
mental picture overall becomes vivified and textured. Even if the reader's
depth of reading is not as intense as this, it is perhaps likely that the poetic
effect of the writing leaves a lasting impression at a more vague and atmospheric level.

Further patterns that are evident to a stylistic analysis but must be scaled
to correspond with the degree of reading intensity include features in the
passage that might be recalled by the reader for later significance in the novel
as a whole. Clearly these are especially noticeable on a second reading of the
novel, but even on a first reading, a highly attentive reader might have their
attention taken by some of the following features. The emphasis on these
throughout this passage (and continuing throughout the novel) can easily
lead to them being thematised as significant resonant patterns in the work as
a whole. For example, there is a clear drawing of attention to the division of
heaven and earth, both as geographical zones and as ideological areas of
contest. Both domains are drawn in the lexis: 'sky', 'cloud', 'heath', 'vegetation', 'astronomical' and 'gravitate' on the modern descriptive side, and with
a more religious or antique tone, 'heaven', 'earth', 'hereon', 'firmament',
'Titanic' and 'the final overthrow'. As mentioned above, there is a clear
theme in the novel that sets tradition and religious faith against a more
agnostic fatalism, and this ground is being set up right in the opening passage.
Hardy takes an ambivalent view, however, on the loss of religious faith and
the modernity of his main characters, captured in the opening in the phrase,
non-committal either way, 'alas, if times be not fair!' Eustacia Vye and
Damon Wildeve are in the end destroyed both by tragic circumstance and
also by their own actions and decisions. The water in which they drown is on
the heath but is an artificial weir-pool controlled by cogs, sluices and winches.
The cause of tragedy – nature or man – is left very much ambivalent in the
novel. In the opening passage, the very strong personification of the landscape is tempered throughout by individually subtle yet cumulatively powerful reminders that what could be a literalization remains in fact an explicit
metaphor: several of the metaphorical terms are introduced with 'seemed',
'appeared' or 'might' rather than 'was', or are cast in simile or comparison

form 'as a tent', 'accordant', 'like man', 'as with some persons', in which the act of comparing is explicit ('congruity', 'combined', 'in like manner', and the repeated formula 'more x than y'). And of course the unremitting repetition of the extended metaphor of landscape as human throughout the entire chapter serves to foreground its metaphoricity too, as extended metaphor is the most visible form of metaphorical mapping (Stockwell 1992, 2000a: 170–2), making it a powerful attraction for attention.

Other precursors that might have a resonance for an intense reading in the context of a typical Hardy novel include the references to 'lover' and 'friend', 'instinct' and 'emotion', 'sublimity' and 'beauty', 'wed' and, of course, least subtly, 'tragical possibilities'. Even the phrase 'instalment of night' might have a resonance for the original readers of the novel, published in twelve serial instalments in *Belgravia* magazine every month throughout 1878. The emphasis on night throughout the opening passage also prefigures the introduction of Eustacia Vye in a chapter entitled 'Queen of Night', and she is constantly presented alongside lexis of night-time and darkness. Light and dark, of course, are a key organising feature of the opening passage. Here again the writing serves to work in tension with the cognitive norm which would have brightness as the strong attractor. The emphasis throughout the passage is on the transition point between light and dark – the text continually draws attention to the edge of the 'normal' figure of sky and light, in order to push attention towards the dark of the heath. The textual organisation thus enacts a non-normal figuration of the dark landscape throughout the passage.

This landscape attractor resists distraction in all the ways I have outlined so far. However, it is also important to look at what those failed distractors are, and it is significant that in many cases here they are people. This is in line with the disruption of the empathetic recognition principle mentioned already: the landscape is more human than the humans who appear marginally in the opening passage. People are marginalised as omitted agents of passivised verbs ('unenclosed', 'be felt', 'be seen', 'could be perceived', 'unmoved') – it is clear that the actions predicated here are human ones, but the explicit agency is removed. On the few occasions where humans are lexicalised and topicalised, they are rendered by role ('the ascetic') and by indefinite article ('a furze-cutter', 'some persons'), or they are made indefinite subjects of a lexical verb denoting the reception of action rather than wilful activity ('Men have suffered from the mockery of a place'). Otherwise, emotions are disembodied into abstractions: 'shaking and dread', 'mockery', and 'oversadly tinged'. Humans are thus anonymous, missing from direct reference and largely sketched only by their predicate, perceptual or emotional traces; presented here as edges (as negative lacunae), they are attached to and defined by the heath ('a furze-cutter') as mechanical cut-outs.

Similarly, the darkness resists all attempts to brighten up the scene. In order to overcome a reader's natural attraction to the light, the passage places reference to the darkness in overwhelmingly prominent and dominant textual positions. Where lightness threatens to distract attention, the dominant and non-normative figure of darkness is quickly re-established: 'whitish cloud' is followed by 'shutting out', 'pallid' and 'darkest'; 'dawn' and 'noon' collocate with 'retard' and 'sadden', and are followed by a 'moonless midnight'; and phrases that might invoke lightness and colour ('smiling champaigns of flowers', 'fair prospects', 'colours and beauties') are rendered dim and distant by being placed inside hypotheticals ('hardly', 'if times be not fair', 'so far subdued'). The passage even begins by invoking enclosure (and does it negatively, in 'unenclosed', which produces a different effect from its alternative apparent synonym 'open'), and places the whole scene that follows from sky to earth inside a closed tent.

Resonant texture

In Oakley's (2004) terms, attention is very much clamped to the landscape and sustained by the textual organisation, resisting what might otherwise be normal cognitive distractions towards people, lightness or a change of scene. Oakley makes a further distinction within sustained attention between *vigilance* and *search*. The former relates to being attentive to details over time while being located in a particular place; the latter relates to being attentive to a shift in scene. Again, the strength of vigilance and search will be dependent on the depth of intensity produced by the reader's disposition, but it is plausible, I think, to suggest that the heavy emphasis on the stability of place in the opening passage leads to an emphasis of attentional focus on specific details within the world in hand – in other words, the passage encourages vigilance and a fine-grained intensity of reading, while the readiness for search (shifting scene or world) is continually deferred. This delay in a change of scene and thus denial of a readerly search is, I argue, what gives the long-lasting resonance of Egdon Heath its persisting character throughout the novel.

The final element in Oakley's framework is a crucial reminder again that readerliness works with textuality. Given all the features that the passage offers in terms of attraction and neglect, readers must find their own configuration of attention by which they organise their view of the passage into sense: this is their *control*. Control is a mechanism for budgeting mental effort. While in general, the greater intensity in the reading, the greater the perceptual resources available, for any reading there must still be a limit to how much significance can be perceived. Significance is a figure/ground feature since not everything can be uniformly significant in an array. How the reader deals with the general thematic meaning of the opening emphasis on the heath is a matter of prioritising certain parts of the attentional landscape and diminishing, ignoring or simply not noticing others. This is how local details of style connect with global outcomes of interpretation.

We are now in a position to redraw in more detail one side of Oakley's framework (from Figure 2b above).

The textual organisation of attractors and the reader's individual and social disposition (off-left of Figure 2c) determine the level of intensity of the reading. Effects of resonance, lasting impression and the establishment of tone and atmosphere are then a direct correlate of the level of intensity. These effects are configured specifically by the selection of features for attention (a matter of particular textual style), the sustenance of attention both within the world at hand and across any world-switches (a matter of textual organisation at a more discourse level also involving readerly decisions), and the control of the field of attention (by a reader with particular preoccupations or expectations). Very roughly, this scheme constitutes an analytical breakdown of the mechanics of attention from local style to global theme in a literary reading.

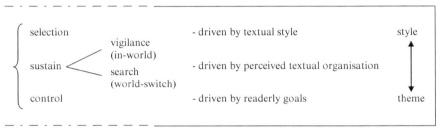

Figure 2c The relationship of style and theme, in attentional terms

This chapter has travelled from the detailed description of the stylistic features of attention to the global assignment of theme. I began by outlining a general model of resonance, based on the cognitive psychology of attention, and spent the first part of the chapter working out the stylistic correlates of attentional features. A guiding typology of what makes a good attractor was produced by combining the psychology of attention, gestalt principles, and cognitive grammar. I described how, in applying this model to a range of texts, literature often exploits the exponential power of attractors being aligned, to create forceful resonant effects in the reader both at the time and after the text is put down. The nature of attentional neglect and occlusion was explored through the resonant notion of a *lacuna* in the reading. Further resonant effects of increased granularity from attentional zooming were discussed.

Resonance seems to correpond with intensity, and together, these assist in the establishment and memory of the tone of a literary text. Though these effects are most observable in dense poetic texts, the same features are apparent in prose fiction too, where the stylistic causes of resonance are more likely to be below the level of consciousness because the intensity of reading is typically not as strong. The global sense of resonance and tone persists as a sense of thematic texture, which has been connected in this chapter to the detailed stylistic patterning established at the beginning.

Reading

The term *resonance* has been used loosely by literary critics from serious scholars to new age impressionists, but never particularly defined: its attraction is its ineffability. For a taste of this range, see Clark and Timmons (2000), Fredericks (2008), Greenblatt (1990), Hollander (1985) and Klenburg (1996).

For the cognitive psychology of attention, see Posner (2004), Purves et al. (2008), Styles (2005, 2006) and Wolfe et al. (2006), and its application to literature and visual art, see Scarry (2001) and Stafford (2007). The work of Sanford and Emmott (Emmott et al. 2006, 2007; Sanford et al. 2006) provides psycholinguistic evidence for the stylistics of attractors.

For further applications of my model, see Stockwell (2002b, 2003, and 2009 on lacunae). The stylistics of foregrounding is addressed in van Peer (1986), van Peer et al. (2007), and Miall (2007), and its relationship to theme in Louwerse and van Peer (2002).

3 Sensation and Empathy

A key principle of embodiment in cognitive linguistics is the notion that there are continuities between physical experiences and higher level conceptual experiences. In the previous chapter, I sketched out the way that visualisation can be seen as the base on which conceptual texture and attention are extended. Though the human capacity for projection from physical to abstract is clearly involved here, cognitive linguists generally claim that the relationship between bodily feeling and abstract thought is real, systematic, socially shared, and explainable in evolutionary terms: in other words, it is more than simply a metaphor or an arbitrary explanation. This chapter begins with an even closer connection between physical feeling and literary experience, captured in the term *sensation*. Some experiences of literary reading can feature actual physical responses, such as laughter, chuckling, smiling, smirking, or shivering, hairs-prickling, catching of breath, or heart-racing and quickness of breathing, or bodily shying away, moving the book to arm's length, arousal, a lump in the throat, or crying, and so on. These are all clear physical manifestations of emotions and feelings that are immediate and direct. Texture, in this chapter, is treated as the point at which physical and conceptual sensations become identical.

Later in the chapter, I connect sensation to readerly empathy and sympathy. Where sensation in literary reading can be understood as a 'feeling of . . .', sympathy is an extension of sensation along a cline of projection towards a 'feeling for . . .', and empathy is a final shift along the cline to a 'feeling with . . .'. In spite of these differences, the fundamental premise of this chapter is that all three affective responses are basically the same aspect of the embodiment principle to varying degrees of projected abstraction. It seems even to be the case that the advancement from physical contact through social connection to individual empathy matches the developmental sequence from infancy to adulthood (Ricard and Kamberk-Kilicci 1995; Lerner 2002; Commons and Wolfsont 2002). Here, however, the cline is primarily an organisational device for the chapter.

Sense and sensation

Since the seventeenth century, a distinction has generally been made between sensation and perception (according to Ben-Zeev 1984), such that sensation is regarded both popularly and in the philosophical literature as primary and passive, and perception is a secondary cognizance of the sensed stimulus. Sensations, in short, just happen to us, and they are then processed, categorised, assigned values and understood. This view underlies Cartesian duality between mind and body from (of course) Descartes ('Nothing more . . . should be assigned to sense, if we wish to distinguish it accurately from the intellect' (1641: 252)) to Bertrand Russell ('the essence of sensation . . . is its independence of past experience . . .; to arrive at what is really sensation, . . . we have to pare away all that is due to habit or interpretation (1921: 144, 140)). Pointing to a range of thinkers in between, Ben-Zeev (1984) argues that the sensation-perception distinction arose because of a distinction made between rational minds, exclusive to humans, and the natural and physical world, and also because it seems plainly causal that a stimulus should lead to a response, rather than the environment being mentally constructed, or causality being looped.

The sensation-perception distinction might be regarded as being all-pervasive beyond the discourses of philosophy as well. In popular conversation, the sensations of the body are seen as features that are ascribable to the environment or to external stimuli. We commonly talk about our conscious awareness as that which makes us human. Separating impulse and 'raw' sense from rationality and consciousness absolves humans of some responsibility for action, and it regards living in the world as an immersion into sense-stimuli that must be 'made sense of' by conscious work.

Modern cognitive linguists, in challenging the mind-body distinction, also therefore challenge the mental passivity involved in seeing a disjunction between sensation and evaluative awareness. Cognizance of the world is our only access to the world, and so our habits of thought and our human condition are partly constitutive of that world as we share it in common discourse and perception (this is experiential realism). There are many examples of evidence for the power of a subjective human mental faculty overcoming measurable intersubjective facts, from the experience of what people will call miracles, uncanny coincidences, luck, fate, tragedy or ironic circumstances, through to the proven rejuvenative and healing power of happiness and determination. In the medical literature, there is a long tradition of research into the phenomenon of 'phantom limbs', in which pain or other tactile sensation is still felt even in arms, legs, fingers or toes which have been lost by surgery or traumatic accident (see Ramachandran and Blakeslee 1998; Ramachandran et al. 1995; Halligan 2002). Vilayanur Ramachandran has demonstrated that this phenomenon is not a product of inflamed nerve-endings, as was previously thought, but is a product of cross-mapping of function between adjacent areas in the brain: in other words, an interpretative matter rather than a matter of false stimulus.

Literary senses

There is an obvious and direct sense in which there is a sensation in reading a literary text: books, screens, theatres and human voices all have a material and textural quality that is often intimately associated with the richness and pleasure of the reading experience. A theatrical production, a film or a television version of the same basic text can all feel very different in almost every respect. The sensations of holding a paperback, crackling open a hardback spine, smelling the dustiness or sharpness of old or new books, even suffering a paper-cut are all real and significant elements in the resonance and sensation of literary reading. However, in this chapter, I will instead be concerned with more interpretative aspects of sensation. There is an interesting experiment conducted by Yamamoto and Kitazawa (2001; see also Kitazawa 2002), in which people were given drumsticks to hold and the tips of the sticks were then tapped in various sequence. The sticks were held first in parallel, then crossed over, or the arms were crossed and the sticks were held straight, or the arms and the sticks were all crossed. What was intriguing about these and related experiments is that the informants seemed to regard the tips of the sticks as the edges of the tactile range of their bodies. In their cognitive fields, the tools had become a material and sensual extension of their awareness. In this chapter, I am arguing that literary texts – books, papers, screens and other media – are analogous tools by which the human sensorium can be extended. Furthermore, I suggest that the sensation within that extended field is not merely artificial, apparently imagined or vicarious but is experienced at the time as being authentic, primary and personal. The literary critic I. A. Richards (1924: 1) cannot have realised how literal his words were when he declared, 'A book is a machine to think with'.

The physicality of literary reading is something that we tend to have a diminishing sense of in the early twenty-first century. Most of the texts examined in this chapter were written before the beginning of the twentieth century, the time from which the move to universal primary education across Europe was starting to produce mass literacy. Before this time, literature (especially poetry) was largely written to be read aloud, in formal readings or as informal parlour entertainment. After this time poetry became more graphological and silent once more, except where lyric shifted into the recorded music industry. Traditional written poetry, apart from the odd poetry reading, has become silent on the page. Nevertheless, the biological primacy of speech and the cultural legacy of literature aloud has meant that the sound-effects of reading are still effective, even if interiorised, and so we must still apply our best understanding of phonological principles to their analysis.

Cognitive linguistics treats phonology as part of general cognitive grammar (Langacker 2008: 19–20), and cognitive grammar insists on the non-distinction between grammatical patterns and meaningfulness. All constructions in language – whether morphemes, words, phrases or clauses – are symbolic and necessarily *bipolar* in that they are comprised of a semantic pole and a phonological pole (Langacker 2008: 15). Individual sounds have a pure, non-symbolic value: in themselves, sounds are *unipolar* (Langacker 2008: 174). They only share in a symbolic value when they are combined with semantics, in other words when they form part of constructions with a natural use. In some traditional literary criticism and often in impressionistic accounts of literary texts, a strong link will be made between a sound and a meaning, so that a prevalence of flat back vowels /ɑ/ is regarded as tortured, or a collection of /s/ and other sibilants is regarded as snake-like hissing, or a dominance of plosives is seen as aggressive, and so on. These judgements are *phonoaesthetic* and it is easy to show that a direct link is false simply by reading through the 's'-initial or 'd'-initial words in a dictionary.

The cognitive linguistic fact that sounds in themselves are unipolar explains why it is wrong to take a strongly phonoaesthetic view: any suggested semantic content attached to sounds is a product of the larger construction in which the sound occurs. A text about contemplation – 'Thou still unravished bride of quietness, thou foster-child of silence and slow time' (Keats' 'Ode on a Grecian Urn') – lends shushing to sibilants, and the /s/es then take on a symbolic value; a comic-book text about fighting makes the plosives in 'bam' and 'kerpow' take on a belligerent symbolic value, and so on. It is in the readerly interaction and assignment of symbolic value that pure sounds take on aesthetic significance. This even applies to so-called onomatopoeia, which does not strictly exist: the real referents of 'roar', 'miaow', 'squelch', and 'Houyhnhnm' (Swift's attempt at a horse's neigh in *Gulliver's Travels*) do not sound like these spoken words.

In cognitive linguistics, a principle of prototypicality also applies to the articulation of sounds. In traditional phonetics, for example, sounds are objectively distinguished on the basis of binary features: /d/ is a voiced version of unvoiced /t/, /z/ is a voiced /s/, /t/ is a plosive version of sibilant /s/, /b/ is a plosive bilabial and /m/ is its nasal version, and so on. In tests, though, respondents take a much more fuzzy view of these categories, avoiding binary distinctions in favour of 'more-or-less' judgements. Though both /m/, /z/, /w/ and /b/ are certainly all voiced consonants, people seem to regard /m/ as most voiced and /b/ as least voiced along a scale (Jaeger and Ohala 1984; Evans and Green 2006: 34), and of the voiceless consonants, fricatives like /f/, /θ/ and /s/ do not seem as voiceless as the plosives /t/, /k/ and /p/. This seems to be a phonological instance of the general cognitive principle that, given the right context and possibly temporarily, any member of a category can be made to operate as an example – for better or worse – of another category (Gibbs 2003).

Sound and sense

How can we use these insights in order to discuss the interiorised sound-effects of literary reading? In order to proceed, please read the following out loud, with a self-conscious awareness of what your mouth is doing.

In a Gondola

The moth's kiss, first!
Kiss me as if you made me believe
You were not sure, this eve,
How my face, your flower, had pursed
Its petals up; so, here and there
You brush it, till I grow aware
Who wants me, and wide ope I burst.

The bee's kiss, now!
Kiss me as if you enter'd gay
My heart at some noonday,
A bud that dares not disallow
The claim, so all is render'd up,
And passively its shatter'd cup
Over your head to sleep I bow.

Robert Browning (comp. 1842 in *Dramatic Lyrics*)

This is a much-anthologised extract (for example, in Quiller-Couch 1913: 268, and many subsequent other collections) from a longer dialogue of the same name. The extracted passage is preceded by 'She sings', so the material musicality of the excerpt is already heightened, and the poem originates at a time of spoken literary performance in both a public and domestic setting.

A brief analysis of the articulatory patterns that this text produces in the mouth suggests a repeated attempt to create pouting or pursing lips in the speaking reader. Matched with the semantic content of the poem, this physical gesture is inescapably a kiss. For example, there are a number of words in the first stanza that require open, rounded lips in their articulation: 'moth's', 'first', 'you', 'You', 'were', 'sure', 'How', 'your', 'flower', and, of course, most pointedly, 'pursed'. The other main articulatory feature around these is spread lips, as in 'kiss', 'me', 'if', 'believe', and 'eve'. Spreading is not as easily assignable iconically to a facial gesture as the kiss, in this context, though it could be regarded as a smile, I suppose; but in fact I think in this text it serves a contrastive purpose to focus attention particularly on the foregrounded kiss. It is noticeable that the 'kiss-words' listed above are alternated with or preceded by prototypically spread words: 'kiss first', 'if you', 'believe You', 'eve You', 'had pursed', and others. Most brilliantly, 'wide' is spread wide and 'ope' is rounded and open, articulately. Often, the preparation consists of several spread words before a kiss-word: 'Kiss me as if you', 'made me believe You', 'this eve, How'. Furthermore, the most common vowel shift involved in these is from high front vowels (/ɪ/ and /i/ in 'kiss', 'this, 'if' and 'me', 'believe', 'eve') to relatively lower mid-vowels (/ə/ in 'the', /ɜ/ in 'first', 'were', 'pursed'), relatively backed vowels (/u/ in 'you'), or the semi-vowel glides /w/ and /j/. These last occur after the diphthong /aʊ/ in 'how' and 'flower' (a transition from low /a/ to high back vowel /ʊ/), or straightforwardly before the highest back vowel /u/ 'you'. It is even likely that a mid-nineteenth century southern English accent (Browning grew up in Camberwell, London) would have pronounced 'sure' closer to the high-back /ʊə/ than the mid-back /ɔ:/ of a modern southern accent. The spread words have an especially high fronted tongue position, compared with the back, mid and low positions of the tongue in the kiss-words. My point here is that the reader is being forced into kissing their way through the text, with the kiss-words made extremely prominent by preparatory contrastive grounding.

The patterns I have drawn out above are not perfect, though. The lead-up to the first kiss-word, 'First!' has an immediately preceding high front vowel /ɪ/ with spread lips ('kiss'), but the two vowels prior to that are central /ðə/ and extremely low back /mɒθs/, and though 'The' and 'moth's' do not have a pursed lip position, neither are they particularly spread. However, if the conclusions above about phonetic prototypicality are right, then it seems that a reader is likely to allow something more than poetic licence here. The pattern is established so strongly across the stanza, I think, that these near-examples of the pattern are likely to be heard eventually as correspondences with the pattern too, rather than as failures or dissonances.

The articulated consonants in the first stanza are as follows:

ð	m	k	s	f	st				
k	m	z	f	j	m	ʔm	b	l	v
j	w	n	tʃ	ð	v				
h	m	f	s	j	fl	h	d	p	st
ts	p	t	ls	p	s	h	n	ð	
j	br	ʃ	t	t	l	gr	w	w	
h	w	nts	m	nd	w	d	p	b	st

Analysing broadly in accordance with the fuzzy edges of phonetic prototypicality, the most voiced sound in the first few lines is /m/, occurring most noticeably in 'me' twice, and 'my'. The stanza tends to a whisper in the middle when the lips are most 'pursed', in the voiceless sounds of 'pursed Its petals up'. Then it ends with stronger voicing, again especially by contrast with the preceding voicelessness, in /b d gr/. The most striking emergent sound towards the end of the first stanza, though, is /w/, occurring in vocalic combinations that emphasise very strongly the kissing of the lips. At this point, it seems to me, there is a correspondence between the poetic persona's emerging awareness of the possibility of a kiss and such a prominent readerly kissing, four times on the /w/s, that the tactile sensation becomes palpable.

The emphasis on these patterns as I have described them seems to me to diminish the impact of the rhyme scheme in the first stanza. This is further assisted by the fragmented nature of the phrasing, often broken up with appositions. If a reader were to assign any value to this pattern, it might be hesitancy or uncertainty in the context. Indeed, the line which raises the possibility of an uncertain communication ('Kiss me as if you made me believe') is also the only irregular syllabic line in the poem (nine syllables where all the others are eight, or four in the stanza-initial lines) – with the second 'me' seeming by repetition and normal redundancy to be the foregrounded word responsible for the jarring. As if to point up the irregularity, the corresponding second line in the second stanza has a graphological elision ('enter'd') as if to show a shortening to fit the rhythm.

The second stanza generates its effects because all of these symbolic correspondences of the sound patterns have been established by the first stanza. A trace template has been pressed into the reader's sub-conscious mind by hearing this permutation of sound. The second stanza emphasises even more strongly the alternation of spread and rounded lip movements, with the preparatory ground being even more contrastively defined: the 'bee's kiss' offers two high front vowels to the one in the 'moth's kiss', so that the pursing on 'now!' is even deeper (and semantically urgent, of course). The pivotal /w/ moment at the end of the previous stanza, signifying emerging confidence and emotional awareness, is affirmed with /w/ being placed very prominently in heavy rhyme position ('now', 'disallow', 'bow'). Appositions in this stanza are diminished and so do not distract from the end-rhyme. Instead, strong voicing immediately precedes every line-ending rhyme: 'now', 'enter'd gay', 'noonday', 'disallow', 'render'd up', 'shatter'd cup', 'I bow'.

The transition from the first stanza to the second is one from delicate anticipation to passionate physicality, and even violence. This is carried, of course, semantically in the lexical and phrasal constructions in which the poem is composed, but it seems to me that the sound-patterning as I have described it takes on a symbolic value – at least temporarily for the duration of the reading – that turns unipolar sounds into bipolar icons in the intensity and physicality of a literary reading out loud.

A sense of richness

It should be clear from the previous chapter that intensity and depth of reading produce a sense of richness around a particular reading experience. Since richness is a product of readerly disposition and the investment of emotional resources (see also later in this chapter), the feeling of a richly textured literary work can be correlated very directly with a sense of readerly involvement. A reader can 'get into' a text, and get more out of it as a result. Richness, then, is not simply a textual or linguistic feature alone, nor is it simply a matter of the volume of condensed material: richness is not (necessarily) the same as density. For example, T. S. Eliot's 'Whispering lunar incantations dissolve the floors of memory' (1917: 20) is richer than 'My impression of the moon seems to make me forget things', or any other possible version of what it might mean, not (only) because of its volume of premodification but because of the interaction of metaphorical elements, and the context in which these lines occur. Any other synonymic re-versions are not as rich in this sense: 'Murmuring moonly songs remove the basis of recall', 'Quiet satellite mantras melt the ground of recollection', and so on. The original line has a richer texture than these because of the effects of its cognitive mechanics, which here are organised around complex metaphorical mappings. The final line of Orwell's (1949) *Nineteen Eighty-Four*, 'He loved Big Brother', is rich too, even though it is grammatically much simpler than the Eliot line, taking its rich texture from the simple horror of the situation and the implication that the reader must inevitably invest in this simple sentence. Sparse stylistic realisations can be as rich as those texts that are highly wrought. Richness might be said to be the accompanying feeling of literary resonance.

Intensity and loading

Of course, it is entirely possible for texts to be too rich. Some readers (for example, young students new to Eliot's poetry) consider lines like his impenetrable and they abandon their readings by closing off further interpretative work. The *loading* offered by a literary text to a reader represents a band in which the degree of textual features seems to match the disposition of the reader to generate satisfactory meanings or effects (see Figure 3a). A text which seems to have very little to it will appear inconsequential even if a reader is highly disposed towards it. An ill-disposed reader will regard a text as inconsequential no matter how great its density of textual features. There is a happy middle ground within which a text will feel rich if it has a reasonable density of textual features and if the reader is reasonably disposed towards the text to generate a set of resonant effects. If both sides of textuality and disposition are high within this band of acceptability, then the feeling of richness will be high too.

However, a literary work can appear overloaded to readers if the density of textual features outstrips the reader's highest levels of disposition. This can be seen to have happened especially with highly stylistically experimental texts such as, for example, James Joyce's *Finnegans Wake* (1939), which is largely only read by academics with an artificially pumped-up level

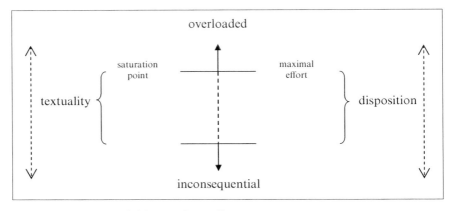

Figure 3a The sense of richness of a reading

of disposition. Overloaded textual experiences feel too rich. In the case of scholarly readings of the Joyce novel, close and detailed analysis of short passages or even isolated phrases can cover several pages (for example, McHugh 1980; Wales 1981; Milesi 2003). Clearly this represents a level of intense reading that goes far beyond what a non-academic reader is likely to engage in, having rather an exclusively scholarly value.

A similar level of intensity of reading can be discerned in my analysis of the opening of Hardy's *The Return of the Native* at the end of the previous chapter. It is worth saying that I do not consider the high granularity of that analysis to be anything that an ordinary reader might undertake, nor that such an analysis is necessary for the passage to be effective in a reader. The highly grained texture of that opening passage appears more and more pronounced under an increasing intensity of gaze, but it must be noted that there is a difference between explicit analytical intensification and a more intuitive intensity of reading. The detailed cognitive analysis allows us to see in intricate detail the potential workings of many different features in the reading. I argue that these features also generate effects in non-academic readers which they might articulate in vaguer, more impressionistic or looser terms. In other words, the artificial cognitive analysis brings to analytical attention those features that are below the level of initial conscious awareness of a natural reading. I argue nevertheless that the effects of these features are genuinely felt naturally. (Hartley and Turvey (2003) provide lots of examples of natural readers articulating their own responses in reading groups.)

The distinction I am trying to make here is between three different sorts of intensification of attention. Primarily, there is the natural attentional dimension of a reader reading: the default situation. Then there is the necessary intensification that an analytical account of that reading renders: this is artificial and part of the scientific process of investigation. Most of this book is comprised of examples of this sort of scrutiny. Lastly, there is the intensification of attention that a traditional, non-cognitive and non-systematic literary critical account would carry with it: this form of intensification is actually a reading as type one masquerading as a reading as type two.

Granularity in reading

In traditional literary criticism, and since the days of I. A. Richards (1924) and others, the practice of 'close reading' represents a wilful intensification of attention to the stylistic texture of a literary work. In this tradition, close-reading is generally impressionistic and amateurish, uninformed by much in the way of linguistic knowledge beyond some elementary grammatical and rhetorical concepts. Close attention to the language of the literary text has become gradually rarer in literary scholarship over the last forty years, and detailed linguistic knowledge has dwindled as a necessary professional skill for literary critics, prompting Henry Widdowson (even in 1975) to comment that linguistics was a discipline and 'English' had become a subject.

The poverty of technical training in supposedly professional literary researchers is scandalous, and is one of the faults against which this book sets itself. Nevertheless it is rife in contemporary literary criticism, and it leads to a misunderstanding about the nature of detailed analysis as I have just suggested. For example, Terry Eagleton (2008) criticises Tom Paulin's (2008) introduction to poetry, *The Secret Life of Poems*, as follows:

> Paulin has a passion for language and a marvellously sensitive ear for its textures and cadences. In fact, he reads so closely, slowing a poem down to a sort of surreal slow-motion, that it becomes in his hands a strange cacophony of plosive, guttural and sibilant noises. He is wondrously nimble at tracking a pattern of sound through a text, though the process rapidly becomes repetitive and over-technical: 'There are three ih sounds in the next stanza, two in the next stanza, along with two i sounds. Then in the last stanza there are a total of nine ih sounds and three i sounds . . .'
>
> You can, in short, read too closely, just as you can squash your nose up against a canvas until the painting fades to a blur. In a legendary analysis of a Baudelaire poem, the French structuralist Claude Lévi-Strauss found all sorts of ingenious combinations of phonemes in the text. It took another critic to point that most of these sound-patterns were far too intricate to be perceptible to a reader. Which raises the question: how far back from or close up to a work of art should we be standing? Would a reader pick up, even unconsciously, some of the

acoustical effects Paulin identifies, and would they contribute to the poem's meaning?

(Eagleton 2008)

There is no question here that Paulin demonstrates, in the lines quoted by Eagleton, a poor command of simple accurate technical terminology. The point I would like to make, though, takes issue with Eagleton's comments in the second paragraph that confuse technical analysis with natural reading. Paulin's undisciplined account nevertheless represents a very high level of intensity of reading, to the point of overload, but a natural reader does not need to have an explicit analytical description for the effects of what is there to be felt, at however intuitive a level.

This is where detailed stylistic and cognitive poetic analysis differs from the literary critical tradition of 'close-reading'. The question is not whether rich features are there in the text, but whether they are potentially available to a reader disposed to look hard enough. (And whether an author intended to place features there or not is irrelevant to any effects rendered in a reading.) Even a reader with a relatively low level of reading intensity might have a vague and loose impression of the textured effects of, say, Hardy's opening passage, that will form a tone that is carried into the rest of the novel. The purpose of a detailed and disciplined analysis is to bring all the potential mechanics to the point of open scrutiny.

Saturation

There is, of course, an upper limit on the degree of granularity and richness in a literary work, a point at which the reader feels overloaded. According to my scheme in Figure 3a, this occurs when the perceived density of features being offered by the text overloads the maximum degree of attentional effort that the reader has devoted to the reading. Such texts are regarded as too rich, too dense, or overloaded. Many non-academic readers of *Finnegans Wake* regard this text as saturated with a density of features that overwhelms them. 'There are few novels in world literature more unapproachable than James Joyce's *Finnegans Wake*', begins a review of a new audio recording of the novel in *The Independent* (25 November 1998). Reading groups which tackle the novel are full of self-deprecating or disparaging comments:

> Actually picked up Finnigan's Wake a few days ago at a book sale for $1. As someone who has only a passing interest in literature, it's almost entirely unapprochable to me. Does anyone have any good references for getting through it, because it really is nothing like The Dubliners.
> 'Nick' at <http://www.37signals.com/svn/posts/633-lszl-moholy-nagys-visual-representation-of-finnegans-wake>

Finnegans Wake, though – he spent decades writing it, and expected his readers to spend the same effort reading it. I've spent decades not reading it, which doesn't amount to the same thing. :)

> 'Skott Klebe' at <http://www.37signals.com/svn/posts/633-lszl-moholy-nagys-visual-representation-of-finnegans-wake>

Seattle, Washington
Allforabit Funferall
Fourth Sunday of every month in Kent.
We call ourselves the world's slowest Finnegans Wake reading group. We have been meeting since November 2005, and in two years have read less than 40 pages. Our emphasis is on extracting all the heady goodness we can from the Wake while having fun doing it. Bring your laptop -- Fweet, Google, and Wikipedia are your friends. So-called 'fanciful' interpretations welcome!

> < http://finneganswake.org/ReadingGroups.shtml>

It also seems significant that many of the search links for 'Finnegans Wake reading groups' result in closed-down webpages, sites that have not been updated, empty links or abandoned groups. One of my colleagues in stylistics has been in a *Finnegans Wake* reading group for thirty years, though the group has transformed into a drinking club, an informal psychotherapy session, a marriage support club, and finally a group that meets to discuss why the participants wanted to read the novel in the first place.

Though *Finnegans Wake* is an extreme example of textual density, there are many examples in which the perceived density of texture might lead readers to regard richness as approaching saturation and overload. Syntactic complexity, multiple creative metaphors, neologisms, allusions and intertextual references are all textual features that might normally be regarded as contributing to density.

Some cognitive constraints might also play a part. For example, it seems that the effort required to pay attention to an attractor in a reading leads to a momentary period of attentional exhaustion immediately following. This is known as *attentional blink* (Styles 2006: 175). In experiments, informants who had just focused on an attractor were unable to focus on newly arriving distracting elements until the first figure had settled into focus (a 'blind spot' in attention of up to half a second). It seems plausible to suppose that ultra-dense and texturally rich literary passages have a higher potential for generating attentional blink beyond their saturation points. In other words, readers will miss elements, or parts of the passage will seem to blur into indistinction. These overlooked elements might be picked up on a second or analytical reading, and thus contribute overall to a prolonged sense of richness in the text.

It is important to realise that neither overloading nor a sense of inconsequentiality will necessarily lead to readers abandoning reading. Saturation can be framed as a general quality of complexity: as happens with *Finnegans Wake*, the detailed tracking of what's going on tends to be replaced either by a general sense that impenetrable complexity is the point itself, or that the text should be enjoyed *purely aesthetically*. Many of the reading groups recorded online seem to consist of meeting to read the novel out loud, in order to enjoy the texture of the sound. Several were working through the book only a few pages at a time in this way, over the course of several years.

Density and elegant variation

There are competing explanations for the phenomenon of attentional blink: there is a bottleneck in the single channel that links perception and cognition that clogs up and delays further attention; or there are multiple channels but there is interference when closely related attractors arrive for processing; or there seems to be a delay in processing similar figures (such as a number followed by a letter, where both are purely symbolic) but dissimilar figures (a number followed by an image of a face) seem not to be a problem (Styles 2006: 177). This last finding (from Awh et al. 2004) has implications for literary reading: a dense sequence of attractors that are all very closely related are not likely to be regarded as conveying richness. (*Repetition blindness* (Kanwisher 1987) seems to be closely related to attentional blink.) Such passages will simply seem repetitive, in a qualitatively negative sense, and monotonous. By contrast, a passage that has a high density of varied features is more likely to be perceived as rich.

I can demonstrate this with a reading of a famous minor poem by Percy Shelley, originally entitled 'To ———'. The composition is dated 1821 in Pisa, and the blank is conventionally taken for his wife Mary Shelley who edited the collection after the poet's death the following year, though given Percy's several relationships in the preceding years there is some doubt about this. In spite of this provenance, the text is currently very popular as a love poem, most commonly retitled as the opening line 'Music, when soft voices die'. It has been set to music numerous times, for example by the jazz musician Brian Christopher Madigan, by the English songwriter Roger Quilter, by the American composer John Harbison, and many others. There is even an avant-garde electronic piece inspired by the text by Roderik de Man. It is clear that some of the more traditional musical settings are popular with choirs and at recitals.

To ———

Music, when soft voices die,
Vibrates in the memory—
Odours, when sweet violets sicken,
Live within the sense they quicken.

Rose leaves, when the rose is dead,
Are heaped for the belovèd's bed;
And so thy thoughts, when thou art gone,
Love itself shall slumber on.

Percy Shelley (1970: 639, published 1824)

The main structural pattern that is immediately noticeable here is a three-part
repetition followed by a fourth iteration that breaks the pattern. Figure 3b
shows this most clearly.

NP	[conj	NP (pre-mod+N)	VP]	VP	prep	NP
Music	when	soft voices	die	Vibrates	in	the memory
Odours	when	sweet violets	sicken	Live	within	the sense they quicken
Rose leaves	when	the rose	is dead	Are heaped	for	the belovèd's bed

Figure 3b Established syntactic structure of Shelley's 'To ——'

There is syntactic repetition here, in the form of a brief initial noun phrase >
followed by a relative clause with a conjunction 'when', a pre-modified noun
phrase and a verb phrase > followed by a main verb phrase > and ending with
a prepositional phrase consisting of a preposition and a noun phrase. There is
also some parallelism across the semantic relationships of these lines. For
example, the initial NP emerges from the NP in the relative clause (music
comes from voices, odours come from violets, rose leaves come from the
rose). There is, of course, some variation within these basic repetitions: the
lexical realisation of the initial NP ('music') is not repeated; though the conjunction 'when' is repeated, the later preposition is varied ('in, within, for');
though the final NP always begins with a determiner, the rest of the NP is variable. An intense reading can examine the significances of the variation. For
example, the semantic progression across the initial NPs goes across the
senses from sound ('music') to smell ('odours') to a combined sight and touch
('rose leaves'), and this progression scales from most intangible to most material. Furthermore at an iconic level, the single senses are referenced with a
single lexical item here while the doubled sense is referenced with two words.
A particularly intensive reader might even notice that the synaesthetic blending of sight and touch is iconically matched by the potential multivalence of
the nouns 'rose' and 'leaves' as active verbs, where there is no such potential
in the single-item occurrences 'music' or 'odours'. This potential, I think, if
noticed, would even so remain unrealised at this point, though as we will see

in a moment, the presaging of noun/verb confusion is taken up later in the poem.

A further close repetition and variation can be seen in the embedded NPs. All three phrases consist of a pre-modifier and a noun, but the first two are closely parallel: 'soft' and 'sweet' are semantically related and phonetically echoic, 'voices' and 'violets' are anagrammatically close permutations, and both NPs are plural. By contrast, 'the rose' is only syntactically parallel as a pre-modifier + noun. The embedded VPs are all drawn from a contiguous semantic field (illness and death), but there is a significant variation in predication here. The first iteration ('soft voices die') is clearly a metaphorical usage of the verb, conventionally referring to the diminishing sound at the end of a song. 'Sweet violets sicken' is also a metaphor, mapping disease in a human lexicalised form onto a flower, though this is such a conventional metaphor that it might barely be noticed as metaphorical: in any case, it is more conventional than the first iteration. The third parallel verb 'is dead' is highly conventional; it is, appropriately, the most dead metaphor of all. Oddly, this progression from most metaphorical towards (but not reaching) the literal has an interesting inverse rendering in the sentences as a whole. The first sentence (with the most metaphorical embedded verb) can be read entirely as a literal description of the sensation of music coming to an end – 'vibrates' here is literal. The second sentence, with the more conventional verb metaphor, seems overall rather more metaphorical than the first sentence, with the personifying value of 'live'. The third sentence, with the most dead metaphor of all, has the most overall metaphorical potential in that 'the rose' (in 'the rose is dead') can be taken as a symbol for the dead lover herself: she is the rose lying on the rose leaves. There is some hint of preparation for this sense, in the conventional feminine attachment typical of 'soft' and 'sweet'.

The richness of the sequencing as set out above can be understood as a series of attractors, sustained by the elegant variation of the patterning, with potentially distracting elements resisted and placed into the background. For example, 'Music', the first attractor, could potentially have been occluded by 'soft voices' (after all, they invoke empathetic recognisability on the human scale), but that potential distraction is instantly backgrounded by the verb 'die', and by the main active verb that immediately follows, 'Vibrates', which acts as a maintenance device and is further strengthened by capitalisation and line-initial positioning. Similarly, the even more vibrant colour of 'sweet violets' could occlude the initial 'odours', but again the embedded verb 'sickens' serves to fade them, and the initial attractor is reinstated with the verb 'Live', similarly capitalised and placed prominently. Within this basic figure-ground landscaping, there is a further dimension of richness in the final grounding prepositional phrases. In the first iteration, the now textured music is placed inside the mind ('in the memory'); in the second, the textured fragrance is placed within the body's senses; in the third, the textured rose leaves are placed on 'the belovèd's bed'. The movement is from interior to exterior, and the prepositional choices reflect this: 'in', 'within' (alongside) and 'for' (here meaning 'on top of' or 'to constitute'). Lastly, there is a parallel scale across these from past (memory) through present immediacy (senses) to prospective future ('for . . .').

In other words, although there is a prominent sense of regularity on the surface of the poem, I think, there is also an underlying but undeniable current of contrary patterning and variation to make up the texture of the poem. Even in the prosody, an apparently simple set of four rhyming couplets are in fact comprised of a complex pattern of syllables – 7, 7, 8, 8, 7, 8, 7, 8 – and a corresponding variation in the rhythm. I suggest that the subtle variations serve to prevent the repetitions becoming monotonous: instead, there is enough incoming richness in each step through the text to maintain and enhance a reader's attention. Furthermore, the establishment of pattern represented in my discussion of Figure 3b above constitutes a habituation of the reading so far in the poem – this pattern is then disrupted in the closing two lines, though as I have sketched above, elements in the oncoming disruption have been hinted at in the first six lines.

Grammatical chains

So far, this description has drawn on my model of attentional resonance couched in traditional stylistic analysis. However, it is worth noting that the syntax available for Shelley's choice is a consequence of the cognitive constraints of the grammar. I will develop a fully applied version of cognitive grammar to literary reading in Chapter 6, but it is worth pre-empting that discussion for this poem.

Work in cognitive linguistics has extended the fundamental forms of creating figure and ground in terms of grammatical features of language. For example, the conceptual event denoted by a clause always involves an object in focus (the figure) acting upon another object (ground) or acting in another domain (background). This is true both of material events ('Peter kicked the ball', 'Ada raced across the floor in the toy car'), perceptual events ('Joanna watched the bird fly away') and relational or attributive events ('Edith is the small one in the red hat'). All objects represented linguistically in clauses (usually by noun phrases) can be given a *role archetype* as an acting wilful agent ('Peter'), a patient that receives the action ('the ball'), an instrument through which the action is conveyed ('in the toy car'), an experiencer which perceives the action ('Joanna'), or a mover which is relocated by or with the action ('the bird'). Some referents can involve several roles ('Ada' is an agent and a mover). In Figure 3c, participant roles are listed vertically by the words in the diagram, and thematic relationships are represented horizontally by the brackets. Our common conceptualisation of these roles can be discerned in the ENERGY TRANSMISSION metaphor that we typically use to describe them, and so a clause can be regarded as an *action chain* involving the set of

Figure 3c Roles and thematic relationships in the clause (after Langacker 1991)

participants. The action of influence exerted by each participant on another can be represented in terms of ENERGY transferred between them. It is plain to understand how 'Peter kicked the ball' literally involves a conceptualisation of energy transfer from Peter to the ball, which almost everyone reading that sentence would understand to result in the ball moving away from the scene. However, in 'Joanna watched the bird fly away', there is also a metaphorical transfer of action from Joanna to the bird, as well as an embedded and more literal shift of energy in the bird taking wing. All of these participant roles, generalised here as archetypes, can be understood as different configurations of figure and ground in a conceptual field.

Since all linguistically-articulated participants fundamentally have existence and attributes, however minimal these might be, there is also a zero role by default, where no energy has been transmitted in an action chain. Existential clauses ('I exist', 'The sky is blue') can be said to have only zero roles because the participant does not do anything, and no energy is transmitted. In addition, sometimes a participant can be unchanged by the action chain ('the floor' in 'Ada raced across the floor in the toy car' above), in which case it is said to be in an absolute role. Finally, when an event seems to occur all by itself ('The glass broke'), the role can be regarded as a theme, where the action chain is implicit or summarised in the verbal element (the broken glass will have been caused by an agent doing the breaking, possibly in a clash with an instrument, perhaps with some other moving object, and so on). Themes subsume all the other roles, since the same thematic event can be represented in a variety of different ways to draw attention to different roles ('Peter broke the glass', 'That was the glass that got broken', 'The glass smashed on the floor', and so on).

Action chains represent fundamental schematic experiences gathered in early childhood (things exerting force on other things). The energy source (the agent represented in a clause) transfers force to the energy sink (the patient in a clause). Agent and patient can be further schematised as a *trajector* and a *landmark*, respectively, and these are instances of the basic conceptual capacity for figure and ground. Of course, stylistic variation encodes different perspectives on this basic assumed event, and this too is a matter of attention within the clause. For example, the difference between an active clause and a passive clause can be understood in terms of two different viewing positions of the same original event, one of which figures the agent as being prominent whereas the other focuses on the effect on the patient.

Different parts of the action chain can thus be *profiled* in the reader's frame of attention, and the consequence of profiling one part rather than another is the readerly *construal*, or interpretative sense, of the clause. (See Chapter 6 for a further explanation and elaboration.)

In the Shelley poem above, the first three sentences generate action chains in the reader's mind. The basic scheme being invoked at the most abstract level is the same in each case: X, at the end of its trajectory, does not cease moving, but persists. The lexical choices in the poem, though, do something odd with this basic action chain. In the default scheme of our everyday senses, a moving object loses momentum and gradually comes to a standstill – its speed diminishes and fades away. In the poem, though this basic scheme is invoked in the embedded clause (where tailing momentum is captured in 'die, sicken, is dead'), the main verb choices ('Vibrates, Live, Are heaped') seem to increase the strength of the object's movement, especially by contrast with the interposed embedded clause, and they are iconically strengthened by capitalisation. So vibrancy and life go on after dying and sickening; the 'belovèd's bed' is enlarged ('heaped') by the actions of an unseen agent. The passive form here ('Are heaped') develops the disembodiment that has been a function of the poem from the point at which only 'voices', 'memory' and 'sense' point metonymically to the (missing, unprofiled) complete person. Equally, the progression from sound, to smell, to sight and touch outlined above profiles human senses rather than any human being themselves. The person to whom the poem is addressed is blanked in the title, possibly metaphorised as 'the rose', or embedded in a literal syntactic and metonymic sense in 'the belovèd's bed'. The speaker reduces himself to the richness of his senses. Neither agent, patient nor experiencer are directly lexicalised in the poem, and all of the stylistic features that I outlined in the discussion above are consequences of the repeated particular profiling of these action chains.

I have left the final two lines of the poem to the end of the discussion. Having established particular patterns of habituation in the reading, the poem disrupts them rather jarringly, though as I have suggested repeatedly above, there have been several subtle hints that prepare the ground for this so that the final quarter of the poem remains in connection with the rest of the text.

On a first reading (see Figure 3d), the now-established pattern (Figure 3b) seems to repeat, with the NP 'thy thoughts' followed by an embedded relative clause ('when thou art gone') that matches the habituated parallels. Already, though, there are departures from the established pattern that might alert the reader to an imminent shift: the sentence begins 'And so'; the noun phrase in the embedded 'when' clause is a simple pronoun 'thou' instead of a premodified noun; the full embedded clause 'thou art gone' shifts from a previously fairly conversational register to a second person pronoun and verb form that was archaic even in the early nineteenth century and had developed by then a self-consciously 'poetic' sense. In spite of these signals, whenever I have made students read the poem aloud, they almost always stumble on a first reading,

NP	[conj	NP (pre-mod+N)	VP]	VP	prep	NP
And so thy thoughts	when	thou	art gone			
Love						itself
				shall slumber	on	

Figure 3d The disjunctive close of Shelley's 'To ———'

when instead of the next expected main verb, they get 'Love'. Even if there is a temptation to read 'Love' as the start of a transitive verb 'thy thoughts love x', this is immediately deflected by the recursive 'itself', which confirms that 'Love' is actually a noun here rather than a verb. Readers search for the actual main verb, which is then 'shall slumber on' – but this leaves the predication of 'thy thoughts' hanging verblessly. The syntax serves iconically again to disembody the thoughts from any action, and in the process leaves those 'thoughts' nowhere. It is as if the poem dangles the comfort that your mental faculties and consciousness, like echoing music, persisting fragrance or the symbolism of roses, will live on, only to whip that prospect away so that the relative clause 'when thou art gone' really means what it says absolutely. The poem ends by replacing the sensual with the abstract, 'Love', utterly self-consuming and static. The very strong action chain of the first three sentences, with their positive dynamic, is replaced conclusively by a syntactic severance of the chain in leaving the first subject verbless, with a weak transfer of energy in the last line ('shall slumber') ending at rest ('on').

The poem resists attempts to read the ending any differently. You could try to maintain the established pattern by reading 'Love' as the continuation of 'thoughts' after 'thou art gone', so the energy transfer is sustained, but the poem still puts your conscious awareness to sleep. You could try to read 'slumber on' not as the phrasal verb that it prototypically seems to be, but as a verb plus preposition: so instead of 'love sleeping on forever', you have 'love shall sleep on thy thoughts', just as the belovèd's body sleeps on the rose leaves. But again this reading simply points back into the poem and confirms the sense of ending.

On a different tack, you could begin to thematise the disjunction so that you re-read the poem not as an addressed love lyric but as a statement asserting the persistence of the spiritual over the material. This approaches a religious affirmation, and if you are a reader who identifies the poetic voice as being close to Shelley himself, then your possible knowledge of his atheism might rule this out. 'Rose', as a past participle of 'risen' serves to close off the (Christian) resurrection which the poem would otherwise invoke. Adapting this, you might re-profile the poem by making more prominent the iconic and symbolic features, so that the text comes to be about the persistence of art (the word 'art' is in the second last line) and is about 'itself'. Even then the final feature of slumbering is hardly triumphant or energetic, and though the poem offers no propositional comfort as an argument, the sensual sound patterns throughout have a soporific and numbing ease that is indicated in the ending: this is aesthetics for its own sake. Alternatively you could historicise the text and notice the theme of diminishing impact and tailing transformation: the choice of violets, for a contemporary reader, would allude strongly to Napoleon ('corporal violet'), who took violets from the tomb of his belovèd Josephine into exile with him. His supporters adopted violet as their colour, but there is an irony in the politically disillusioned Shelley's use of violets as a symbol of faithfulness to the Bonapartist cause – the republican turned despot. Shelley composed a withering blast against Napoleon on hearing of his death in 1821, the same year as this poem, and both were published in the same 1824 volume. (As an aside, while I was researching the symbolism and historical provenance of violets, I discovered that their fragrance in the substance ionone is very closely chemically related to beta-ionone in roses, and ionone has the property like a fragrant attentional blink of blocking the ability to sense any other smell for a few moments after experiencing the sweetness of violets.) Finally, you might shift the poem out of Shelley's voice to read it as a dramatic monologue: the blank in the title then becomes universalising; the present tense assertions take on proverbial and generic values; and the abstracting that is the main feature of your reading culminates in a sense of the sustaining idea of love – the poem moves from the level of material nature to the level of sublime idealisation.

Poetic trajectories

All of these possibilities represent different attempts to construe the disjunction in the action chain pattern that the poem presents. 'To ———' is rich because of the density but variability of its attractors. I think the soporific construal of the poem, amongst those outlined above, is difficult because this variability maintains richness of texture rather than attentional loss. A more repetitive text will highlight this by contrast:

To One Singing

My spirit like a charmèd bark doth swim
  Upon the liquid waves of thy sweet singing,
Far far away into the regions dim

   Of rapture – as a boat, with swift sails winging
Its way adown some many-winding river,
Speeds through dark forests o'er the waters swinging . . .
      Percy Shelley (1970: 541, composed 1817, published 1839)

This, too, is a short poem by Shelley concerning music and composed only a few years previously. It is not as famous or popular as the other poem, and I suggest that one reason for this is that relatively it is not internally variable enough, though it has its own appeal. Overall, the poem suffers from the closeness of subsequent attractors and the straightforward ongoing dynamic of its extended action chain. Its main texture lies in its sound effects, and beyond that, it is relatively untextured.

For example, the initial attractor in the poem, 'My spirit', is instantly turned into a metaphorical blend with the figure of a boat ('a charmèd bark'), and the blended figure of the boat-like spirit is then maintained by a continuation and repetition of the verb and the metaphor throughout the rest of the poem. There is no pause in the extended action chain across the whole poem, not even at the end, where the tailing ellipsis ('. . .') gestures at the continuing momentum of the sense beyond the end of the text. (This is the 1817 version; Mary Shelley deleted the whole final line for the 1839 edition, and also reduced 'Far far away' to 'Far away', thus destroying the poem's main effect and ruining the interlocking *terza rima* scheme a-b-a, b-c-b.)

There is some variation in the path of the 'spirit/boat' trajector as it progresses through the poem – it moves 'upon', continues 'far far away', moves 'into', is enhanced 'with swift sails', continues 'adown', then 'through' and finally 'o'er'. This dynamic variation, though, only serves to emphasise attention recurringly back onto the constant attractor that is being profiled. Several of the landmarks against which this trajectory is described consist of embedded attractors such as 'the liquid waves of thy sweet singing' and 'the regions dim of rapture'. In both these examples, the prepositions point to image-schemas of a completed state of partition: 'of' evokes a breaking off of a trajector from a landmark, where the final resting position of the figure-ground partition is profiled. As potential distracting elements, these are neglected into the background as the main attractor (boat-spirit) sweeps on. Unlike in 'To ———', there is no looping and repetition of the main clause. Even where the stanza break threatens a moment of pause in the trajectory, the syntax is maintained across the space, and the first of two adjective-noun reversals ('regions dim' and 'waters swinging') serve to signal the end-directed nature of the poem's movement. Viewed as a transfer of energy across an action chain, the first poem repeats the pattern four times with increasing variation, whereas 'To One Singing' sustains the constant momentum of energy across the entire text and suggestively beyond the ending.

My own sense is that this poem is not as successful as the first, because the governing feature is more often the sound-effect of the text rather than any other element. The 'spirit-boat' blend is maintained only by focusing on the boat element, so that by the second stanza the notion that the main figure was 'My spirit' has been almost completely lost, I think. Several of the alliterative phrases are only achieved through clumsy literal repetition (you can see why Mary Shelley might have edited 'Far far'), or are necessarily divided ('regions

[dim] of rapture') to sustain the trajectory but destroy the sound-effect. Some of the rhyming and prosodic patterning is only maintained by resort to a highly self-conscious archaism ('adown') or malapropism ('waters swinging'). Overall, 'To One Singing' is too unidirectional in its attentional patterning, and too one-dimensional in its sound-effects, relative to the first, more popular poem.

This is not to say that a strong and sustained attractor cannot be immensely powerful. The opening of Coleridge's 'Kubla Khan' has a comparable action chain structure to Shelley's poem:

In Xanadu did Kubla Khan
A stately pleasure-dome decree:
Where Alph, the sacred river, ran
Through caverns measureless to man
   Down to a sunless sea.
Samuel Taylor Coleridge (1950: 157, composed 1797, published 1816)

Tsur (1987, 2006) demonstrates the cognitive mechanics and effects of this poem in great detail, and Benzon (2003) shows how different senses are prominent successively across the text. The prepositions that activate image-schemas in this opening are more textured than in the Shelley poem: 'in, where, through, down' all in these few lines generate a closely physical orientation. The primary attractor (the human, agentive, eponymous speaker Kubla Khan) is quickly occluded by the named active river, and then by the measureless caverns and sunless sea. These last two attractors are interestingly anomalous, figured as negative lacunae, as specific indefinites, and with human agency sidelined. The overall sense of the opening is of a powerfully resonating texture, reinforced by the tactile value on the tongue of reading the rhythm and alliterations aloud.

It is important to emphasise that the different texturally-mediated sensations discussed in this chapter are experienced as *real* sensations. There is no physical difference between feeling anxious in life and feeling anxiety in a fictional situation; no difference between feelings of love or attachment evoked by a lyric and those evoked in everyday life; no material difference between sadness that brings tears during a literary experience and the sadness of a life-changing event. Arousal, excitement, anxiety, and crying are all physically authentic. Gripping the pages of a book at a 'gripping' moment in the plot of a thriller, crying when an established character is killed off, feeling queasy at a gory description or anxious alone at home after reading a horror narrative – all these responses are *at the moment of experience* real, natural, primary and necessarily authentic. It is this fact that above all gives literature its extraordinary resonant power.

This is not to say that, for example, the death of a fictional character is equivalent to the death of someone you know in reality. The difference, though, I would argue, is a difference at a higher cognitive level. The fictional emotion is 'tagged' as fictional after the initial experience, and this framing serves to assign a value to the initial sensation. There is clearly an ethical and moral difference between a real death and a fictional one, and even subjectively the feeling of missing a person from your life is different from missing a fictional character who never materially existed in the first place. The distinction is made by mature adults in general (most children develop this distinction by early adolescence – see Woolley and Cox 2007; Sharon and Woolley 2004), though of course there are some adults for whom a close identification of the fictional in their lives approaches the level of a pathology. For example, at the 1986 funeral of Pat Phoenix, who played the character Elsie Tanner in the long-running British television soap *Coronation Street*, there were numerous wreaths from members of the public with messages for the fictional Elsie Tanner. People used to visit the 'real' home of Sherlock Holmes at 221b Baker Street in London, even when it was the branch of a bank (it is now a museum of the fictional detective). Film settings and television drama locations are particularly susceptible to the frisson of excitement generated, for example, by standing in Harry Potter's school, on the platform of *Brief Encounter,* on Juliet's Veronese balcony, in Dracula's Whitby or on a bridge in Batman's Chicago-Gotham City. How many little girls believe they actually are princesses, thanks to Disney's output of role-play costumes, magazines and accessories? The pathological end of the authenticity scale can perhaps be seen in the more committed enthusiasts of re-enactment societies, role-play gatherings and, increasingly, avatar-based online virtual environments (where the tagging itself might be socially de-emphasised as part of a carnivalesque inversion: Bakhtin 1941, 1984). The willing escapism of much of this is the basis of the thrilling tension in the tagline 'Based on a true story' attached to a fictional dramatisation.

Such pathologies are merely the exaggerated functioning of normal experiential processing, which at its closest to this tipping point constitutes an authentic and deeply felt intimacy with the literary work. I will develop this phenomenon of readerly identification in the next chapter, but here I go on to examine the connections between sensation and empathy.

Experiential metaphors of reading

Where sensation is largely located in individual subjectivity, empathy is a social matter. However, this crude distinction disguises the connections between the two. Individual sense experiences are partly shaped by our socialised sense of acceptable responses and appropriate articulations, from a very early point in processing. This socialisation is an inherent part of learning to read, from a period very soon after the skill of decoding grapheme-sound pairs has been learned. Reading seems solitary but we are only capable of it on the

back of a long and intersubjective process of learning to read as a social practice. Solitary reading is thus threaded through already with social design.
Mostly this happens automatically below the level of awareness (a character in
a novel is morally upright because of normally socially sanctioned actions), or
sometimes it can be manifest as an aware self-censorship (you are appalled at
your own enjoyment of a violent scene and resolve never to admit it out loud).
The development of empathy in later adolescence is partly shaped also by the
extended domains of experience offered vicariously by literary fictional
scenarios.

How best to talk in principled terms and in compliance with cognitive
theory about the process of empathy in literary reading? The way forward, it
seems to me, is to explore the conceptual metaphors by which people in
general talk about their own involvements in literature, and generate theoretical and analytical accounts from those natural mappings. In order to do
this, it is important to look at natural forums of reading. In observable terms,
reading is evidently social when it forms part of a group discussion, such as
for students in literature classes, for participants in book clubs, or in the
course of everyday conversation about a recent good read. These observable
arenas of reading offer a great opportunity for insight into the social mechanics of private reading, and the enormous increase in the popularity of non-
academic reading groups in recent years has been matched by scholarly
interest in their activities. A very useful point of entry into the sensation of
reading lies in the constitutive metaphors by which these non-academic
readers describe their own experiences.

In the small central English county of Nottinghamshire, with a population
of just under 800,000, for example, there are at least thirty reading groups
who meet in libraries, each with a membership of between five and thirty.
Alongside these 'official' groups are certainly even more that meet informally
in pubs, cafés and private houses. Even allowing for the fact that some
individuals belong to two or more groups, it is clear that these sorts of
numbers scaled across the UK (and then worldwide) mean that many tens of
thousands of people are engaged in actively social reading outside academic
institutions such as schools, colleges and universities, scholarly and critical
journals and the arts media. Many reading groups either exist entirely online,
with discussions posted in the form of an ongoing blog, or record their conversations on a website. The data that can be gathered from such sources
have not been set up as part of a reading experiment, and so there is no prior
interference from the analyst.

It is difficult to produce quantitative descriptions for reading group data
gathered in this way, since the total reading group population is a matter
of guesswork, and much of the statistical information that would be carefully delineated in a laboratory-based empirical study is not available after
the groups have posted their discussions. Groups are often also transient
and recording accurate data is not the main concern of the club secretary

as it would be for an investigating discourse analyst. However, any scan of the online reading group data that is currently available reveals very evidently that there are three main organising discourse metaphors being used:

- reading as transportation
- reading as control
- reading as investment.

Very roughly, my sense is that the most popular articulation is the transportation metaphor, accounting for perhaps half of the ways in which people in general describe their own reading. Readers say things like: 'We follow the boy on his journey round the world', 'There are quite a few battle scenes which I found slightly heavy going', 'I really got lost in this after the first few pages', 'Persist with it and it will carry you off', 'It takes a while to get into but eventually you get taken along with the action', and so on. The notion that literary reading transports the reader was most fully developed by the psychologist Richard Gerrig, who argues as I did at the end of the previous section that 'there is no psychologically privileged category "fiction"' (Gerrig 1993: 197), that fictional transportation of the reader's mind is basically the same sort of projection as other non-literary discourses, and that (contrary to Samuel Taylor Coleridge's famous 1817 contention), there is no 'willing suspension of disbelief', but rather a real engagement in a literary work. This engagement is a form of readerly identification (see further Chapter 5 below).

The other two metaphors comprise roughly equally the other half of the discourse of reading groups. Readers who describe their literary experience as a form of control tend to see the direction of control as coming from the book or author, with themselves as readers being the entity controlled. These people say things like: 'The weave of the daughter's life in modern San Francisco and her mother's life in China holds you right to the end', 'It's gripping stuff', 'I couldn't put it down', 'It's action-packed and it doesn't let go till the very last page'.

The final organising metaphor is the most overlooked. Many readers describe their reading as a form of investment, and it is particularly noticeable that this metaphor seems exclusively to be used to articulate experiences of emotional or empathetic senses. People say things like: 'By the end I was emotionally drained but rewarded by it', 'It rewards your effort with a great payoff at the end', 'Well worth the investment – emotional and financial!', 'You get more out of it on each reading', 'If you can take a chance by putting a lot of energy into the first half, then the rest of the book is a real page-turner', 'Worth the effort', and so on.

It should first be noticed that reading as transportation and reading as control are both bidirectional: in both cases, the reader is either the one controlling or the one actively doing the travelling, or alternatively is the one controlled or the one who is carried off on the journey. It is possible, perhaps, to see these two metaphors as specifications of a larger conceptual metaphor READING IS A JOURNEY. At an even more general level, this might even be seen as a particular version of the almost universal conceptual mapping LIFE IS A JOURNEY, where the idealised cognitive model of READING is placed as either an analogue of the cognitive model of LIFE or as a metonymic particularisation of it. By contrast, reading as investment is unidirectional in the sense that the reader is modelled as an active participant with no alternative of acting in a passive or purely receptive role. In the rest of this chapter, I offer a means of examining reading as control and transportation on the one hand, and reading as investment on the other. The first part of the discussion concerns identification and empathy and prefigures further work in Chapter 5; the weight of discussion here is given to reading as investment.

Reading laments as a control of emotion

In order to explore these three organising metaphors, I have been collecting texts that are very successful at provoking a physical and therefore observable emotional reaction in readers. These might be called 'tear jerkers', except that the term has pejorative connotations in general, and many of my poems are regarded as canonical high art. These texts come from a long tradition of lament poems, unfortunately often concerning the death of children, and I have discovered that reading these poems in seminars or at other events often provokes tears in the audience. There are, of course, cultural variations in the physical response: some of the texts discussed below caused a largely Japanese audience in Kyoto to react with a frown of deep concern, American audiences tend to fill up with tears, English audiences tend to fulfil their stereotype by stifling back crying with deep breaths, averted gaze and tight lips. A mixed European audience at a conference in Finland displayed several of these outward manifestations. Note that the criterion for inclusion of texts in this corpus is primarily based on effect, and only secondarily on formal features or historical accident: I am claiming a degree of 'naturalness' in the data in some respect here.

The lament is one of the oldest forms of literature, no doubt with precursors in oral forms of the expression of loss and grief (see Suter 2008). The Sumerian *Lament for Ur* – about the destruction of the city – and the Old Testament *Book of Lamentations* of Jeremiah are two very early examples (from 2000 BC and 500 BC respectively). Laments also feature strongly in the Anglo-Saxon tradition (the elegiac tenth century poem *The Wanderer* is a lament for the speaker's lost lord and family) and throughout English literature, with motifs alluded to and adapted down the ages.

A very early and influential example was brought to me at the end of a seminar in which I had read some more modern laments. This is from the Roman poet Martial (Marcus Valerius Martialis, AD 40–c.103):

Hanc tibi, Fronto pater, genetrix Flaccilla, puellam
    oscula commendo deliciasque meas,
paruola ne nigras horrescat Erotion umbras
    oraque Tartarei prodigiosa canis.
Impletura fuit sextae modo frigora brumae,
    uixisset totidem ni minus illa dies.
Inter tam ueteres ludat lasciua patronos
    et nomen blaeso garriat ore meum.
Mollia non rigidus caespes tegat ossa nec illi,
    terra, grauis fueris: non fuit illa tibi.
                                    Martial (*Epigrams* Book V, no. 34)

There are many translations of this into English, such as a closely literal
version by the librarian and collector Henry George Bohn (1796–1884), a
modernised version by the British author and translator Peter Whigham
(1925–1987), a rather sentimentalised version by the American writer and
teacher Rose Williams, an elaborated version by the Australian poet Peter
Porter (b. 1929), and many others. The following version (one of his several
variants, this being the closest to the Martial and the most successful, I think)
is by the English novelist Robert Louis Stevenson (1850–94):

Epitaphium Erotii

Mother and sire, to you do I commend
Tiny Erotion, who must now descend,
A child, among the shadows, and appear
Before hell's bandog and hell's gondolier.
Of six hoar winters she had felt the cold,
But lacked six days of being six years old.
Now she must come, all playful, to that place
Where the great ancients sit with reverend face;
Now lisping, as she used, of whence she came,
Perchance she names and stumbles at my name.
O'er these so fragile bones, let there be laid
A plaything for a turf; and for that maid
That swam light-footed as the thistle-burr
On thee, O Mother earth, be light on her.
                                    Robert Louis Stevenson (1998: 44, composed c.1880)

There are some striking sets here of poetic iconicity in the cognitive linguistic (rather than semiotic) sense of phonological and lexical parallelism, and
also conceptual and visual emblematising (see Nanny and Fischer 1999;
Muller and Fischer 2003), and also departures from iconic norms. For
example, the three main principles of iconicity are exploited richly in this

poem. According to the *quantity principle*, formal complexity corresponds to conceptual complexity. Here are many examples of phonoaesthetic parallelism, principally the way Stevenson sets up an iconic representation of the little girl's lisping voice. The line, 'Now lisping, as she used, of whence she came', places very close iterations of /s/ and /ʃ/ in close proximity with approximants such as /l/, /j/ in the initial articulation of 'used', and /w/ perhaps even voicelessly breathed as /ʍ/ in 'whence'. The next line echoes some of these patterns with /tʃ/, /s/, /ʃ/, /z/ – 'Perchance she names' – and then the girl's stumbling voice is echoed in the close collection of /n/, /m/, /b/ and the consonant clusters – 'names and stumbles at my name'. The next two lines switch to dentals and labiodentals /t/, /d/, /f/, in order to set up a contrastive ground against which the final line-and-a-half again echoes the lisping voice: '. . . as the thistle-burr On thee, O Mother earth', with its /s/ and /l/, and alternating voiced /ð/ 'the', voiceless /θ/ 'thistle, voiced /ð/ 'thee' and 'Mother', and voiceless /θ/ 'earth'.

In a similar vein, there is a poetic play of alliteration and repetition when play and place are mentioned. The heavy emphasis on 'six', repeated three times for the bathos of falling short of her sixth birthday, is followed by the very regular rhythm of the iambic pentameter, 'Now she must come, all playful, to that place', with its repetitive alliteration. This iconic formal playfulness contrasts sharply with the next serious and stern line, composed of formulaic phrases ('Where the great ancients sit with reverend face'), no alliteration, and a disrupted pair of offbeats at the beginning. Even the repeated diphthong /eɪ/ from 'playful' and 'place' are here embedded in the stern phrasing 'great ancients . . . face'.

Further in line with this iconic matching of form and concept, the phrasing becomes short and appositional whenever the little girl is invoked directly. For example, from the mention of 'Tiny Erotion', the next two lines are halted by appositional phrases and the punctuation: 'who must now descend, A child, among the shadows, and appear' – the syntax then running on and underlined by lexical repetition once the focus switches to 'hell's bandog and hell's gondolier'. The effect is to invoke the hesitancy of the little girl's speech. Similarly, in the 'playful . . . place' line quoted above, 'all playful' interrupts the syntax, whereas the 'great ancients' line is uninterrupted; and again 'as she used' makes the syntax of that line iconically stumble. The pattern is set for the final, moving line, where the interjection 'O Mother earth' makes readers literally catch their breath. The poem ends with a physical sense-effect generated by the phonetic and prosodic patterns that it has established.

There is another, more general pattern established in the patterns of syntax across line-endings that can also be regarded as an iconic evocation of sighing breath and its close physical association with grief. The first four lines of enjambed syntax must be read in a continuous flow of breath, with the mid-line pauses between appositional phrases not long enough to draw breath and sound fluent. Having allowed this release of breath, the middle six lines are all heavily end-stopped. Only the line ending 'to that place' might have allowed a pause, but the proleptic-facing deictic 'that' suggests that there is a further continued specification to follow in the next line, and so it proves. Where the initial four-line flow is released, the central six-line completions represent a clipping of emotion. This leaves the final four enjambed lines as a final sighing out of grief.

The iconic *proximity principle* – where linguistic distancing matches conceptual and emotional distance – is also exploited in the poem. There is a down/up directionality, paralleled with dark shadows and light, and blended in the girl's lightness. Firstly, there is a conventional generational vector established in the family outline: up a generation to 'Mother and sire', and down a generation to the child 'Tiny Erotion'. The grandness of the address is in contrast with the diminution of the 'Tiny' girl, whose name is already a diminutive Latin form meaning 'little loved one'. The child's descent into the underworld is conventionally paralleled 'among the shadows'. This physical movement which is conventionally deictically drawn is followed by a temporal movement, carried in the deictics of the verb-phrases: 'had felt . . . lacked . . . must come . . . sit'. This approaching perspectival view (distant past > near past > modal imperative present > continuous present) is rapidly reversed in the next line: 'Now (present) lisping (continuous), as she used (continuous near past), of whence she came (originating past)'.

The suggestion of temporal disruption enacted in these lines serves to presage the final four lines, where the established conventional iconicity is disrupted with a more complex sequence of up/down gestures and temporal texture. In the order of reading, the first phrase ('O'er these so fragile bones') sets out the level of the bones and focuses attention on the future level above, where 'a plaything' is to be set in the next line. The proximal deictic 'These' places the bones in the close present, in contrast with the remote deictic 'that maid' in the past, though in reading sequence the past follows the present. The completion of the sentence in the final two lines, however, restores the temporally natural order: from past descriptive ('swam') to present imperative ('be light'), which also of course points into the future. At the same time in the up/down scheme, the maid who walked 'On thee' will be covered by 'Mother earth' – both the physical soil ('turf') and a return to the higher generational 'Mother'. The particular human mother of the first line (Flaccilla in Martial) becomes a general personified mother of nature in the last line. In the beginning, the 'Mother' is capitalised by accident of the line opening; in the last line, 'Mother' is significantly capitalised by choice. Simultaneously and furthermore, the complexity of these last lines is increased again by a breathless heightening of fragility and lightness (carried echoically by the multiple repetition of /l/) in 'fragile', 'light-footed', the evocation of the 'thistle-burr' blowing in the wind, and 'be light'. This final phrase locally means 'light' as weight, but it can also be contrasted with the 'shadows' of the beginning.

Some of these comments overlap with the *sequential principle*, which is also richly played out. We have seen already how the natural temporal sequence of life is reconfigured in the poem. This is matched by the point of view being established not in chronological sequence but in an indirection of addressivity: in the first four lines the poem is addressed to the mother and father. These could be read in Stevenson's version as Erotion's parents, standing by the graveside. Fronto and Flaccilla were in fact the names of Martial's parents, who died in his youth, and so are co-referential with 'the great ancients' in the middle of the poem. There is speculation that Erotion was a slave-girl known to Martial after his move from his native Hispania to Rome in AD 64. Either way, a reader might naturally assume that the middle six lines are similarly addressed to the parents. However, the last four lines end with a disarming switch of address in the last line to 'Mother earth', and a point of view switch back from the underworld to earth.

Such textual manipulations are often described – both positively and negatively – by my students as 'manipulative' in emotional terms. They feel they are being controlled by the poem and the poet, and this control appears to them as being more or less intense, depending on how many of the textural features I have just outlined they perceive for themselves. They often describe the interlocking parallelisms of the poem as 'tight' in construction and highly wrought – there is a strong sense that there is a controlling and manipulating voice governing the effects of the poem. It is clear from their use of the 'control' metaphor that they see this sense of being manipulated as gradable: texts (as avatars for their creators) can exert greater or lesser control over their readers. This sense of a gradation in control can be demonstrated by comparing readings of two further such poems. The following is a loose version of the lament by Ben Jonson (who also translated Martial's epigrams), influenced perhaps only in the last few lines.

On My First Daughter

Here lies to each her parents' ruth,
Mary, the daughter of their youth:
Yet, all heaven's gifts, being heaven's due,
It makes the father, less to rue.
At six months' end, she parted hence
With safety of her innocence;
Whose soul heaven's queen, (whose name she bears)
In comfort of her mother's tears,
Hath placed amongst her virgin-train:
Where, while that sever'd doth remain,
This grave partakes the fleshly birth.
Which cover lightly, gentle earth.

Ben Jonson (1984: 35, composed c.1593)

Readers with whom I have discussed this poem note the empathetic effect generated in the last line, which contrasts with the religious convention and third person distancing of the previous lines. The first six lines consist of three sets of rhyming couplets, which seem conventionally contained and restrained. There is a middle sequence in which enjambment figures prominently, and then the final two lines return to the initial couplet format. This pattern is the opposite way round to Stevenson's organisation of his poem. Partly for these reasons, my students comment that they regard the Jonson poem as sounding very like a gravestone epitaph. They do not see it as particularly manipulative or involving, especially when compared with the following poem by the same author, composed some years later.

On My First Son

Farewell, thou child of my right hand, and joy;
    My sin was too much hope of thee, lov'd boy,
Seven years thou wert lent to me, and I thee pay,
    Exacted by thy fate, on the just day.
O, could I lose all father, now. For why
    Will man lament the state he should envy?
To have so soon 'scap'd world's, and flesh's rage,
    And if no other misery, yet age?
Rest in soft peace, and, ask'd, say here doth lie
    Ben. Jonson his best piece of poetry.
For whose sake, henceforth, all his vows be such,
    As what he loves may never like too much.

                  Ben Jonson (1984: 43, composed 1616)

My readers generally describe this as more intensely moving than the first lament. They do not regard it as emotionally manipulative, but recognise that it does exert some force on their empathies. Most interestingly, several readers comment that the poet barely seems to be in control of himself, to the extent that he comes very close to complaining about God's judgement.

In an earlier extended analysis (see Stockwell 2002a: 60–4), I adapted Langacker's (1991) prototypicality model of the topicality of subject in order to demonstrate the cognitive poetic features of control in this poem. There are many features which serve to discomfort a reader in this text, not in a radically shocking way but in ways that are much more subtle. For example, there is no single prototypically actualised sentence. Instead, there is a vocative address 'thou child'; an attributive clause with 'my sin' as subject; a passive 'wert lent'; a declarative which is lost in both an exclamatory 'O' and a verb-reversal 'could I lose' that makes it look like a question; a real 'why' question; a non-finite extension of the question 'to have 'scap'd'; two imperatives 'rest' and 'say'; and a final existential clause 'vows be such' that the prepositional phrase 'for whose sake' connects as if it is an extension of the previous imperative. It is easy to thematise this avoidance of declarative forms in the loss and uncertainty evident in the subject-matter.

The consequences of this non-actualisation, together with other ambiguities throughout the poem such as 'Ben. Jonson his best piece of poetry' (where the son's name was also Ben), render uncertain the distinctions between the child and the poem. There is a readerly switch in addressivity, as in Stevenson's version of the Martial lament above: 'Rest in peace' seems at first to be addressed to the son, but the second linked imperative, 'and, ask'd, say here doth lie', cannot be addressed to the dead child. Instead it can only be attached to the reader of an epitaph at the graveside, or the reader of these lines. The reader and reading are being implicated in the poem. There is an iconic quantity principle (in which formal complexity matches conceptual complexity) operating throughout the poem, but perhaps most clearly in the grammatical disjunction in the exclamation, 'O, could I lose all father, now', where 'father' is placed in a slot where an abstract quality would be expected. The effect is to empty his role as a father into an abstraction, which of course captures exactly the emotional sense of the poem.

Readers discussing these Jonson poems with me consistently regard the 'Son' poem as more controlling and manipulative than the 'Daughter' poem. They tend to hold the 'Son' poem in higher esteem, describing it as more moving and emotionally involving, but they also often point to the impression that the writer of the 'Son' poem seems almost not to be in control of his own reading of his son's death, blurring agency and recipient, son and poem, human accountancy and divine justice, and losing his syntactic and semantic skills in the middle of his writing.

Understanding reading as control necessitates the reader paying close attention to the stylistic texture. Broadly, it seems that the tighter the parallels in iconicity at various different levels, the more successful is the sense of manipulation of emotion. In other words, the richer the perceived text and the greater intensity of the reading, the greater the sense of control.

Lamentation as transportation between worlds

Readers who described the controlling features of the Jonson poem as 'moving' are also clearly drawing on the metaphor of reading as transportation, most fully researched by Gerrig (1993; see also Gibbs 2002; Andringa 2004). The notion that a reading mind is 'transported' in a literary work involves a projection of identity into another mental world, in which all the deictic references and attributes of the observing consciousness are shifted to the imaginary landscape. This is by far the most common metaphorical casting of the experience of reading in the online book group data. The ability to shift one's perceptual viewpoint by an act of projection is a natural capacity that is evident in a range of discourse situations other than the literary fictional, for example in jokes, gossip, imagined future hypothetical outcomes, unrealised parallel possibilities, and many others. Since these imagined alternative positions almost always involve the viewpoints of people, Gerrig emphasises their function as a form of identification: a process of setting the reader's self-aware personality traits against those of projected characters, in order to resolve both the similarities and differences. It is easy to see how this line of thought represents a specification of empathy.

In a review of Gerrig's work, David Miall (2000) queries the use of 'identification' to refer to this readerly involvement, preferring his own term of 'self-implication' (Miall and Kuiken 1994; Kuiken, Miall and Sikora 2004) leading to a readerly 'self-modification' (Miall and Kuiken 2002) of personality. Whatever the precise nature of the psychological effect, there is agreement around the notion that there is a readerly projection into an alternative deictic landscape, where the alternative viewpoint is mapped back and forth with the readerly viewpoint – a process which alters both the readers' perception of the character and also sometimes the readers' sense of themselves.

It is possible to sketch an analytical account of the discourse metaphor of reading as transportation using text world theory (Werth 1999; Gavins 2007), which sets out conceptual deictic spaces as different linked 'worlds', with their own rich attributes, within the discourse world shared and jointly constructed by the reader and writer. Text world theory is a deictically-driven discourse analytical model, and is particularly useful for an analysis of texture because it does not neglect the stylistic level alongside the conceptual level of worlds (which can be roughly seen to correspond with earlier notions of possible worlds, schemas, frames, scenarios, and mental spaces: see, respectively, Ryan 1991, Schank and Abelson 1977; Fillmore 1985; Langendoen 1969; and Fauconnier 1994).

The idea of transportation is captured in text world theory as a *world-switch* from the discourse world of reader and author into the text world which is constructed in the reader's mind using the text itself and appropriate text-driven knowledge. Further world-switches within the first text world projection are triggered by, for example, negations, flash-forwards, flashbacks, hypotheticals, metaphorical situations, and any modalised proposition. In a hypothetical situation, for example, a character in the text world imagines what would happen to them in an embedded speculative world: in this case, there are two versions of the character to monitor, each with different traits and attributes. These two (or more) versions of the character are called *enactors* in text world theory (Emmott 1992, 1997). Clearly there are interactive connections in the form of a trans-world mapping between associated enactors, and if an enactor in the text world is also mapped closely by the reader onto him/herself, then this part of the theory also captures the notion of identification and transportation.

Similarly to the proximity principle of iconicity, world-switching in the Ben Jonson poems above can be regarded theoretically as a calibration of conceptual and emotional distance. A text world analysis can account quite well for the deictic positioning that underlies the feeling of transportation in literary reading, and specifically here it can explain quite well the emotionally involving differences between 'On My First Son' and 'On My First Daughter'.

In the 'Son' poem, there are many world-switches, reflecting a complex deictic positioning; in the 'Daughter' poem, there are hardly any – the world remains fairly constant throughout the poem. For example, the 'Son' poem begins in the present, switches to the past seven years, returns to the 'now' present but places it within a conditional world-switch 'could', then it asks an apparently future-set question ('why will man lament'), before returning to the present moment, switching to direct speech with 'I' switched to the third person 'Ben. Jonson', and ending with a modalised ('may'), negated ('never') and future ('henceforth') flood of world-switching.

There is also ambiguity in the poem that a text world analysis reveals. 'If no other misery, yet age' can be read as a continuation of 'escape' (with only a brief negational world-switch) where age is a bad thing – a type of misery – and escaping it is good. Alternatively, 'if' can be read as a full hypothetical world-switch: if you escape social upheaval and bodily disease, and avoid any other misery, then you will age. Here, 'age' is a good thing, set against the memory of the death which has cut off its possibility.

Like the Stevenson poem, there are four lines of direct address to the boy, middle lines of generic address, and then the last four lines blur the address from the text world to the discourse world. It is not clear whether we are participating in an accessible discourse world or eavesdropping on an inaccessible text world: unlike ambiguity, it cannot be both. Who is 'ask'd'? The boy / the poet / the bystander (reader)? And 'whose' in 'For whose sake' is ambiguous between son and father. The third person switch and this discourse world / text world uncertainty distances the poet emotionally and ethically, and is uncomfortable for the (Christian) reader.

Furthermore, the *accounting* metaphor, especially in the beginning, creates a world-switch, but the mapping (in Gentner's 1982 terms) is rich rather than clear: there are multiple possible mappings that equate financial loss, physical volume, emotional volume (grief), feeling (hope), the boy and 'father-ness'. Overall, the effect is of a very rich and dense set of interlocked and embedded worlds.

By contrast, even though the consistency of world maintenance affirms a strong religious comfort offered by the 'Daughter' poem, the distance between discourse world and text world undermines any emotional closeness. The distance is especially remote for a modern readership who, even if Christian, would not perhaps share the same expression as used in the poem.

From these brief two examples, we can see that the tactile sense of texture is a product of crossing world-boundaries. The deictic projection and shift that is the necessary component of world-building forms the uneven texture between one world and another, which is experienced dynamically as the reader reads. A simple analogy, along the lines of understanding reading as a journey, would be to consider the textural difference between riding a bicycle over smooth consistent ground and riding over cracked and fractured rocks. Not only does consistency feel more solid, it also requires less effort and attention to negotiating your way over the points of disjunction.

For a final theatrical example, here is a moving passage in which the speaker mourns the loss of her son and attempts to communicate her grief to the others in the room, and the theatre audience. In the middle of Shakespeare's play, *King John*, Prince Arthur has been imprisoned as a threat to his uncle John's claim to the throne of England. Arthur is presented as a child in the play, though historically he was around fifteen years old at the time of these events (in the year 1203). Though he is not yet dead, his mother Constance prefigures her own grief upon his death – in fact Arthur is killed later in an accident while trying to escape.

> *Constance:*
>   Grief fills the room up of my absent child,
>   Lies in his bed, walks up and down with me,
>   Puts on his pretty looks, repeats his words,
>   Remembers me of all his gracious parts,
>   Stuffs out his vacant garments with his form;
>   Then have I reason to be fond of grief.
>   Fare you well. Had you such a loss as I,
>   I could give better comfort than you do.
>   [*She unbinds her hair*]
>   I will not keep this form upon my head
>   When there is such disorder in my wit.
>   O Lord, my boy, my Arthur, my fair son,
>   My life, my joy, my food, my all the world,
>   My widow-comfort, and my sorrow's cure!
>   [*Exit*]
>   William Shakespeare, *King John* (III. iv. 93–105, first performed 1596)

The capacity for theatre to fill the senses of an audience member is very often articulated as a form of transportation: 'Top ten performances that trans-ported me' (Robert Faires in *The Austin Chronicle*, 7 January 2005); 'Prepare to be transported into a terrifying and ghostly world by *The Woman in Black* as the West End smash-hit returns to Bath' (*The Wiltshire Times*, 1 October 2008); 'Be transported to the lively heart of London in this timeless tale of the making of a lady' (*My Fair Lady* at the Theatre Royal, London, October 2008); 'Get ready to be transported to a magical, wonderful world! . . . We are instantly immersed in the glamorous, hilarious tale of a celebrity bride and her uproarious wedding day, complete with thrills and surprises that take both the cast (literally) and the audiences (metaphorically) soaring into the rafters' (*California Music Theatre*, 1 October 2008).

While the expressive and experiential reality of transportation seems evident, the question remains of how we can investigate the readerly sensation of transportation in cognitive poetic terms. Since transportation seems to be a form of projection of identity, or at least a close comparison of an alternate state of affairs, a worlds-based analysis seems to be the most promising technique to deploy. I will sketch this out briefly here, and return to it more extensively in Chapter 5.

Constance's emotions are being belittled by King Philip (who triggers this speech by observing 'You are as fond of grief as of your child') and by the Pope's messenger Pandolf ('Lady, you utter madness, and not sorrow'). In her speech, she complains about their failure to sympathise, and of course in the process she evokes sympathy in the theatre audience. She presents a delusional world in which her dead son Arthur is grotesquely impersonated by Grief, a world in which she also implicates herself, and this world is collapsed onto the actual reality of her life at that point in the play. A text world diagram (Figure 3e) illustrates this structure clearly.

In the discourse world (DW) of the theatre, a text world (TW) is jointly constructed in a viewer's mind by Shakespeare, the production crew including the actor playing Constance, and the audience including the individual viewer. In the speech quoted above, Constance presents a world-switch (WS) in which she describes her perception of Grief acting out Arthur's role. Strictly speaking, there is a two-step world-switch involved here, since there is a hypothetical situation being imagined (Arthur is already dead), and a personification metaphor being used. The embedded switched world presents an enactor of Constance ('me'), a deluded version of herself: the underlining in the diagram (see Figure 3e) here indicates a close identification of entities. The delusional world (WS) comes to overlay Constance's actual world (TW) in the course of her speech.

Constance sets out her delusional state of mind in the world-switch. The

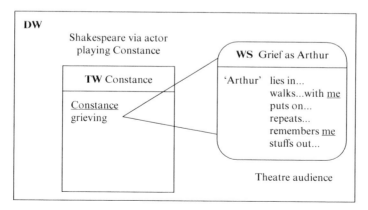

Figure 3e Text world diagram of Constance's speech

fact that the audience treats it as delusional has already been suggested by Philip and Pandolf's comments, but in her speech itself she signals the fictionality directly with an obvious volumising active verb ('fills . . . up') creating a personification of grief, and then more subtly in the potential double meaning of 'lies'. Grief stands as a replacement for Arthur, and takes on his attributes in a series of function-advancing verbs. The repetition of these without repeating the agent ('Grief'), it seems to me, works gradually to neglect the focus on Grief and replace it in audience attention with Arthur – the syntactic arrangement of these agentless clauses works to enact in the audience too the delusion that Arthur has gone and his place has been taken over. The effect, though, is of Arthur as a ghostly absence, the focus of attention but displaced by the strength of emotion.

The loss of Constance's sense of reality is marked iconically by the odd transitivity of the verb in '(Grief) Remembers me of all his (Arthur's) precious parts'. Given that a listener needs to take in the world-switch in order to keep track of what Constance is saying, from the vantage point within that switched world, the conclusion 'Then have I reason to be fond of grief' is naturally logical, but the mismatch between this statement and the audience's position in the discourse world is plainly evident. Constance has taken leave of her senses, and as if to underline this, she bids 'fare . . . well' immediately. Her speech foregrounds the ontologically alternate complexity of her mind in the next lines ('Had you such a loss as I, I could . . .'). This is another small world-switch (not diagrammed in Figure 3e), which again involves variant enactors: the first 'I' of the line who has the loss is the same deluded 'I' as the 'me' in the original world-switch, since the loss has not actually yet been suffered, and the second 'I' of the line is a further switched enactor, complete with all her reason, who would be giving comfort to a deluded Philip and Pandolf. The rhetorical patina of logic on top of this complex chaos is further discomfit for the audience. To emphasise the sense even further, Constance then draws explicit attention to symbolism itself by unbinding her hair with a commentary that mentions the disorder in her head. She ends her speech with a series of world-building noun-phrases ('my boy, my Arthur, my fair son') that become increasingly metaphorical ('My life, my joy, my food') and non-normally grammatical ('my all the world'). The final phrase ('my sorrow's cure') is a richly embedded metaphor (SORROW IS A DISEASE) that defies causality and temporality: Arthur, who is not dead, if brought back to life, would be the solution, if he were dead, to her sorrow at him being dead. Arthur is both there and not there. The noun-phrase listing simply emphasises that there are no function-advancers in Constance's world. She is paralysed and delusional with grief, and her only action left is to absent herself finally from the scene. She never returns to the play.

My brief analysis here draws out a situation of sympathy. The audience feels for Constance, but in general we do not feel actual grief – in any case, Arthur is not actually dead. The overlaying of the delusional world (WS) onto Constance's sense of the real world (TW) is watched by the audience, but there are sufficient textual and physical cues in the situation for an audience not to match Constance's emotional state. Here the analysis reveals a limited transportation: the audience is transported to the court and environment of the characters (in fact, placed in correspondence with the onlookers Philip and Pandolf in the scene), and is moved by Constance's display of feeling. But the world-switch she enacts is a matter of observation for the audience, rather than participation, and our transportation is not complete. This is sympathy. To end this chapter, I will consider a final framework for accounting for empathy.

Lamenting as emotional investment

The foregoing worlds analysis illuminates the constitutive readerly metaphor of a sense of transportation quite well. A text world account draws very clearly a correspondence between the emotional distance involving individuals and the ontological distance between worlds in the framework. As part of its discourse world level, it also provides a technical means of including readerly positioning in the account, and delineating the relationship between a reader and the world participants such as characters in the text worlds. It seems to me that a text world account draws a neat distinction of the dissimilarities between Ben Jonson's 'Daughter' and 'Son' poems that goes some way to explaining the commonest sense of their affective difference. The analysis also suggests how sympathy – especially in a theatrical setting where there is a real human voice articulating the text – can be regarded as a deictic distance from the reader. In text world theory terms, sympathy involves a reader in the discourse world observing a character in a text world and their world-switches; empathy, by contrast, involves a bidirectional trans-world mapping between the discourse world reader and the character in the embedded worlds.

However, a plain worlds-based analysis cannot easily get at the depth of emotional vulnerability, nor the power of the reading effect nor the sensed quality of feeling. These qualitative sensations underlie the constitutive readerly metaphor of investment. The transportation model of reading – though it too is generated from naturally-occurring discourse metaphors – does not cover all reading response articulations (such as control or investment). It also models the reader as a single unified entity, where the entire stable identity of the reader moves on the occurrence of literary reading. The reader, in this model, tends to be rather passively constructed, one who is transported elsewhere. It is clear that the most affecting moment along the transportation metaphor is the moment of return, where the physical text is closed and emotional resonance begins. An analytical representation of this moment is not easily achievable in current text world theory. Lastly, a model of analysis needs to account for the variability of response. I mentioned earlier that I have encountered cultural variation in audiences' manifestations of emotional responses when the texts which appear in this chapter were read in different settings across the world. However, I also discovered a curious consistency in the effectiveness of each text. For example, there are two poems that I will explore in the rest of this chapter. In readings of the first, by Tony Harrison, around two-thirds of the audience were observed to be physically affected by the poem. As I said earlier, this outward manifestation varied, but the rough two-thirds to one-third proportion seemed to be consistent from Japan to Argentina. By contrast, the second poem below, by Jon Silkin, had an even higher rate of affectivity: crudely, more people cried. In fact, this poem seemed to affect almost everyone in the room. I would like to be able to account for the inter-cultural consistency of each text, and also for the variability of readers in each separate reading.

The constitutive metaphor READING IS INVESTMENT offers a means of adapting a worlds-based account to give a deictically rich model of readerly engagement. As indicated above, readers commonly talk of their involvement in a literary text as an investment, where the currency of the investment is figured as time, emotional attachment, intellectual effort, or even actual cash. A conceptual net can be drawn to represent the idealised cognitive model (Lakoff 1987) for INVESTMENT (see Figure 3f).

The diagram in Figure 3f represents the key aspects, I think, in most people's schematised concept of investment. Mapping this to an emotional domain, as readers do when they use the source domain (INVESTMENT) to discuss their literary experience (READING), results in a series of commitments and encourages a particular view of reading, involvement and identity. Investment involves an assumption of an ownership of resources that are available to be invested (the reader does not arrive in the emotional literary marketplace as a blank slate). These resources are transferred in the transactional process of reading, an engagement which involves a potential loss, and therefore a risk. In emotional involvement, this risk can be perceived as wasting time (through a linked metaphor of TIME IS MONEY) or as opening up a vulnerability. The invested resources are understood to be at work, with an anticipation of a return on the investment that will outdo the initial loss. Clearly there are matters of risk and faith inherent in the investor, and a flow of resource to and trust in the object of investment. Investors look to the object in anticipation of an improvement in themselves.

There are interesting resonances in regarding individual investment as the adoption of literary stance by a reader and understanding sympathy as a form of social investment. In economic and management theory, the metaphor is explicitly theoretical in the notion of 'emotional capital' (derived from Bourdieu's (1972) notion of 'social capital', defined in economics as 'sympathy'). This stands in contrast to 'intellectual capital' – that is, knowledge – so information and aesthetic attachment are viewed as forms of capital value that can be transmitted, shared, put to work, and operate in production. The return on readerly investment can be regarded as empathy. In

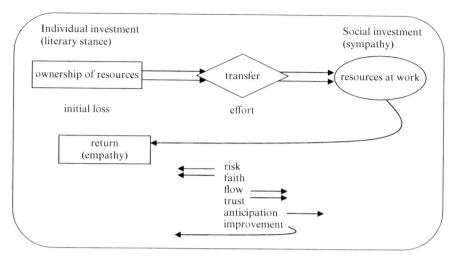

Figure 3f A conceptual net for INVESTMENT

Figure 3f, sympathy is modelled as a distance from the readerly stance, which accords with the distancing between worlds drawn in relation to Constance's speech in *King John* above. The feedback loop that produces empathy as a return on investment indicates a shift back, as a result of the mapping, towards a realignment of the readerly stance. I will show some examples of this below. It is plain from this model that there is a directly proportional scaling between perceived effort invested and the degree of empathy felt, with the stylistic patterns of the literary work serving as a multiplier in the process.

A model of reading drawing on emotional investment has several advantages. It retains the *in/out* metaphor implicit in the notion of transportation and explicit in text world theory in order to talk about depth of involvement. It explains the ratio of effort to payoff in literary reading. It accounts for readerly difference as variation in emotional investment. Vulnerability is figured as personal identity risk, especially in a social setting where face (Goffman 1967, 1981; Brown and Levinson 1987) plays a part. And it involves a notion of personality as multi-faceted and socially constructed, able to be fragmented into smaller resource packets that can be proportionately committed to the task in hand. In relation to the contrasting readerly effects of Jonson's 'Daughter' and 'Son' poems above, a view of the reader's emotional investment foregrounds the degrees of reader effort and engagement necessary for an emotional effect. The imaginative deictic positioning, especially in the 'Son' poem, requires the adoption of a literary stance that in turn requires a movement of identity. Having shifted to map with a speaking 'I' in this poem, the text forces a shift in the last four lines to a third person, disembodied sense. In the 'Daughter' poem, only the final two words enact this shift into the speaker's mind. And, of course, neatly for my argument here, the 'Son' poem explicitly includes the ACCOUNTANCY metaphor to underline the investment of emotion in its reading.

How does this view of reading work dynamically? In my collection of 'tear-jerkers', one of the most successful in terms of having my audience in tears is this famous poem by Tony Harrison.

Long Distance

Though my mother was already two years dead
Dad kept her slippers warming by the gas,
put hot water bottles her side of the bed
and still went to renew her transport pass.

You couldn't just drop in. You had to phone.
He'd put you off an hour to give him time
to clear away her things and look alone
as though his still raw love were such a crime.

He couldn't risk my blight of disbelief
though sure that very soon he'd hear her key
scrape in the rusted lock and end his grief.
He *knew* she'd just popped out to get the tea.

I believe life ends with death, and that is all.
You haven't both gone shopping; just the same,
in my new black leather phone book there's your name
and the disconnected number I still call.

Tony Harrison (1978)

In many readings and discussions of this text across the world, I have found that roughly but consistently two-thirds of the audience are visibly physically moved by the poem (this manifests itself in different cultural kinesics across the world, from the Japanese facial frown of extreme concern to the American quiet tears). I even think that most people begin to exhibit this observable emotional reaction at the word 'You' in the third-last line, though it is difficult for me to be certain given the problem of observation. I am not saying, of course, that the other one-third of people who appear unmoved actually *are* unmoved, simply that they do not display their emotion physically at this point. It must also be observed that there is a natural empathetic connection made in listeners from hearing the human voice (mine) read this poem aloud, which lies at one remove in printed text; one audience member (in Finland) also commented to me that my northern English accent contributed to the poem's effects (though my accent is from some sixty miles away from Harrison's native Leeds).

Applying an investment model to a reading of this text involves, firstly, an understanding of the personal resources committed by readers, and where the poem draws on universal shared resources. All readers have, or have had, parents, and the experience of their deaths may be a painful memory or a painful speculation. Memory rather than anticipation seems to be a significant resource for investment on this occasion, since, if there is any social factor that seems to characterise the two-thirds group it is that they appear to be over the age of thirty – roughly the point at which the older generation are likely to be dying off or a point at which individuals start to think about their parents' mortality rather more, perhaps. At the same time, there is a social investment (sympathy) and an individual investment (empathy) being made here: the degrees of perceived similarity and difference between the poetic world and the reader's world are relevant to the intensity of the empathetic connection. There are certain particularities concerning a twentieth-century northern English working class context here, such as slippers and gas-heating, the use of hot water bottles in non-centrally heated houses, the bus pass for pensioners, the rusty lock and 'tea' – the evening meal, not the warm drink. These particularities locate the immediate context of the poem very precisely in cultural terms, and this is confirmed if the poetic voice is assigned very closely to that of Tony Harrison himself: other work by him addresses directly his place as a grammar school educated man with a northern English voice, and the tension between his working class roots and his status as a poet and playwright. For a reader, recognising a specific positioning in the naming of 'mother' and 'Dad' and these other specificities is a form of investment as complicit understanding, and the monologic form increases believability, trust and good faith in the poetic voice.

The poem foregrounds the feeling of different moments through a manipulation of time-sequencing. Chronologically, the events are:

T1: Father/mother/son, going shopping, popping out to get the tea
T2: Mother dies
T3: Two years later, son regards father: re-iterated events, with micro-shift of 'one hour'
T4: Father dies
T5: Son writes poem.

However, the sequence presented in the poem to the reader is:

(T2 world switch) – T3 text world – T5 discourse world – (T4 world switch).

The major shift in perspective is T3 to T5, with T1 a brief gesture. T2 and T4 are world-switch 'asides' from the main T5 discourse world. There is no need to sketch this as a diagram to realise that there is a rich texture of worlds involved in the poem, with cross-world mappings between the different enactors of 'my', 'I' and 'you' at different times in the speaker's life: 'you', among other referents (see below), can mean the speaker too. The fact that the deictics in the poem move closer temporally (mother's death to the moment of writing), spatially (from his father's house to his own), and perceptually ('you' to 'he' to 'I') supports the establishment of empathy. A greater distancing effect would be created if the time sequence were to be reversed, with the poetic voice starting with an admission of missing his father, who missed his mother. In the sequence of the poem, the act of missing moves closer to the reader.

The other main location for emotional investment is the set of inter-related belief worlds that the reader is invited to activate imaginatively. The father's viewpoint is signalled three times by the ontological shifter 'though', and the son's viewpoint by the discoursally equivalent 'just the same':

> 'Though my mother was already two years dead'
> 'as though his still raw love were such a crime'
> 'though sure that very soon he'd hear her key'
> 'just the same, /in my new black leather phone book there's your name.'

There is, of course, a mismatch between the father's and son's belief worlds and their wish worlds, and the reader is required to invest some emotional resource into all of these worldviews in order to make sense of them. Investing in them involves buying into their painful dissonant consequences.

The poem also matches this conceptual configuration with an iconic additive syntax as a flow of grief, stopped up with matching clause endings and line endings. The additive syntax is cleverly done: across the first three stanzas, the lines appear to end at complete constituent boundaries, allowing a brief reading pause before the absence of a full-stop punctuation and the continuation of the sentence in the next line forces the revised reading to run on. The pattern breaks in the final stanza with 'and that is all'. Of course, that is not all, and the final three lines release the syntax and the grief in one single onward flow in the reading. It seems to me this is the moment of payoff, and the return on the emotional investment is signalled very directly with the line-initial capitalised 'You'. The two 'You's of the second stanza are generic 'one' as used in most colloquial and northern English dialects, blended with this specific son, whereas this last 'You' denotes both his dead parents: it is a shock here to jump forward and realise his Dad has died too, and also I think the emotional identification up to this point encourages a suggestion of reader-address in 'You' as well.

Eavesdropping, even necessarily, on the poet's interior emotions is uncomfortable and intimate, and all of this works so well because of the depth of emotional investment that the poem has required up to this point. Activating the multiplicity of deictic possibilities for 'you' in relation to the different world-enactors of 'I' and the complicit outward readerly address of 'you' is a complex and rich investment of emotion that produces the observable physical effects of empathy in an audience sharing a reading. My suggestion is that those one-third of people who appear unmoved, and specifically the sub-set of this group that actually *are* relatively less affected, have not been led to make the same level of emotional investment, so the payoff in empathetic response is lessened. Why should this be? Drawing on my framework in chapter 2, it could be, of course, that the intensity of their reading is not as great as the emotionally-affected group. Their level of attention might simply be lower, which could be caused by all sorts of idiosyncratic factors distracting them to other things at the time. This would mean that they were simply unaware, even at a sub-conscious level, of the working of textual patterns in the poem. Alternatively, the specificities of age and culture that the poem draws out might simply be too distant for these readers, rendering a gap between their discourse world and the poetic text world that is bridged by sympathy but not closely mapped for empathy. Of course, by contrast, recognition of these cultural specificities in an involved reader will enhance even further the empathetic closeness of the mapping, and heighten the return on the emotional engagement.

The final text I would like to explore in this chapter has a very high trauma rate for my readers. I suggest this is because, even though its subject-matter is ostensibly more specific and less universal than the loss of parents, it is textually configured in a way which makes it appear rhetorically more universal than the Harrison poem. What I mean is that there are very few culturally specific evocations that could distract potentially non-involved readers.

Death of a Son
(who died in a mental hospital aged one)

Something has ceased to come along with me.
Something like a person: something very like one.
   And there was no nobility in it
      Or anything like that.

Something was there like a one year
Old house, dumb as stone. While the near buildings
   Sang like birds and laughed
      Understanding the pact

They were to have with silence. But he
Neither sang nor laughed. He did not bless silence
   Like bread, with words.
      He did not forsake silence.

But rather, like a house in mourning
Kept the eye turned in to watch the silence while
    The other houses like birds
        Sang around him.

And the breathing silence neither
Moved nor was still.

    I have seen stones: I have seen brick
But this house was made up of neither bricks nor stone
    But a house of flesh and blood
        With flesh of stone

    And bricks for blood. A house
Of stones and blood in breathing silence with the other
    Birds singing crazy on its chimneys.
        But this was silence,

    This was something else, this was
Hearing and speaking though he was a house drawn
    Into silence, this was
        Something religious in his silence,

    Something shining in his quiet,
This was different this was altogether something else:
    Though he never spoke, this
        Was something to do with death.

    And then slowly the eye stopped looking
Inward. The silence rose and became still.
The look turned to the outer place and stopped,
    With the birds still shrilling around him.
        And as if he could speak

He turned over on his side with his one year
Red as a wound

He turned over as if he could be sorry for this
And out of his eyes two great tears rolled, like stones, and he died.

                                        Jon Silkin (1954)

This has been described as 'probably the most moving and sad elegiac poem of this century' (Booth 1985: 154), and my own experience of reading it to an audience is indeed of a high level of manifestly observable empathetic response. More people, wherever they are in the world, cry at this poem than any other text I know. Yet there are mercifully few in my audiences, I would like to imagine, who have actually experienced the death of their one-year old son in a mental hospital, so the deep empathy involved here is a matter of emotional work rather than instant identificatory recognition.

Unlike the culturally-specific references in the Harrison poem above, this text draws on metaphoric sources that are truly universal: buildings, bread, bodies, birds singing, sound and vision, and death. At the same time, and most suitably for the subject of the poem, it draws on basic image-schemas of motion and stasis, container and contained, inside and outside, and noise and silence that are the first to develop in human cognition even before birth. There are projections of these basic sources into abstractions, but often the projection is confused, stuttering and unstable, and there is a failure of the adult mind to make sense of the incomprehensible thing that, until the very end of the poem, has not yet quite become a person, incapable of communication, inarticulate and difficult.

Unlike the Harrison text, the Silkin poem tells the reader in the title and sub-title what the poem will be about. However, it goes on to confound expectations of the sort of description that you might be anticipating from the Martial, Jonson, Stevenson or Shakespeare laments previously discussed in this chapter. The poem begins with vagueness: 'something', repeated several times throughout the entire poem. In the first two stanzas, the 'something' is the boy; later in the poem as the boy slips further away, even this word becomes more abstract – 'something else', 'something religious', 'something shining', 'altogether something else', 'something to do with death'.

Image-schemas are basic to human cognition, with the physical properties of objects in motion and friction, inertia and stasis developing early and forming the extended basis in later cognitive development for trajector-landmark relations of grammatical verb-chains and abstract relationships. In this poem, though, the basic elements of such image-schemas are invoked and then contradicted or denied by two main world-switch triggers: negations and metaphors. For example, in 'Something has ceased to come along with me', the invocation of basic movement along the universal and conventional conceptual metaphor of LIFE IS A JOURNEY is almost instantly switched by the negational verb 'ceased'. At the same time, the two people (described son and speaking father) are delineated into separate but linked text worlds, and the spatial deixis in 'to come along' positions the viewpoint with the father, leaving the son adrift and motionless in the switched world. Almost at the same time, metaphoricality is introduced, and we can see here that metaphor is a close relation of negation: for X to be Y, it cannot in the same world still be X. The painful irony here is that the metaphorical mapping is expressed in a way that makes the metaphor highly visible (Stockwell 1994) in the use of the simile form 'like a person'. This, and its intensified reiteration – 'something very like one' – serves simultaneously to undermine the assertion even in the moment of uttering it. Of course, there are also multiple ambivalences in 'one' as an elided form of 'one person' and 'one year old', and 'one' meaning the generic universal and reader-directed 'you'. The double-edgedness of metaphorical and negational switching in motion and stasis is captured in the centre of the poem, where the silence 'neither Moved nor was still', and of course the moment at which life stops at the end is marked by 'He turned over', repeated twice, and his tears which 'rolled, like stones'.

The image-schema of containment, with its basic relationships between container and contained, and the related abstractions inside and outside, is also exploited in the poem. This conceptual scheme underlies the prepositional phrases with 'in' ('no nobility in it', 'a house in mourning', 'in breathing silence', 'a house drawn into silence', 'religious in his silence', 'shining in his quiet'). As this progression of examples shows, the poem moves to make this underlying concept explicitly metaphorical. Combined, the spatial relationships generated by motion and containment image-schemas have the potential to define the locations of invoked noun-phrases ('the near buildings', 'the other houses like birds / Sang around him', 'on its chimneys'), but of course these locating features shift constantly throughout the poem, as the target metaphorical domain (the boy) is joined with alternating and fleeting and protean source domains. So from being 'very like' a person, he becomes 'like a one year / Old house' (the line break causing a stutter in reading and drawing attention to the metaphoricality), with 'the near buildings' by consistency of the metaphorical mapping standing then presumably for the other babies in the hospital ward, crying 'like birds'. The simile forms in this part of the poem ('like a one year old house', 'like a house in mourning') represent a weak commitment to the truth-value of the metaphor, but this strength varies as the poem progresses. The other children lose the simile to become simply 'the other houses', implicitly figuring him too as a house; this metaphorical strengthening of commitment is made to seem natural immediately by the closely following simile that distracts attention away from the anomalous metaphor ('The other houses like birds / Sang around him'). Notice too, here, how the mapping in the simile (birds are capable of singing) is transferred, with the sleight of hand of the line break, onto the house and thus the other children. These metaphorical slippages are too fast and numerous and skilfully distracted for the reader to disentangle their illogic in the moments of reading.

Once figured as a house, the metaphor is later unconstructed ('this house was made up of neither bricks nor stone'); though it has 'flesh of stone / And bricks for blood' and becomes reconstructed as 'a house of stones and blood'; though it later still has 'chimneys'; though the other children in the mental ward ('birds singing crazy') are perched on them. All of this confusing shifting is drawn into a lacuna with only vague and ill-defined edges ('This was something else') and the ghostly memory of previous attempts at definition ('though he was a house drawn / Into silence'). This dismantling of metaphor is the outcome of the dual technique of metaphorical and negational world-switching, and the moving in and out of these transient, fragile, precarious worlds creates the sense of instability across the poem. The sense of the child's stillness in contrast with the perceptual anguish of the father, who turns over different schemes for coming to terms with what is happening, is an effect of these shifts, and the implied conceptual motion of rapid attentional shifts in the texture of the poem parallels the in/out motif across the text: in breathing, in silence, in the child's eye looking inward and then outward, in turning over, and in the tears rolling 'out of his eyes'.

Inarticulacy is the brilliant cumulative effect of the poet's carefully articulated struggle for definition. Even the conversational vagueness and the indented graphology of the lines are stuttering. There are many turns to religion for comfort: resurrection, trans-substantiation and penitence in 'bless silence like bread', 'house of flesh and blood', 'something religious', 'the outer place', 'sorry for this' at the end, and the rolling away of stones after the 'Death of a Son'. But these are world-switched away from the present moment, negated ('did not bless'), metaphorised ('like bread'), or finally analogised, hypothesised and modalised ('as if he could be sorry'). After this last preparatory grounding of shifting complexity, the only simple, unmodified clause in the entire text world of the poem is the final phrase, 'and he died'.

It seems to me that the highly-grained micro-texture of creating world-switches and almost immediately dismantling them in several different ways offers a reader an enormously rich opportunity for depth of effort. The disruption of patterning – in metaphor, in negation, in variable line-lengths and the fragmentation of stanza forms, in the variation between end-stopped lines and continuations, and in the reconfiguration of image-schemas, the most basic and naturalised forms of cognition – all these disruptions take the reader across a rough ground of texture. Readers who engage with this, who invest their emotions in trying to 'come along' with the poetic viewpoint, are rewarded, if that is the right term, with one of the most moving and affecting experiences in literature. The degree of involvement which is necessary for this effect defines the experience as empathy.

Sense and sensibility

This chapter began by asserting a continuity between physical and virtual sensation, not as an arbitrary or allegorical connection but as an unavoidable implication of taking cognitive embodiment seriously. I began by noting the different sorts of physical manifestations that literary works can give rise to, including external facial and bodily signs as well as internal state-changes in feelings, emotions and dispositions. There is no question that some literary encounters involve deep feelings and reactions in readers, whether these are physically observable and measurable or not, and also no question that the same text can produce a variety of responses in a group of readers, depending on their disposition and intensity of engagement. I set out various ways in which these effects can be accounted for.

Those people who read this chapter in draft reported to me that reading the last two literary texts in the chapter was a moving experience in itself, but following the analysis closely further enhanced the sensation of sadness and loss. It can easily be objected, though, that literary feeling is not the same as genuine, authentic, natural feeling. However deeply my readers respond to the lament poems featured in this chapter, there is still something more authentic in real-life grief than literary grief, even if that literary representation has reality for the authors (as in most of the laments in this chapter).

Langacker (2008: 536–8) points out that all language representations involve some degree of *simulation*, the principle of cognitive projection operating on the traditional notion of linguistic displacement. Even face-to-face online commentary on the shared situation involves grammaticalisation and assumptions about shared embodied experience, and so has a small degree of simulation in this sense (see further Chapter 6 below). For Langacker, this means that expressions are to a greater or lesser degree *attenuated* from the direct reality (though, of course, that pure reality is not attainable at all except through some experiential representation). Attenuation, nevertheless, is a thread of connection along which sense and sensibility can be mapped. Some literary works close the simulated distance to a greater degree than others, never becoming identical, but still achieving such minimal attenuation that the difference is barely noticed at all.

This was brought home to me very affectingly recently when I attended the funeral of a husband of one of my colleagues, and one of the readings was from John Donne:

> Sweetest love, I do not goe,
>   For wearinesse of thee,
> Nor in hope the world can show
>   A fitter Love for mee;
>   But since that I
> Must dye at last, 'tis best,
> To use my selfe in jest
>   Thus by fain'd deaths to dye.
>
> John Donne (1985: 62, composed 1611)

The death in the poem is a metaphor for departure, but in the funeral context it was literalised again. Almost everyone in the church was crying at this point, not because of their literary sensibility (actually, only a handful of us there were literary academics), but because the poem's simulation brought home most articulately the tangible feelings present on the occasion. There was no sense of attenuation at all, just an empathetic feeling with our friend who was saying goodbye to her husband for the last time.

The conclusion, for me then, is that simulated literary feeling and original non-literary feeling are both authentic, are both in fact the same thing. They are both caused by perceiving and representing an experience to consciousness. They both involve the same physical effects. They both produce sensations that feel the same. The difference between original (minimally simulated) and literary feeling is one of degree or volume rather than type. We talk of the minimal simulation as 'raw' emotion, and we mean it is closest to what we think of as reality; it is least attenuated. The sense of attenuation itself is what makes us think that literary emotion is less authentic, but it is only this sense that makes the difference.

Reading

I have avoided getting into the debate differentiating between emotion, feelings, dispositions, and so on. See LeDoux (1998), Opdahl (2002), Miall and Kuiken (2002), Oatley (1992, 1994, 2003, 2004), Oatley, Keltner and Jenkins (2006), and Niedenthal, Krauth-Gruber and Ric (2006).

For more on empathy from a cognitive poetic perspective, but with a different argument from mine, see Keen (2007). For the relationship between sensation, perception and cognition, see Wolfe et al. (2006) and Goldstein (2006). For cognitive approaches to phonology, see Durand and Laks (2002) and Välimaa-Blum (2005). For work on iconicity, see the collections in Nanny and Fischer (1999), Muller and Fischer (2003), and Willems and De Cuypere (2009). For interesting work on synaesthesia and poetic effects, see Shen and Cohen (1998, 2008), and Tsur (2006).

4 Voice and Mind

At the conclusion of the previous chapter, I suggested that a major factor in the sensation of texture lies in the process of crossing world-levels. In this chapter, I will elaborate on that argument with a closer exploration of the cognitive mechanics that readers must engage in when experiencing fictional literary works and the beings which inhabit them. Though narrative fiction will be in focus in my discussion, it is important to remember again that literary discourse occupies a position of continuity with all other non-literary forms of discourse, in most respects. Literature is the complex artistic extension of our everyday linguistic and cognitive capacities. Literary genres and registers are assigned a global value – as comic, as novelistic, as lyric, as lament, or as literary, and so on – and this general frame does affect the way in which the work itself is experienced. But aside from this general assignment, readers do not suddenly become non-human beings when confronted by the literary.

Asserting the continuities of the textual options and the commonalities of cognitive faculties between the literary and the non-literary does not exclude a recognition that exploring literary reading can tell us more general things about our conceptual make-up. Literary texture often exploits everyday patterns and processes, foregrounds them, makes them appear odd, heightens readerly awareness so that we notice things we might not otherwise notice in a non-artistic setting. There is thus an everyday payoff in cognitive poetic investigation, as well as a better understanding of what makes the literary work work. However, in this book I am particularly, and even only, interested in the workings of literary encounters. These encounters primarily involve people: readers, authors and characters. From the perspective of literary reading, all of these entities (even the first) are refracted through the reader's consciousness: so characters are people with a life inside a reader's mind; authors are people whose ideas and traits are assembled in a reader's mind; and readers themselves are sets of stances that a reader is more or less aware of in different circumstances. The ontological differences involved here are products of the assignments of value: characters are generally not real; authors are generally real but not known well; reading is a self-reflexive activity consisting of a real integrated personality mediating a partial avatar of themselves. This conceptualisation will inform this and the following two chapters of this book.

The texture of edges

Texture is felt when the mind is aware of the body moving from one medium to another (sand to water, grass to gravel, novel to newspaper, sans serif to italics), or from one quality of ground to another (smooth to fractured, granulated to liquid, narrator's voice to character's voice) or when the ground changes its reference points (ascending in a lift, sliding down ice, jumping in a flashback, unmasking the monster as the villain). These senses are all to a greater or lesser extent physically-focused conceptualisations or conceptually-focused physical analogues, along a scale of sensation. What they all have in common is the flow of experience across a transitional moment. The essence of texture, then, is in edges.

Returning to what we know about the perception of physical objects, Smith, Johnson and Spelke (2003) demonstrate experimentally that objects with regular predictable edge-boundaries achieve a unity in perception more readily than objects with ragged or misaligned edges. Furthermore, when these objects move against a background or are occluded by other objects, the misaligned edges are harder to track and call for greater effort and attention. Peterson and Enns (2005) observe too that expected edges are easier to track in motion, and that past experience of similar objects speeds up the rate of edge processing. Though edges are a transitional concept, this experimental work shows that any particular edge is regarded as 'belonging' to the figure rather than the ground (see also Carstensen (2007) and my discussion of lacunae in Chapter 2), and the edge has what I will call a *vector* value. A vector is the combined value of the magnitude (size or length) of an entity plus its directionality or orientation. In Euclidian mathematics, the end-point of a vector is its 'sense'. An edge of an object thus has a shape (such as smooth or grainy, straight or crooked) and a directionality (it both points towards the figure and is regarded as part of it). Peterson and Enns (2005) refer to the set of qualities of object-boundaries as the *edge complex*. This set requires particular processing effort, and they also note that edge complexes appear to be processed more efficiently in the linguistic left hemisphere of the brain.

There are consequences of these insights for the texture of literary reading. For example, it is clear that reading across different attractors in the course of a text correlates with our cognitive faculties for understanding motion. As well as stylistic elements denoting actual motion, the forward directionality of reading across a texture generates a sense of virtual motion that is handled in the same way, I argue. Motion is fundamentally a matter of the interaction of a viewing point and space. SPACE, then, is the basic source domain for all of the related conceptual metaphors involved in point of view and perceived motion. In relation to point of view in a (literary) text, Fowler (1986) delineates four basic types: spatial point of view, temporal point of view, point of view on the plane of ideology, and point of view on the psychological plane. The first of these seems clearly the most literal use of point of view as SPACE, with deixis and other locative expressions encoding a particular physical relationship with the objects perceived in the text world. The same deictics and locative expressions are used metaphorically to represent time as space, though (as Evans 2003: 57–77 points out) two further sub-metaphors provide alternative vectors: the 'Moving Time' mapping (which, strictly, is a 'moving object' mapping, as in 'Christmas is coming') and the 'Moving Ego' mapping ('we're getting close to Christmas'). Psychological and ideological point of view are, in practice, hard to distinguish and might better be treated as the same thing.

Psychological and ideological point of view are, of course, also metaphorical mappings based on SPACE, in these cases both involving a virtual shift into the imagined mind of a different perceiver. Simpson (1993: 43) argues that spatio-temporal point of view is best regarded as a sub-set of psychological point of view, since the place and time of perception is anchored to the *perception* itself. The governing factor for Simpson is the effect of modalisation in allowing the reader to reconstruct the viewpoint of the speaker. It should of course be noted that even spatial point of view in a literary context involves a displacement from the reader's physical setting, and so can be seen as being only relatively literal. Chilton (2004), in developing an ingenious three-dimensional model of viewpoint with spatial, temporal and modal axes, still relies on the spatial metaphor for the analytical framework, as well as *space* as one of the factors of point of view. Nevertheless, in general it seems reasonable to observe that all forms of virtual viewpoint encoded in texts are analogues of spatial relations and motions.

As Palmer (2004) sets out in detail, the governing feature of fiction of any sort is the reader's construction of alternate minds, in the forms of author, imagined author, narrator, various characters, and even group or generalised minds such as in gossip, public opinion, common morals or the expressions of any other body of people (see also Palmer 2005, 2007). He calls this basic feature of narrativity *intermentality*, also drawing implicitly on the spatial metaphor of one mind moving into another. Palmer's is a cognitive poetic approach that combines stylistic analysis with an inescapable sense of the reader's mental construction of another persona. The most natural assumption in encountering language is that someone has produced that language, and this approach simply projects that basic intuition into the imaginary and virtual realm. The fact that this is reader-centred means that – at a primary level of the reader's encounter – it does not matter whether the author, narrator, character or any variants of these are as real as the reader or not. Furthermore, since the minds of others are indivisible parts of the bodies of others (a cognitive linguistic principle and a basic premise of human experience), there is a very strong (perhaps even unavoidable) inclination to generate a sense of physical existence in textual and even fictional characters, narrators and authors. Curiously, this even goes for group-discourse as in Palmer's (2007) examples from George Eliot's *Middlemarch*: 'Many people believed that Lydgate's coming to the town at all was really due to Bulstrode'; 'the town knew of the loan, believed it to be a bribe'; 'There was a general impression, however, that Lydgate was not altogether a common country doctor', and many other examples. Here, the notions of collective, political or public 'bodies' achieve a group dynamic that is still recognisably human and physical. Of course, the town of Middlemarch, or its common gossip, is a less prototypically apt manifestation of an embodied mind than a single character (Lydgate, Bulstrode, or the others), but the perceived difference, I argue along with Palmer, is one of degree. The difference, ontologically, is also irrelevant, since both group minds and character minds are, strictly speaking, equally fictional.

Viewpoint as vector

The crucial relationship between reader and fictional entities is at base a spatial one, which is then extrapolated and projected into higher-level and more complex social, emotional and ethical relationships. Distance, and the crossing of distance (motion), and the orientation in space (vector), gives the possible dimensions that a spatial scheme can entail as *distance, direction, pace*, and *quality* of movement (see Figure 4a). Firstly, the perceived distance between reader and fictional entity (whether the sense of author, narrator, character, and so on) can be calibrated deictically. The spatial distance evoked by locative proximity or deictic distals or alienating lexical choices is rooted in a sense of physical space that lends a tactile sense to emotional or ideological remoteness. For example in the previous chapter, the distance between reader and Constance (in *King John*) is further than the distance between reader and Silkin (in 'Death of a Son'), in terms of world-boundaries crossed by switching, and the emotional distance corresponds directly with this sense. Perceived distance is the key to a sense of authenticity, trust and intermental engagement.

The relative orientations of the reader to the characters' worlds in these cases add in the vectored directionality: in everyday terms, a reader comes face to face with different aspects of a character, and feels a 'connection' with that person. Characters that are directly presented (where the reader is faced with the direct viewpoint of or on the character) are likely to generate a closer connection than characters which are presented indirectly, where the readerly gaze is averted or distracted by other prominent features or other characters. For example, Constance offers her own direct viewpoint; the persona in the Silkin poem offers his own direct viewpoint on his son; but in the opening to

Hardy's *The Return of the Native*, discussed in Chapter 2 above, the view-points of actual humans in the landscape are averted from the reader's scrutiny by the textual techniques of generalisation and indefiniteness. There is clearly less likelihood that a reader will connect emotionally with such backgrounded characters in a passage like that.

The vector between reader and character (R to C in Figure 4a) also has the property of *pace*. A sense of speed in the presentation of viewpoint is a consequence of how fast a reader perceives their access to a character (the distance of R → C over a sense of time). For example, a narrative technique in which the stream of consciousness of a character's thoughts details every flickering instant of her life is likely to be regarded as a 'fast' connection with that character. Pace in a spatial source domain invokes that part of the basic image-schema that is profiled as speed of motion. Higher-level extensions of this in literary reading might be felt as a sense of paciness in a narrative conveyed through this viewpoint, or noisiness, or, most abstractedly, busy-ness, stress, excitement or anxiety (see the correspondences between fullness, brightness, noisiness and active motion in Chapter 2). By contrast, a sense of a calm, peaceful or contemplative character and the scene viewed through her can be modelled here as a perceived slowness of pace in the relationship between reader and character.

Lastly, a model of viewpoint in spatial vector terms needs also to take account of the sense of quality in the reader-character relationship. A character-accessible world that is heavily modalised and a character-accessible world that is heavily metaphorised or negated or hypothetical involve a reader crossing very different sorts of world-edges. The nature of the relationship alters accordingly. The four properties of the relationship between

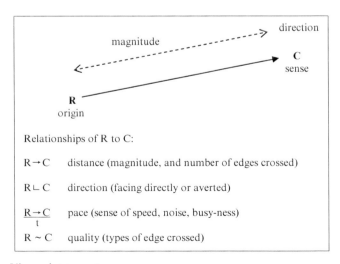

Figure 4a Viewpoint as vector

reader and fictional entity (in Figure 4a) will inform the discussion of readerly stance towards the end of this chapter. First, though, some comments on the 'sense' end of the vector terminal: the character.

The prototypicality of character

In cognitive prototypical terms, the best example of a person is, tautologically, a person, especially if that person is yourself. The next best example is someone else located near to you. A less good example of a person is someone you are told about, or someone you met once a long time ago, or a friend of a friend of a friend. Ontologically speaking, a fictional character ought to be a really poor example of a person, having neither historical physicality, nor an actual mind, nor an actual body. However, the switch across a fictional edge does not seem to work like this. Readers commonly talk about fictional characters in very similar terms to their discourse about friends and acquaintances, and though for the most part they know that fictional people are not real people, many of the textual negotiations involved in reading characterisation are extrapolations of real relationships.

The scale of extrapolation can be regarded as a graded set of prototypicality judgements, even within the fictional domain. For example, the best examples of a person in a fictional work are likely to be those in which there is a strong vector relationship between reader and character. An example would be a character who is textually prominent, such as by being the narrator or primary focaliser, who filters most of the world-switches through his own consciousness, who presents a rich set of sub-worlds within the fictional text-world, and whose perceptual system is foregrounded by explicitly being the filter of events. The reader's relationship with such a character would be close, direct, pacy and qualitatively rich, in the terms sketched out above.

By contrast, the poorest examples of people in fictional worlds are the non-character elements such as abstractions; landscape objects; immovable objects; human-scale objects such as tools; machines with moving or display parts; plants; animals; and groups or ill-defined people (this sequence in approaching order to the radial centre of a prototypical domain). By 'groups or ill-defined people' I mean the sense that 'the market' or 'a German' are less good examples of a person than a named individual. Most of the early examples in this list consist of such bad examples of persons that they could only be rendered personable by an unnatural, shocking or innovative narrative technique. For example, the most common forms of unnatural scaling up of a poor prototype are the personification of abstractions and the anthropomorphisation of animals. Common personifications of abstractions include Death as a grim reaper, old Father Time, Mother Nature, the three Fates Clotho (the spinner), Lachesis (the measurer) and Atropos (the cutter of the thread of life), Britannia as a trident-wielding national personification of

Britain, and Uncle Sam as a figure of the US government. Anthropomorphised animals are even more common in literary works from the earliest recorded oral folktales to contemporary literature. The usual means by which animals are scaled into people are by wearing clothes (Rupert the Bear), having the power of speech (the Town Mouse and the Country Mouse), having rational skills of goal-planning (Brer Rabbit) and other non-natural cognitive capacities (Lassie, Trigger, Aslan), and frequently combinations of all of these.

As a readerly connection from selfhood to character is made along a vector, the first boundary crossed is the edge of the text world, into the fictional domain. In line with my comments above, the directionality of this virtual motion is inward, towards the character, and the edge also belongs to the character-domain. Engaging with fictionality, then, first involves some degree, however small, of readerly effacement, as consciousness is 'pointed at' character along the process of characterisation. Engaging with the vector of viewpoint involves looking away from the self. The terminal end of the vector (the 'sense') is the textual realisation of the character-entity, where the textualisation of the character's selfhood is asserted. These textual moments can be analysed in three related dimensions: physical description, psychological description, and social description. Following Egri's (1960) dimensions for dramatic personae, a character's physiology is carried by their physical appearance, their gait and their clothing; their sociology is signalled by the status they are accorded by other characters, their occupation and apparent and described relationships; and their psychology encompasses signs of their mental and emotional states, their intelligence, motivations, current thoughts and general temperament. In prose, the first encounter with a character – especially in genre fiction – is usually a description of physical appearance. Often, in fictional art, each of these dimensions (especially physical appearance) serve as emblems of the others, and collectively they are often emblematic of the thematic significance of the character in the work as a whole.

For example, in Yann Martel's (2002) *Life of Pi*, the central narrative concerns a sixteen-year-old Indian boy, Pi, who survives adrift at sea in a lifeboat with a companion called Richard Parker, who, it emerges, is in fact a large Bengal tiger being shipped from Pi's parents' zoo to North America. It is not immediately apparent, after the shipwreck, that Richard Parker is a tiger. The novel up to this point has very carefully avoided this crucial piece of character information, without the narrator actually acting in bad faith. For example, on the second page of the narrative proper, told from the retrospective position of later life in Canada, the narrating Pi says,

> Richard Parker has stayed with me. I've never forgotten him. Dare I say I miss him? I do. I miss him. I still see him in my dreams. They are nightmares mostly, but nightmares tinged with love. Such is the strangeness of the human heart. I still cannot understand how he could

abandon me so unceremoniously, without any sort of goodbye, without looking back even once.

Yann Martel (2002: 6)

The conventional and western name is the obvious stylistic device that deflects the characterisation of the entity as a human person (another huge tiger, which Pi's father shows killing a goat as a warning to Pi of how dangerous tigers are, is called 'Mahisha'). However, this is also reinforced more subtly by the delineation of a personal relationship that is social and expressed in psychological, emotional terms. The power of conscious awareness and potential for speech are assigned to Richard Parker in the final sentence, albeit subordinated to the negated and non-factive verb form 'I still cannot understand'.

Later, an old photograph is produced by Pi for the imagined author of the book, 'Yann Martel':

> The photo is crowded with people. [. . .]
> On the same page there's another group shot, mostly of schoolchildren. He taps the photo.
> 'That's Richard Parker', he says.
> I'm amazed. I look closely, trying to extract personality from appearance. Unfortunately it's black and white again and a little out of focus. A photo taken in better days, casually. Richard Parker is looking away. He doesn't even realize that his picture is being taken.

Martel (2002: 86–7)

Again, and even in a photograph, physical appearance is mentioned but not described. Instead, co-referential chains are left implicit ('schoolchildren' suggests that the 'person' tapped next is one of them). The agent of the photography (Pi's father) is deleted by passivisation ('A photo taken . . .'), but his psychological demeanour remains ('casually'), and the very next reference entity is 'Richard Parker', who is looking away, both wilfully and (resonantly) casually. Again, in the last sentence, a negated verb introduces the misdirection that attributes conscious realisation to the tiger.

The central section of the novel concerns Pi's 227-days adrift on a lifeboat with Richard Parker, a zebra and a hyena, and Pi's attempts to avoid being eaten. For almost three pages, the ship's sinking is described, and Pi's attempts to save Richard Parker by casting him a rope while speaking directly to him, and asking him philosophical and religious questions. Throughout, Richard Parker is assigned consciousness and wilfulness, and his physical appearance is only mentioned with words like 'nose', 'eyes', 'mouth' and 'legs' that are also common to humans. Only the odd repetition of the full name 'Richard Parker' suggests that the creature in the water is anything other than another person. Only when he is aboard the boat is the character's identity revealed:

> Truly I was to be the next goat. I had a wet, trembling, half-drowned, heaving and coughing three-year-old adult Bengal tiger in my lifeboat. Richard Parker rose unsteadily to his feet on the tarpaulin, eyes blazing as they met mine, ears laid tight to his head, all weapons drawn. His head was the size and colour of the lifebuoy, with teeth.
>
> Martel (2002: 99)

Here at last is a physical description. Several readers I have discussed this passage with have commented that they still did not make a co-referential link in this excerpt between 'three-year-old adult Bengal tiger' and 'Richard Parker', persisting in assuming that Richard Parker was another human survivor in addition to the tiger, and it was only the detail of 'ears laid tight to his head', and the focus on the teeth, that caused their view finally to be revised.

The novel overall generates a richly textured vector between a reader and the characters of Pi and Richard Parker. There are three general world-boundaries to cross: an italicised foreword purports implicitly to be written by 'Yann Martel', a novelist searching for a new story to tell. There are bio-graphical and fictional elements blended here. He meets a Francis Adirubasamy, who says, 'I have a story that will make you believe in God' (Martel 2002: x). The novelist hears the story in summary from this man, and then tracks down Pi Patel in Canada for the first-hand account. Secondly, the main part of the novel is told in the first-person as if by Pi Patel, but with continuing interspersed italicised shifts back out to the 'authorial' voice. Richard Parker saves Pi from being murdered by another castaway with a French accent, who is eaten by the tiger. They wash up on a wooded island, but the island turns out to be carnivorous by night, so they escape and finally land in Mexico, where Richard Parker disappears into the forest. Pi recounts this story to two Japanese shipping investigators – this third part of the novel is told as a recorded transcription. When they tell him that they do not believe the story, he gives an alternative account in which Pi's mother, a French chef and a wounded sailor are in the lifeboat. The sailor is killed and eaten by the chef, who then kills the mother, and Pi then kills the chef and eats him. It seems apparent that this more realist story represents a trauma that the boy has allegorised into the animal story as a psychological defence.

Represented like this, the experience of reading *Life of Pi* already involves tracing a set of shifting viewpoints across different types of worlds edges: authorial foreword, recount of experience, casting into fantasy, bureaucratic report. However, the novel ends with Pi asking the investigators which version they prefer, since neither explains what sank the ship. They, like most readers it seems, prefer the animal story which covers almost the whole of the

319 pages of the novel, compared with the nine pages (Martel 2002: 303–11) devoted to the alternative, psychosis story. Interwoven throughout the novel are choices which line up imagination, allegory, life, the major religions and God against literalism, brutality, bureaucracy, and commerce. Even outside the novel, intertextual allusions and tricks foreground literary artifice over literal artefacts: 'Richard Parker' is the name of a young sailor who is eaten by castaways in Edgar Allan Poe's (1838) *The Narrative of Arthur Gordon Pym of Nantucket*, and there are other coincidences of the name in the context of cannibalism and being adrift at sea, both fictional and historical. Furthermore, it seems likely that Martel himself is playing an elaborate but thematically consistent extra-textual trick in drawing the basic story from a Brazilian writer, Moacyr Scliar, who is credited but within the faked foreword, leading to a set of criticisms of plagiarism after Martel won the Booker prize for the novel. Martel's defence included an invented review of Scliar's book by John Updike (Martel 2008). All of this rich inter- and intra-textual edge-crossing sets up a sensitivity to choosing the viewpoint vector through Pi which has its terminal sense in the allegorical world rather than the realist one as the choice that 'will make you believe in God'.

Impersonation as embodiment

In most respects, Richard Parker behaves like a naturally territorial and brutal tiger. But in order for a tiger to be perceived as a character, its terminal sense at the other end of a viewpoint vector from a reader needs to be *impersonated*. Prototypically poor examples of character along the scale suggested above (abstractions > landscape objects > immovable objects > human-scale objects > machines > plants > animals > groups > ill-defined individuals > specific persons (hearer > speaker)) can be moved rightward, or in towards the radial centre of the prototype, by a rich textual manifestation of social, psychological and physical traits as I have described (see also Langacker 1991: 305–29; Stockwell 2002a: 61). The quality of impersonation depends on the readerly sense that there is a direct and facing connection with the fictional person being constructed, a sense of richness that crosses the threshold of plausibility.

Plausibility and authenticity do not depend upon realism or believability, of course. Richard Parker, for many readers, is a plausible character, though clearly not believable in any natural or literal sense. Equally, Pi Patel is plausible and authentic, though his name (short for 'Piscine' – swimming pool – and mispronounced by his teacher as 'pissing') points to the ratio of a circle's circumference to its diameter, the ratio 22/7 (he is adrift for 227 days), rendered in a decimal sequence beginning 3.14159265. . ., which is endless and incomprehensible. The filtered narrating viewpoint is thus richly layered and prominently symbolic, rather than literal.

For a character to achieve the threshold of impersonation (for a solid line to be drawn between R and C in Figure 4a), their physical, social and psychological traits need to be sufficiently richly delineated or implied as to feel plausible and authentic. In relation to African ritual and drama in general, Ukala (2001: 133) asserts: 'In performance, the character's physiology, sociology and psychology are bodied forth by means of impersonation'. This embodiment can be applied to prose characterisation. When characters reach the threshold of impersonation, they acquire a mind with their body, and a life beyond the book, and an intermental relationship with the reader as a person. Though of course the sense of where exactly this threshold lies is a subjective matter, in practice readers as social beings tend towards general agreement about those characters that seem authentic and those that fall short of impersonation. Non-impersonated characters and entities do not achieve an intermental relationship along a reading vector, though of course they can function significantly in a literary work as ciphers, symbolic characters, plot-device mechanics, background crowds, or everyman tokens. In general, though, such sub-personal entities do not seem to have a life beyond the book.

By contrast, impersonations constitute what is currently a key canonising feature in both scholarly literary criticism and for natural readers. Most online and book group discussions of narrative fiction move quickly to debates about the motives and the ethical status of characters. People talk and think about impersonated fictional characters as if they were real because that is the most prototypically natural thing to do in relation to other people. One of the most 'related-to' characters in fiction is Harry 'Rabbit' Angstrom, from four novels and a novella by John Updike (1964, 1971, 1981, 1990, 2001). Rabbit is usually regarded as a realistic anti-hero (see de Bellis 2005), plausible and authentic as a portrait of an unlikable, self-centred and indecisive mid-class American man.

> Who likes Rabbit, apart from his author? [. . .] Sexist, dumb, lazy, illiterate (he spends the whole novel not finishing a book on American history), a terrible father, an inadequate husband, an unreliable lover, a tiresome lecher, a failing businessman, a cowardly patient, a typically 'territorial' male: what kind of moral vantage point is this? [. . .] What redeems Rabbit is that, inside his brutish exterior, he is tender, feminine, and empathetic.
>
> (Lee 1990: 34)

Rabbit clearly reaches the level of a fully impersonated fictional entity, a person, available for judgement, psychological guesswork and empathy. However, he is also an emblem of Americans and America throughout the second half of the twentieth century, and thus has an allegorical or at least symbolic significance as well. Over the course of the first novel, *Rabbit, Run*

(Updike 1964) and then the sequels in each decade, the character is textually impersonated and rounded out (Forster 1927) by being richly textualised in terms of physical, psychological and social description. Rabbit is introduced in the first pages of the novel, in the present tense and narratological style that is typical of the work as a whole:

> Boys are playing basketball around a telephone pole with a backboard bolted to it. Legs, shouts. The scrape and snap of Keds on loose alley pebbles seems to catapult their voices high into the moist March air blue above the wires. Rabbit Angstrom, coming up the alley in a business suit, stops and watches, though he's twenty-six and six three. So tall, he seems an unlikely rabbit, but the breadth of white face, the pallor of his blue irisis, and a nervous flutter under his brief nose as he stabs a cigarette into his mouth partially explain the nickname, which was given to him when he too was a boy. He stands there thinking, the kids keep coming, they keep crowding you up.
>   His standing there makes the boys feel strange.
>
>   Updike (1964: 3)

There is an interesting spatial viewpoint set up here that, in the first few sentences, is fixed at the point where Rabbit will stop and watch the game, though he has not arrived there yet. The disembodied viewpoint sees the boys around the pole, looks down at their legs, hears their shouts, and the sound makes the viewpoint look up past the wires to the sky. Only then does Rabbit Angstrom catch up with the viewpoint ('coming up the alley' to the viewpoint), which he then inhabits psychologically from there on. The physical description at this point leaves him standing there while it switches back to his own boyhood to explain his nickname and physical appearance. The phrase 'when he too was a boy' returns the perspective to the boys in the present, and then it moves inside Rabbit's mind at the end of the first paragraph.

A doubled viewpoint is thus established that remains the hallmark of all the 'Rabbit' novels: a narrating voice ('Updike') who can move in and out of the characters' minds (for example, into the boys' collective feelings at the end of the extract above), and a primary focaliser, Angstrom, whose thoughts are sometimes directly transmitted ('the kids keep coming') and sometimes simply inform the scene that is described. The character traits of the two minds in this doubled viewpoint are being established from this beginning. Rabbit is a physical presence in the novel, materialistic and aware of how others conventionally perceive him. The measurable and precise physical description is prominent in this opening: he is reasonably but not freakishly tall, a former high-school basketball player but not a professional – 'stops and watches' might suggest a 'stopwatch' to gesture towards his athletic history, now separate from his current life in his 'business suit'. This last phrase denotes his physical dress, but is also of course emblematic of his social positioning. The description of his age ('twenty-six') is followed by the initial echo in his height ('six three'), as if he is almost but not quite at a moment of balance in his life. The physical description of his face, with precise named colours, seems to evoke his rational but cold ('white' and 'blue') personality, with the tiny hint of suppressed violence in 'stabs'. The deictic directionality of his direct thought ('there . . . the kids keep coming') is spatially and ideologically self-centred.

The narrative mind is more poetic and articulate. Though the precision of specifying the American sports-shoe brand 'Keds' (the original 'sneakers') would be something that Rabbit would notice, the surrounding style is the narrator's, heavy with alliteration and phonetic echo: /b l p t/ in the first line 'Boys are playing basketball around a telephone pole with a backboard bolted to it', 'scrape and snap', 'moist March', /l/ in 'loose alley pebbles . . . catapult', and so on. The odd choice of 'catapult' is self-consciously suggestive of boys' activities. The literal view and hearing of 'Legs, shouts' is Rabbit's, but the artful verbless expression is the narrator's. The poetically post-modified 'moist March air blue above the wires' is the narrator's style, as is the subtle homophonic hint of 'March hare' that precedes the introduction of 'Rabbit'. The descriptive terms 'pallor', 'irises' and 'nervous' are too lyrical for them to be Rabbit's choices.

In the terms I have developed so far, there is a direct and close relationship between the reader and the character's interior thoughts established from the beginning: the R → C link is firmly connected, and crosses only one text world boundary. The angle of this connection (R ∟ C) is direct, though the interjections of the narrative voice deflect the angle from time to time, placing an intermediate narrating world boundary that filters the reader's single boundary-crossing access to Rabbit. The effect of this is to enrich the quality of the connection (R ~ C). The reader's relationship with Rabbit (and the narrating voice, generally taken to be 'Updike') is developed further over the entire course of the novel, which covers three months in Rabbit's life – and of course it is followed by the rest of his life over the next four decades in the other novels. From being sketched in several of its significant terms in this opening passage, the viewpoint vector between the reader and Rabbit is thus reinscribed throughout the reading experience. This *reinscription* represents the duration of R – C over time, and the sense that Rabbit has a mind that persists as a presence in the reader's conceptualisation of the world of the novels.

Furthermore, as the character evolves, these reinscriptions multiply into emerging diverse enactors (see Emmott 1992, 1997) of Rabbit. In the course of *Rabbit, Run*, he leaves his wife, Janice; has an affair with a prostitute, Ruth; runs back to his wife as she gives birth; later returns to Ruth who is now pregnant, as Janice accidentally drowns their daughter; returns for the funeral and then runs away back to Ruth, who pressures him into making a firm decision about his life; and the novel ends with him running away from that as well. As Rabbit is presented facing and turning over the different possibilities and outcomes of his life, each version sets up an enactor of the character. For example, at the moment when he leaves his wife for the second fateful time:

> Even this late he might have stayed if she hadn't accepted defeat by doing this [crying]. His need to love her is by, so there's no reason to go. He's stopped loving her at last so he might as well lie down beside her and go to sleep. But she asks for it, lying there in a muddle sobbing, and outside, down in the town, a motor guns and he thinks of the air and the trees and streets stretching bare under the streetlamps and goes out the door.
>
> Updike (1964: 249-50)

The two occurrences of 'might' in this excerpt offer world-switches into a hypothetical reality in which Janice does not accept defeat and a parallel and marginally less cruel enactor of Rabbit lies down and goes to sleep. In the rest of the chapter, Janice responds to her emotional turmoil by getting drunk and the baby is drowned in the bath. At this and several similar pivotally decisive moments in the novel, Rabbit makes the wrong decision, but each time the narrative voice explicitly sets out the fact that Rabbit had choices, as at this moment quoted above. As in the opening to the novel, the narrative voice and Rabbit's viewpoint are very closely threaded, but discernible: 'might as well' is Rabbit's vocabulary choice but the narrator's articulation of the parallel alternative; the final perception of the open town is Rabbit's but, again, the poetry of the /s t/ alliterations and echoes and the trailing syntax of 'and' is the narrator's. Throughout the novels, the enacted extensions of the character of Rabbit are all consistent, rather than disjunctive, so they serve as an enrichment of the R – C vector rather than a disruption of it.

Rabbit is clearly an impersonated character, even for his author who realised he had a life beyond the first novel. The mode of writing of Updike's series of novels is realist though some have described Rabbit as an absurdist character (Galloway 1981), given the way fate and his indecision seem to conspire against him to reveal the futility of his life. Placing a character in a realist mode is a plausibility technique in itself, of course, but impersonation can be achieved even in non-realist modes of writing. Impersonation, it must be remembered, has a text-driven but experiential threshold, so children might regard anthropomorphised literary bears such as Paddington, Mary Plain, Teddy Edward, Winnie the Pooh, or Rupert the Bear as achieving the threshold of plausibility for impersonation, whereas adults might not. In adult fiction, too, non-realist impersonation is common in well-written science fiction and fantasy, and other genres.

In Paul Auster's (1999) novel *Timbuktu*, the protagonist Mr Bones is fully impersonated, though he is a dog. The measure of success is not realism, since it is not realistic to presume that the sort of rational and articulate thought that is presented in the novel lies within the capacity of even the most intelligent actual dog. However, the characterisation developed through the novel has a relative authenticity within the fictional frame: if the anthropomorphisation of a dog was literal, then this would be how that dog behaves and thinks. For example, the evident attachment as surrogate pack-leader that domestic dogs form with their owners is commonly read by dog-lovers as canine emotion or affection. Within this belief frame, Auster articulates a plausible sense of feeling. At the beginning of the novel, after outlining the fact that Willy G. Christmas is seriously ill, the novel becomes explicit about the nature of its focaliser:

> What was a poor dog to do? Mr Bones has been with Willy since his earliest days as a pup, and by now it was next to impossible for him to imagine a world that did not have his master in it. Every thought, every memory, every particle of the earth and air was saturated with Willy's presence. Habits die hard, and no doubt there's some truth to the adage about old dogs and new tricks, but it was more than just love or devotion that caused Mr Bones to dread what was coming. It was pure ontological terror. Subtract Willy from the world, and the odds were that the world itself would cease to exist.
>
> Such was the quandary Mr Bones faced that August morning as he shuffled through the streets of Baltimore with his ailing master.
>
> Auster (1999: 4)

The sense of plausibility within the fictional frame suggests a paradox of 'fictional authenticity' around Mr Bones here, but this paradox can be resolved by considering the viewpoint vector between reader and character. The vector R → C crosses only one fictive boundary, but in the dog's text world his thoughts are presented immediately and without any further sense of narrative involvement by a mediating mind. Access to the character is thus oddly direct but also apparently instant and swift. Rhetorical questions as if to himself (as in the opening of this excerpt) are posed plainly, so the reader receives them as the dog raises them. The novel as a whole is told in the normative narrative past (unlike the contrivedness of Updike's narrative present tense), which lends it a non-distracting authenticity. In the quoted excerpt, which is typical of the dog's mind-style in general, the standard past-tense narration is enriched with a variety of modalised, speculative and generic departures that create a complex sense of personality. The rich negational and modal embedding of not being able 'to imagine a world that did not have his master in it' increases the quality of the reader's relationship with the enactors of Mr Bones in those other sub-worlds. Auster has a trademark technique in general of gesturing towards his work's own fictionality by referring to himself and the real world within his fiction, but in *Timbuktu* this technique itself is knowingly avoided in the allusion to 'old dogs and new tricks'. The allusion is literal in this context, of course, where it is metaphorical in its real-world proverbial form, but the notion of proverbial-ness has been set up by the generic sentence 'Habits die hard', so the shift to Mr Bones' perception is less artificial. Though a third-person narrative, the focalisation is strongly articulated from the viewpoint location of Mr Bones, and this dog has a sense of sympathetic self-consciousness ('a poor dog'), the power of speculation ('him to imagine'), a conversational tone ('no doubt'), higher emotional capacity ('love or devotion'), anticipatory anxiety ('dread') and an educated philosophical training ('ontological terror'). By the end of the novel, most readers have developed a close relationship with the character of Mr Bones, and the final pages of the novel, in which he is alone after the death of Willy and ready to run into the road to be dispatched to the afterlife called 'Timbuktu', are extremely poignant, in spite of the fact that all readers know the relationship is fictional and unreal.

Other forms of character are even more unusual, but can still reach impersonation. Greg Egan's science fiction novel *Permutation City* (1994) features the character of Paul Durham, who creates copies of himself within computer software so that he can experiment on his own personality. Running a software consciousness takes up huge amounts of expensive computer processing resources, though, and so is largely the preserve of large corporations and billionaires with terminal illnesses. Within the virtual world (the 'Autoverse'), characters can fall into the 'slums', where they can continue to be computed but at a slower rate, or into 'Slow clubs', where everyone agrees to run at the pace of the slowest computed member, or they may become 'witnesses' to huge spans of history, as each digital computation that constitutes their personalities is separated by long periods of inactivity.

Similarly, in Egan's (2008) *Incandescence*, two characters, Parantham and Rakesh, are converted into information and transported across an alien trans-galactic communications network in order to be re-embodied at the other end. However, the transmission obeys the limit of the speed of light (rather than other science fictional short-cuts like space-warps or wormholes), so their round-trip takes many thousands of years. They attempt to rescue a species of insect-like radiation-hardened creatures living on a unstable asteroid around a neutron star, two of which, Zak and Roi, lead a group who work out their predicament and save themselves.

In Alastair Reynolds' (2002) novella *Diamond Dogs*, the character Richard Swift joins an expedition to explore the Blood Spire, an alien artefact on an isolated planet called Golgotha. The structure is surrounded by the bodies of previous explorers, all ejected from it at different rates. Swift and his fellows work their way through each smaller and smaller chamber in the spire, passing each brutal test only by re-engineering their bodies for each environment, and becoming less and less human the further they progress. Swift becomes utterly transformed in the process.

In Jonathan Carroll's (2003) *White Apples*, Vincent Ettrich returns to life after his death, brought back by his lover Isabelle Neukor to save their son and the universe. In Robert Henryson's *Morall Fabillis* (c.1480), Chantecleir the cockerel is almost outwitted by a wily fox, only to escape death from his own sinfulness. In Ray Bradbury's 'And There Shall Come Soft Rains', the penultimate story of *The Martian Chronicles* (1977, written in 1950), an auto-mated house in California maintains itself for the family who have been vaporised in a nuclear war – their silhouettes are burned onto the outside of one of its walls. The house is a character, a metonym for the family and a metaphor for the technology that caused the war. It makes the breakfast, cleans up, reads the poem of the title to the absent mother of the 'nuclear' family, and is embodied: the house 'is afraid that nobody would' get up, the kitchen 'stove gave a hissing sigh', 'memory tapes glided under electric eyes', uneaten eggs and toast are 'whirled down a metal throat'; 'it had shut up its windows and drawn shades in an old-maidenly preoccupation with self-protection which bordered on a mechanical paranoia'. When a tree falls on the house and starts a fire from the stove, the 'house tried to save itself' but its 'attic brain' is burned, its 'bared skeleton' is revealed, and only one wall is left, intoning the date, '"Today is August 5, 2026, today is August 5, 2026, today is . . ."'. The date is the anniversary of the bombing of Hiroshima, US time.

Mr Bones, Paul Durham, Parantham, Rakesh, Zak, Roi, Richard Swift, Vincent Ettrich, Chantecleir and the house are all characters that achieve the threshold of impersonation, for me. The literary work in each case authenti-cates the person as a character by establishing strong and rich viewpoint vectors between the reader and these text-entities. There are, of course, many more animal, machine and even inanimate characters in literary fiction, such as Richard Parker the tiger and Egdon Heath the Wessex landscape as I have described elsewhere in this book. Even collectivities like the city of London have been characterised, for example by Peter Ackroyd (2001) in *London: The Biography*, a history that becomes a literary work by the force of its impersonation.

Of course, all these impersonations are unusual, serving often as thematic techniques in themselves. Most impersonated characters are claims for peo-ple-like entities. However, the success of odd characters like these is an indi-cation that impersonation is a text-driven technique rather than an allusion to realistic or naturalistic comparisons. However outlandish the world on the other side of the reader's fictional boundary, impersonation and the felt rela-tionship with a character is a cognitive poetic matter and not a matter of realism or plausibility framed in real-world terms alone. Furthermore, there seems to be a mutually reinforcing feedback loop at work: characters that achieve the sense of impersonation feel tangible and physically real. This is not just a matter of the striking description of the physical traits of the character, though that too affirms the sense. Since our default pattern for a communicating mind is a physically embodied person, it is impossible not to attribute something very close to physicality to characters who seem to achieve impersonation.

Edgework and transitioning

Earlier I claimed that the best example of a person is a person, but in literary fiction an extra factor comes into play – what narratologists after Labov (1972) have called *tellability*. This is the motivation for a narrative to be recounted on the basis that it communicates a story that is worth telling. Successful natural narratives are stories that are worth telling, and this motivation is compounded for literary narratives. In literature, the best example of a person is an unusual or interesting person, someone who stands out from the ordinary, like an attractor. When literary narratives feature the ordinary man or the unremarkable woman, there is usually a thematised point being made about banality or daily tedium, or contrarily about the extraordinary moments of epiphany in an otherwise pedestrian existence. The difference between literary and non-literary reading here is the sense of literariness that the reader brings to the text, and its intensification effect on reading (see Chapter 2 above).

Readerly stance is clearly crucial in the vectoring of character viewpoint. Most studies of point of view (Fowler 1986; Simpson 1993) focus on the character terminal of the vector, describing the stylistic realisation of that character's perception of her own position. Such studies treat character viewpoint as an autonomous locus with connections to other characters, the narrator and author. However, I will argue that a character's viewpoint is not free-floating within its text world but can be understood only with reference to the viewing position of the reader. Readers vivify character perception as part of the process towards impersonation. The initial work of the process is the same whether the threshold of impersonation is achieved or not. Culpeper's (2001) study which centres on the knowledge schemas that readers bring to bear in order to psychologise characters is an example of an approach that begins from readerly stance. In this final section of the chapter, I will investigate the detailed mechanics of what is happening at the edge between reader and character, and how we might account for the sense of movement of perception as *edgework*.

Mind-style

In his groundbreaking work on point of view especially in relation to drama, McIntyre (2006) discusses the overlapping terms *worldview, ideological point*

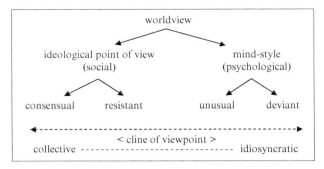

Figure 4b Worldview scheme (partly after Semino 2002)

of view and *mind-style*. All of these, especially the last highly suggestive phrase for cognitive poetics, owe their currency in stylistics to Fowler (1986). Semino (2002; see also Semino and Swindlehurst 1996) draws distinctions between them that bring out different nuances. She sees two distinct aspects to the overall worldview presented in a literary text: ideological point of view is the socially shared, cultural and political position expressed by, say, a character, while their mind-style is the more individual and personally defined subjective viewpoint. I can schematise these in summary as in Figure 4b.

McIntyre (2006: 143) points out that it can be very difficult in practice to differentiate ideological point of view and mind-style, and he suggests that the distinction between them 'should be understood as heuristic. . . only'. We can imagine it might be impossible to say that a person's individual viewpoint is not informed by their culture and politics, for example. However, McIntyre (2006: 144) goes on to make a point that renders the distinction useful again: 'the mind styles likely to be most noticeable and interesting interpretatively are those which in some way deviate from normal assumptions'. Engaging with this point, we can redraw Semino's (2002) distinction into a cline as in the lower half of Figure 4b. In this scheme, we can recognise that some viewpoints occupied by characters are 'normal', and collectively shared. Such viewpoints are often so naturalised and shared that within the collective culture they are regarded as 'common sense'. For example, it is inconceivable, probably universally, that Rabbit's behaviour towards his wife is regarded as normal and unremarkable: I would imagine that the vast majority of readers would adopt a viewpoint stance that would see his behaviour as morally criticisable, to put it most mildly. This is an example of readerly viewpoint located towards the collective end of the scale. The colloquial normality and observational banter that characterises Mr Bones is recognisable as a common view too, and this would place him as a character viewpoint towards the collective left-hand side of the scale as well, were it not for the oddity of him being a dog. This anomalous factor alone serves to shift Mr Bones to the idiosyncratic end of the scale, and the canine perspective makes this mind-style most foregrounded. The disparity between the dog-ness of the narrator and the human ordinariness of his discourse generates the texture that makes the viewpoint noticeable. In other words, what I am saying, along with McIntyre, is that all entities (characters, authors, narrators and readers) manifest viewpoints, but only those viewpoints that are regarded as non-normative and idiosyncratic are actually noticed in natural reading: these odd, distracting viewpoints are mind-styles.

It is also worth noting that the scheme applies to readers and authors as well as characters. Readers and authors have discernible viewpoints that might be collectively shared or idiosyncratic too. The readerly viewpoint of vector points at and faces character, though, so character viewpoint is most usually discussed, but there is no doubt that the position of readerly (and authorial) viewpoint *in relation to* character viewpoint is a crucial matter. This point will be developed in the relation to readerly resistance in the next chapter.

Mind-style, then, can be defined as being the presentation of a highly deviant or at least very unusual worldview, judged of course by a reader against his own set of cultural norms. The evaluation of mind-style is thus relative in two ways: it depends on the reader's match-up or not with the character (the relationship of R to C in Figure 4a above), and it depends on the reader's relationship in his own culture (the locus of R in his discourse world). An absolute correspondence of consensual viewpoint across reader, author and character is rather rare in literary fiction, since there would be no tension at all. There usually needs to be some resistance somewhere amongst these elements for a literary work to have any sort of impact or effect. A good example is the Disney animated film *Cinderella* (Geronimi, Luske and Jackson 1950) and its first sequel *Cinderella II: Dreams Come True* (Kafka 2002). The original hugely successful film follows the classic story fairly closely, with the three characters of the wicked stepmother and two sisters having very strong viewpoints that most viewers would regard as nasty and mean, judged from a consensual context. The sequel, although financially very successful as a straight-to-video enterprise, was critically panned and is a less interesting story because it does not really have any characters with non-consensual viewpoints. Bluntly, there are no villains, and the worst ordeal the new Princess Cinderella has to undergo is to organise a party without much help from a few sniffy servants. The film is as a consequence largely forgettable, even for its target audience.

Engaging with an impersonated character that differs from your own viewpoint involves a textured quality to the R ~ C vector, that is currently valued in literary fiction. In my model, world boundaries are crossed in the process of establishing the vector from reader to character. For illustration of the mechanics of what is involved, here is another dog-impersonation story.

The Falling Dog

Yes, a dog jumped on me out of a high window. I think it was the third floor, or the fourth floor. Or the third floor. Well, it knocked me down. I had my chin on the concrete. Well, he didn't bark before he jumped. It was a silent dog. I was stretched out on the concrete with the dog on my back. The dog was looking at me, his muzzle curled round my ear, his breath was bad, I said, 'Get off!'

He did. He walked away looking back over his shoulder. 'Christ' I said. Crumbs of concrete had been driven into my chin. 'For God's sake', I said. The dog was four or five meters down the sidewalk, standing still. Looking back at me over his shoulder.

(from *Sixty Stories*, by Donald Barthelme 1981: 169, original 1972)

There is a single vector represented in this extract that is deflected through the narrating consciousness, as in Figure 4c. The reader's relationship with the dog is an odd and deflected one. There is nothing in the passage that denotes anything that a normal dog from the reader's discourse world would not perhaps do (though, of course, the fact of being floored by a falling dog in itself has unusual tellability). Nevertheless, this dog seems to have a deviant or at least unusual personality; it seems to have a sullen wilfulness, deliberation and language comprehension skills that go beyond normal dogs in the reader's discourse world. The anthropomorphisation is created by the narrating 'I' character in the first text world (TW1) with which the reader has to engage, initially in the choice of 'jumped', denoting a deliberate, planned act, rather than, say, 'fell'. 'Knocked me down' could be either deliberate or simply an event description, as could the first iteration of 'the dog was looking at me'. However, the repetition twice of this latter phrase with the addition of 'over his shoulder' makes the act more deliberate because more human-like (do dogs have shoulders?).

Similarly, the narrator tells the dog to 'Get off!', and after a paragraph break denoting its sullen-ness or surly pause for thought, it complies. A normal, discourse world dog might do this unremarkably, but this looks more like linguistic comprehension since it follows, 'Well, he didn't bark

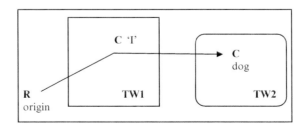

Figure 4c Viewpoint vector in Barthelme's 'The Falling Dog'

before he jumped. It was a silent dog'. The negational world-switch (to a TW3 not sketched in the diagram) invokes a lacuna in which another enactor of the dog barks a warning before he jumps. Even though this world is immediately negated, the echoic effect of a dog capable of considerate and planned thought is already created, and this trait of the occluded enactor is attached to the dog character in general. The humour in 'It was a silent dog' derives from the odd aptness of this phrase in the co-text.

The different enactors of the dog can be seen in the narrator's alternation of 'he' and 'it' to refer to the dog, and the inconsistency of these across the text keeps prominent the sense of crossing perceptual edges. 'It' would be a normal dog, and 'he' would contrastively be an impersonated dog. However, in the sentence, 'It was a silent dog', the return to the relatively normal 'it' is undermined by the lacuna effect of the silence being deliberate. After this point, the dog is treated as a person. Furthermore, the narrator's switching between pronouns is paralleled not only by his uncertainty ('the third floor, or the fourth floor') but also by his failed grasping after irrelevant precision ('Or the third floor').

The historical dog that fell on the narrator exists in TW1, but our access as readers to the character of the dog is almost entirely to the enactor of the dog with the non-normal mind in TW2 (and TW3). The filtering through the narrator is also foregrounded as being unreliable, as indicated above, and also by the self-conscious conversational markers in this written text: 'Yes', as if in dialogic response to the reader's prior question, and 'well'. The dog character is thus rich, possessing both normal dog-like traits (barking ability, implicit physical dog-ness) and person-like traits. The suggested planning capacity of the dog is not, however, explained. There is no explanation for the dog's motivation or objective, so the passage ends leaving a puzzling tone in the reader's mind. Since the vector to the dog has been deflected through the angle of the prominent narrator, returning back up the vector for a resolution simply results in the puzzlement being attached first to the narrator's motivations and, when that is also similarly unresolvable, to the author's motivations back in the discourse world. Note that the author's description of the dog as 'Falling' in the title is further at odds with the narrator's choice of 'jumped'. Tracking back up a viewpoint vector is the mechanics of thematisation.

Deictic braiding

In this Barthelme example, the reader must cross two or three world-edges along the vector to the dog. There is a diversion through the narrator, and the shortness of the passage and its colloquial intimacy both render a sense of a snappy tale rather than a contemplative one. What about the quality of the edge-crossing involved? In the first transition, the reader crosses away from the discourse world and over the edge that belongs to TW1, the narrator's recount of past experience (doubtless fictional, unless Barthelme is being peculiarly autobiographical). This involves an imagined temporary relocation of viewpoint as a deictic shift. In fact, we can examine more closely the single vector line of the model and see it as being composed of braids of deictic dimensions, as I will describe below.

In *deictic shift theory* (as originated in Duchan, Bruder and Hewitt 1995 and developed in Stockwell 2002a, 2006, 2008; McIntyre 2006; and Gavins 2007), the traditional categories of deixis are reconfigured to accord with cognitive linguistic principles. Ever since the pioneering work in the 1930s by Bühler (1982), deictic positioning has always involved a conceptualisation of two ends of a vectored relationship, though the viewing (readerly) end has often been implicit in most studies (see further Lyons 1977; Jarvella and Klein 1982; Levinson 1983; Rauh 1983; and Green 1995). The focus has tended to be on the conceptual field as expressed from the viewpoint of the deictic centre being encoded in the text (the character terminal), rather than in combination with the interlocutor of the discourse. Deixis is always relative to an interlocutor's location, and this in general is captured in the vector line.

The dimensions of deixis in literary encounters are as follows (following Stockwell 2002a: 45–6):

- Perceptual deixis (pronouns, demonstratives, definite articles and definite reference, and verbs of mental states)
- Spatial deixis (locatives, spatial adverbs, distal demonstratives, verbs of motion)
- Temporal deixis (locatives, temporal adverbs, tense and aspect)
- Relational deixis (encoding of social position)
- Textual deixis (self-referential textuality, iconicity, sense of texture)
- Compositional deixis (interpersonal extratextual features).

Each vector line can be regarded upon closer inspection as consisting of a bundle of these six braids. In deictic shift theory (DST), a reader adopts a cognitive stance in relation to the perceptual worlds being presented in the literary work, with each world marking out the boundaries of a deictic field. Since (as Palmer 2004 indicates) all encountered discourse streams imply a mind, a deictic field (or world) is a manifestation of the viewpoint from a deictic centre. The notion of a deictic centre replaces the notion of the egocentric *origo* from traditional deictic theory: the DST version is portable and relativised to the interlocutor's position, and it also accords better with current psychological models rather than analytical pragmatics.

When a reader projects a vector towards a character, the relative deictic braids are threaded inwards towards the terminal sense. In the original DST, each readerly projection across a world boundary involves a 'push' into that deictic field, and each return towards the discourse world involves a 'pop'. These terms originate in the computer programming register that informs much of the initial theory (in Duchan, Bruder and Hewitt 1995). I am deliberately blending the terminology of DST and text world theory (Werth 1999; Gavins 2007) here, in order to show that the deictic signatures of minds that are drawn as text worlds can be viewed dynamically as reader-originated virtual movement. In essence, DST is text world theory viewed 'edge on'.

McIntyre (2006: 109) points out the awkward asymmetry between the terms 'push' and 'pop', where the former is normally transitive and the latter intransitive, so they are not in fact antonyms. This unfortunately suggests that readers actively push into deictic fields but are popped out by authors or texts. In fact, the act of cognition generates the shifting in both directions, and McIntyre suggests that 'shifting in and out' better captures this. Related to this discussion, he cites Segal's (1995a: 14–15, 1995b) work in the original DST book as a conceptualisation in which readers 'get inside of stories and vicariously experience them'. McIntyre (2006: 110–11) questions whether this actually corresponds with readers' genuine experiences: he is particularly interested in experiences of drama. The notion that readers shift into a fictional deictic field and lose their own origins there is explained by Galbraith within DST as a focusing of attention on the shifted deictic centre so that the readers' sense of their own deictic positioning suffers from *decay*. (There are clear analogues between this and my model of resonance in Chapter 2, of course.) This version of DST accounts quite well for reading viewed as the transportation of the reader into an imaginary landscape (Gerrig 1993; see Chapter 3 above), where self-effacement is almost complete.

However, McIntyre (2006: 111) is right to point out that this dissolution of self is only apparent in some literary encounters. In a noisy theatre or on a crowded train, in his example, the viewer or reader might be constantly reminded of their own discourse world. In the terms developed above, the reader continues to hold one end of the braided vector that connects the reading deictic centre with the talking deictic centre of the character in the text, though the reader is looking inward at that character and tracing her deictic field characteristics. Adapting a cognitive linguistic term, the reader is profiling the character terminal of the vector while experiencing the construal effect of being lost in the fiction. The profiling focus shifts back outwards to the reader if, say, the reading is broken off, or the reader goes to make a coffee, or the textual organisation suggests a shift of awareness out to the narratorial, textual or compositional edges. Where the reader is, at any one moment of a reading, can be mapped as the position along the vector that he is profiling at that moment. Incidentally, this adaptation of DST (with the reader holding one end of the braid while the other is anchored within the text worlds) serves as a specification of the metaphor of reading as investment introduced in Chapter 3 above).

The effect of all this can be demonstrated quite neatly by referring back again to 'The Falling Dog' text and Figure 4c. The encounter with a story by Donald Barthelme, either in the book collection *Sixty Stories* or in the extract reproduced above, prompts the reader to adopt a story stance in relation to this author: we are ready and disposed for a shift into another compositional world. The reader's initial encounter with the edge of TW1 occurs as soon as the conversational partner begins with 'Yes, a dog jumped on me . . .'. The first person pronoun and the relational value of the conversational register threads together dimensions of perceptual and relational deixis pointing along a vector towards a narrating character. The reader must adopt the narrator's deictic perspective here, so 'a dog' is introduced as a specific indefinite, and though we would naturally connect the co-reference of this dog and the dog of the title which we have already met, instead we go along with the new introduction of the dog in the narrator's world. The past tense choice locates the story in the past, which is also the most normative aspect for narrativity, and the prepositions 'on' and then 'out of a high window' locate the narrator's spatial deictic position in relation to the objects mentioned.

In this story, the conversational tone (part of the relational braid) serves to prevent the complete decay of the reader's sense of self, since it constantly sustains the sense of interlocution. Aside from the introductory elements mentioned above, the conversational tone is maintained throughout the narrative, by features such as the online correction of which floor the dog fell from, the very short sentences, the use of sentences without main clauses, the informal punctuation (commas used where full-stops or semi-colons would appear in formal writing), and the use of direct speech. All are usual in oral narrative or where writing is attempting to gesture towards orality. However, the artifice of this text compared with a natural oral account is also apparent. This is mainly generated by the further transitioning along the vector into the dog's perceptual and conceptual world (TW2). The dog is prominent in each subject of the clauses in the sentence at the end of the first paragraph ('The dog was looking at me, his muzzle curled round my ear, his breath was bad, I said, "Get off!"'). Though a traditional point of view analysis (such as Fowler's (1986) or Simpson's (1993)) would have this sentence within the narrative focalisation, in fact there is a sense here that the dog's perspective is also being taken: the dog is doing the looking, with 'at me' in the distance; his muzzle is doing the curling, with 'my ear' as the background; his breath is in focus. Even the last clause here ('I said, "Get off!"') consists of what the dog would first see and then hear – and the exclamation mark is a feature of the dog's hearing as much as the speaker's outrage. The reader is being taken into the dog's mind, vectored through the narrator's viewpoint, and this is enacted here largely through perceptual and spatial shifts ('looked', 'at', 'round') and with reference to the dog's body ('muzzle', 'breath').

I can only account for this sort of doubled viewpoint by explaining it as a diverted angle of the vector between reader and dog through the narrator. The effect continues in the second paragraph. The reader needs to shift back out to the deictic centre of the narrator again, profiling the angled point on the vector, to understand the perspective of 'He did. He walked away . . .'. The view of the third person dog is from the perceptual centre of the narrator, and the directionality of the spatial adverbial 'away' confirms this. However, the phrase that follows ('looking back over his shoulder') again allows the dog's view 'back' and 'over' to be felt alongside the narrator's. Again the dog's mental action ('looking') and his body ('shoulder') are focused. The next sentence ('"Christ" I said') is perceptually centred on the narrator, but again is what the dog hears. And the choice of 'crumbs' as a particle of concrete seems more a dog-like perception than human. The story ends with a perfectly balanced doubled viewpoint: 'Looking back at me over his shoulder' braids together both the human's and the dog's perceptual field.

Throughout, the instability of the normal is asserted by the rapid shifting across deictic edges. The dog takes on wilfulness, but the effect is subtle rather than heavily personified: this dog does not actually speak, though the negational shift 'didn't bark' and the lacuna of 'a silent dog' invoke the possibility that he could; this dog does not have simple direct verbs of wilfulness and intention, but he is the subject of almost every clause except the actual direct speech, with 'me' the most common beneficiary of the action. The dog throughout behaves almost, but not exactly, like a normal dog.

The processing of the edge complex at the transition between worlds (or deictic centres, in alternative terms) is *edgework*. McIntyre (2006: 105–6) finds this term problematic, pointing out that Segal (1995b) refers to the processing work that the reader does when identifying deictic shift moments, while Young (1987) first coined the term to refer to the textual markers of the real-fictional world boundary. However, it is crucial that edgework encompasses the single phenomenon whereby the transitioning work that the reader engages in is worked upon actual textual material (this is my sense in Stockwell 2002a: 49). Edgework is work at the edge, which can only be discussed by describing the actual nature of the edge-boundary in textural terms. As we have seen above, examining the textual features without a sense of where the reader and character are located, and where they have come from, will not allow us to explore the sort of subtle effects that lie at the heart of a text like Barthelme's 'The Falling Dog'. It is another example of texture being a holistic phenomenon of cognition and language.

Voicing the mind

In this chapter I have drawn on a range of linked themes – characterisation, point of view, deictic positioning – and placed them into a unified account from a cognitive perspective. Again, though these areas are generally associated with fictional displacement, the only account which makes plausible psychological sense is one that retains a continuity with natural and everyday discourse. There is no difference in the basic mechanics that we use to interact with other people in our world compared with fictional people. The face-to-face scenario, with instant gestural evaluations and interlocution, is the basis for all our cognitive capacities of forming relationships with people, whether they are physically right in front of us, or displaced by telephone, email, text messaging, letter, television, newspaper report, court transcript, biography, obituary, literary fiction, or allegorical mythology, to give some examples in increasing radiality of displacement from the prototypical situation. But all these and other displacements draw on the same cognitive resources that we evolved as a species. The attenuation (Langacker 2008: 536) offered by these displacements from the prototypical situation can be regarded as a projection, stretching out our default capacities and, usefully, rendering their detailed workings to clearer observation.

As I mentioned in the chapter, there is an assumed model of personality, identity and consciousness implicit in this approach. It views personality as contingent rather than an essence. We configure both our demeanour to the world and our internal self-sense according to the situation in hand. This comprises our objectives, our sense of local and general goals, our desire for social cohesion and interaction, our natural adaptation to others, our sense of past experiential configurations and our consistency with them, and so on. Personality, in other words, is also a prototype effect. We have a best sense of ourselves, and less good examples of ourselves that might nevertheless be appropriate in certain circumstances. Social deviance and transgression, or lesser examples of nonconformity, resistance, eccentricity, awkwardness, naughtiness and actions performed 'out of character' are all examples of possibly temporary reconfigurations of personality in varied situations.

Most non-pathological or non-psychotic people have a sense of personal stability in identity, at least in the short and medium term, but this sense is a consequence of habituation: it becomes schematised and then the schema is used to form prototypical consciousness and behaviour. This perception of the mind is then performed, realised and grammaticalised, and given a voice which you regard as your voice. In relation to other people, there is also a socially self-validating effect of mind-modelling (see Leahy 2005 and Chapter 5 below) – we assume others are, in basic mechanics, the same as us, and we anticipate their beliefs, motives, speech and actions accordingly by projecting them in their circumstances. This is to an extent circular and mutually reinforcing, as our anticipations – sharpened experientially by internalised cultural norms and our own encounters – prove generally accurate. Even where inaccurate, we tend to read them as validations of our own accuracy. This 'proof' serves, circularly, to stabilise our own identity and personality as if it too were consistent and unchanging.

Other people include fictional people (Rabbit, Mr Bones, Pi), group people (Middlemarch, town gossip) and metonymically partial or collective people ('give me a hand', 'the White House says . . .', 'public opinion has it that . . .'). But all these people share the same ascribed characteristics as people in our families, houses and workplaces. Our relationships with them all are different only to the extent that we are conscious of crossing boundaries of spatial or temporal displacement, hearsay recounting, speculation, or fictional edges. It is the crossing of world-boundaries itself that generates this sense of texture. In all cases, all we have to go on is our perceptual, often discursive, representations not only of these other people in the world(s), but all the objects and beliefs they seem to have about everything. All style – not just mind-style – is a mental inscription.

Reading

Point of view has been a highly productive area in narratology and stylistics, and all approaches are implicitly and unavoidably cognitive by definition, even if they are not cognitivist in orientation. Narratological approaches include Booth (1961), Prince (1982), Bal (1985), Cohn (1989), Fludernik (1996), and Toolan (2001). In stylistics, Simpson (1993), McIntyre (2006) and Leech and Short (2007) all deal with point of view. Specific work on character includes Suvin (1988), Fokkema (1991), Rorty (2000), and Culpeper (2001). The last reference is an excellent stylistic discussion with cognitive poetic influences. Also in this tradition are Fowler (1986), Phelan (1989) Emmott (1992, 1994, 1995, 1996, 1997) and Montgomery (1993).

The place of deixis in literary contexts is explored initially by Bühler (1982), and then Jarvella and Klein (1982), Rauh (1983), and Green (1992, 1995). Adaptations and applications of deictic shift theory (Bruder and Wiebe 1995; Duchan, Bruder and Hewitt 1995) can be found in Stockwell (2002a, 2006, 2008a), McIntyre (2004, 2005, 2006, 2007) and in Culpeper and McIntyre (2009).

On the performance of character and identity, see Johnson (1980), Maclean (1988), Butler (1990, 1993, 1997), and Parker and Sedgwick (1995). Identity and performativity is a large areas of research especially in sociolinguistics: see Llamas, Mullany and Stockwell (2007) for further work.

5 Identification and Resistance

Readerliness has been the key element in much of the discussion of this book so far. Aside from my introductory comments in Chapter 1, however, a precise account of exactly what is meant by the *reader* in cognitive poetic terms has been left until the present chapter. The notion, of course, has a long tradition of theorising, especially in critical theory and specifically in the traditions of reception theory and reader-response criticism. The reception aesthetics developed initially at Konstanz University in the late 1960s can be seen as a precursor of many of the interests of cognitive poetics. Drawing on the phenomenological work of Ingarden (1973a, 1973b) in the 1930s and later Gadamer (1989), reception theorists like Iser (1978) and Jauss (1982a) situated literary meaning neither immanently in the text nor in an infinite social freeplay of meaning, but in a holistic combination of both. Though much of the actual analysis can appear quite formalist in their work, this emphasis on textual form remained an important commitment of the project at a time when literary scholarship across the rest of the world was in general beginning to turn away from stylistic matters in favour of pure theory. Reception aesthetics placed the meaning-generating function of the reader in the centre of the theoretical account, but the combined complex of reader-text was not treated in isolation. Jauss (1982b), in particular, emphasised the historical influence of successive generations of readings in his framing notion of the 'horizon of expectations'. It is easy to regard this as a common, schema-like thread running from Ingarden through Jauss and into modern cognitive poetic applications of schema theory (Cook 1994; Cockcroft 2002), frames (Lakoff 2002, 2006; Fillmore 1985) and worlds (Werth 1999; Gavins 2007).

In this chapter, I develop a broadly text world theoretical account of the conceptual attachment that readers make with literary works, in order further to specify the nature of the reader-text complex and its cognitive dynamics. The notion of *identification* is crucial as a means of capturing the nature of the relationship that is created between a reader and perceived entities in a text, developing the discussion of reader-character vectors in the previous chapter. However, this term is not without its difficulties, and it is necessary in the discussion below to consider the assumptions about personality that underlie the different approaches to literary readerliness. I consider examples of sympathetic readerly construction, where the experience of reading the literary work seems to be mutually reinforcing. I also consider the contrary scenario where there is a disjunction between readerly disposition and the apparent disposition adopted by the literary text, where there is a sense of *resistance* in the reader towards the perceived ethos of the work.

The personality of the reader

A reader is a person, and a persona is, etymologically, a mask that is worn in drama to indicate a type of role. Defining a reader is thus a special case of the general problem of defining a person. Cognitive psychology has several answers to the question of what it means to be a person: the fundamental apparent paradox that has to be resolved is the presence of variable behaviours and experiences in different circumstances and over time, within a broad sense of the consistency of self-hood.

In psychology in general, there have been roughly two main approaches to personality research (see Ryckman 2008; Engler 2006). For example, the unified personality can be described in terms of types, where these types are broad categories which connect outlook with behaviour. Deriving from psychoanalytical theorists such as Jung (1967, 1970), this approach is popular in business as customer profiling, in psychometrics, and in demographic research. It also seems to be the most populist understanding of personality as a relatively fixed feature of an individual's life: people are invariantly good-natured, or villains, have a heart of gold, or are irredeemable monsters. Alternatively, personality can be regarded as a set of traits. Ultimately, this can perhaps be seen as a derivation of the pre-modern psycho-anatomical model of 'humours' of the body, but in modern times it has resolved into five general traits: a scale of conscientiousness; a scale of openness or intellect; a scale of extraversion or outgoing-ness; a scale of agreeableness or compassion; and a scale of neuroticism or emotional instability. Intriguingly for a linguistic perspective, trait theories of personality developed from the 1930s from a lexical exercise in which English dictionaries were scanned for personality-descriptive words and these were then reduced down to fewer and fewer broad semantic areas. Trait theories of personality also tend to be largely fixed, and they remain mostly descriptive rather than explanatory accounts.

Cognitive theories of personality tend instead to emphasise the fluctuating and inconsistent nature of personality, preferring to account for notions of self-awareness in terms of correspondences between plans, goals and judgements (see Mischel, Shoda and Smith 2004). These conceptual strategies can change throughout life, of course, and the circumstances in which they might be applied at any one point might also vary, so personality becomes a variable matter of configuring expectations, motivations and effective behaviour. As with any abstract conceptual category, prototypical effects apply, so it is reasonable to imagine a mind with a prototypically central sense of itself, aspiring to certain attitudes and dispositions under what it regards as normal circumstances, and with less central instantiations of its typical thinking and behaviour in different circumstances. At the radial extremes, most of us can also imagine exceptional or freakish behaviour that is 'out of character' in imagined extreme circumstances, though we might accept that certain wild actions and thoughts are within our capacities.

The model of personality this suggests, then, is one that has our best sense of ourselves at the centre – a combination of how we would like to be and how we have configured ourselves in the past. There is no bounded edge to the radial structure of our personality, only less and less good examples of how we think of ourselves, right out to our knowledge of psychotic, pathological, immoral and other unattractive characteristics that we would like to think are beyond us, but which, because we can think of them, are always potentially available. At an ethical level, of course, this entails a position of individual moral responsibility, to a great extent. Choice of behaviour cannot be ascribed to a fixed bad characteristic, though an appeal can always be made to the vicissitudes of extreme circumstance.

Nevertheless, personality according to these principles is never entirely stable in itself; it only appears consistent by constant practice of instantiation. Personality is adaptive to the conditions at hand. In literary encounters, if personality were rigid and fixed, immovable and inextensible, then it would be impossible to engage with or appreciate viewpoints that were distant from our own. We would live a literal and limited existence, and would have no need for literary fiction or expression at all. The reader's subjectivity is defined by its points of contact with others, including fictional others, and we might talk of personality as being socially and intersubjectively circumscribed and tested over and over in literature by reinscription.

The consequence of this position on personality as dynamic, provisional and reinscribed is an acceptance that an apt persona is required for different literary contexts. In crude terms, literary works create their own readers. This is close to an old idea from the early days of stylistics as a discipline, which held that readers constructed 'the grammar of a text' in the course of reading, and then used that grammar as a norm against which to generate interpretation (Traugott and Pratt 1977: 24; see also Nowottny 1972; and Cluysenaar 1976). It should be apparent from my formulation of this view, though, that there is a circularity here and an extended sense of 'grammar' that does not seem entirely valid. As I hope to show in this chapter, the situation is in fact more complex than this simple formulation.

The basic position is also comparable with Iser's (1974) notion of the *implied reader*, a construct that sits awkwardly on the borderline between being a textual entity and an extratextual entity. By analogy with Booth's

(1961) *implied author* (the sense of an author created from the entire text in hand, and separate from the historical, physical author), the implied reader is mainly a textual construct that Booth originally called the *postulated* or *mock reader*. This is the notion that a text is often addressed to a certain sort of reader who is ideally placed to make sense of it. Iser (1974) suggests that actual readers adapt themselves towards the implied reader in the course of reading, so the notion is also partly extratextual too. The idea of a theoretical reader has led to the notions of the *perfect reader* (Leavis 1952), the *informed reader* (Fish 1970), the *ideal reader* (Culler 1975), the *super-reader* (Riffaterre 1966), and the *model reader* (Eco 1990). All of these capture different nuances of the sense of a reader who has available all possible readings, or is omnisciently sensitive, or is perfectly matched to the text in hand. Of course, in none of these cases could an actual natural reader correspond with any of them – they are all abstracted and idealised to a greater or lesser extent. They are abstractions of reading rather than embodied reading minds (that is, readers!). None of these abstract entities can be said to have psychological motivation, feeling, or a life outside the reading situation. The textual end of these abstractions, and the confused nature of the implied reader are all rendered redundant by the further and more useful notion of the *narratee* (Prince 1973; Chatman 1978) – the directly addressed and textualised principal target of the discourse (in Robert Burns' 'I will love thee still, my dear', Ray Bradbury's 'You are a child in a small town', Charlotte Brontë's 'Reader, I married him'). As a consequence, the narratologist Uri Margolin (2007) has described the implied reader as 'a ghost. It doesn't exist'.

The reader in this book is primarily a natural reader, a real reader, a reader who could and often does exist, a reader with a mind and a body, with memories, motivations and experiences. Above all, the reader represented in this book is a psychologised reader. In many of the discussions in previous chapters, the reader has been myself, or a contributor to a book group or seminar discussion, or a literary critic, but in all cases a retrievable and traceable person. There are, though, two notions that can survive from my dismissal of previous accounts. The first is the notion of the adaptation of a reader in the course of reading, which is partly a result of textural organisation. The second is the notion that reading involves a personal relationship between natural people out in the world and virtual people inside the world of the text.

Identity and mind-modelling

In the previous section I mentioned the fundamental apparent paradox that personality appears to be variable over time and yet feels consistent in the moment. This is the psychological equivalent of the fundamental problem in linguistics in the fact that language is constantly changing and variable and yet we have internalised patterns of grammar to be able to talk to each other fairly successfully. Both of these apparent problems create a constructional paradox for literary reading: if texts can build readers who are engaged and defined by the work, why do some literary experiences fail? In other words, why don't all actual readers become implied (or ideal, super, model, and so on) readers? I think only a cognitivist view of the literary reading experience can resolve this problem, and I will address it later in the chapter in exploring readerly resistance to literary works.

There has been a great deal of interest in the issues surrounding identity and identification in cognitive poetics. These terms have become bound up with empathy, sympathy, attachment and engagement in various overlapping ways, in different disciplines (as Bray 2007 points out). The term *identity* shifts from its philosophical sense of exact equivalence to a more psychological sense of personal recognition and attachment. Applied to literary fiction, largely in the form of narrative, *identification* comes to refer to this recognition in text world characters of aspects of the reader's own self-aware personality (see Zillmann 1994; Bortolussi and Dixon 2003; Herman 2004). The ontological status of fictional entities has been explored, as has their relationship with readers. The fact of a connection between reader and character has been established empirically in the continuing work of David Miall and his colleagues (Miall and Kuiken 1994, 1999, 2002; Kuiken, Miall and Sikora 2004), where the term *self-implication* is preferred. In this work, readers are observed in a test situation generating feelings from an encounter with a literary text, and these feelings serve as modifiers of self-awareness. Kuiken, Miall and Sikora (2004) show that both metonymic and metaphorical mappings are involved between reader and character, with readers expressing their attachments as similarities and as recognition, respectively. These 'expressive enactments' thus encompass acts of comparison and acts of self-awareness, though the latter can also be seen as part of the process of modification of the self in the reader.

In much of this work, the empirical demonstration of the fact of identification is undisputed, though there are various ways in which it can be modelled. Miall (2005) argues that an empirical focus on feelings produced by literary readings shows that the way readers respond to literary characters is not the same as the way we respond to other people in the world. The literary manipulation of feeling (for example, by techniques such as free indirect discourse or direct thought that have no direct analogues except telepathy), he argues, renders a difference of literariness that makes the whole experience unique. Miall (2005: 151) sees this as a potential problem for the continuity between the everyday and the literary that is a principle of cognitive poetics. Taking issue with Bortolussi and Dixon (2003) and some of my own work (Stockwell 2002a), he argues that the 'assumption that the methods of literary analysis drawn from cognition will be adequate for all tasks, forecloses the possibility of establishing what may be distinctive to the experience of literature'. I am not sure that this is the case, though. I would not want to argue that the feelings of grief generated by the lament texts in chapter 3 above are exactly the same as natural feelings of grief generated by real death, but I think the difference is one of degree rather than kind, and the difference is the sense that a text world boundary must be crossed in the former but not the latter. In both cases, the cognitive mechanics are the same, but the particular effect of the literary experience is different. I can acknowledge the particular distinctiveness of literary reading without having to posit a 'literariness module' in the mind. Miall (2005) is right, though, to argue that cognitive poetics must address aesthetics as well as informational interpretation.

A recent productive and contentious arena for debate about literary identification lies in the use made by literary scholars of the 'Theory of Mind' (ToM) notion. In psychology, the capacity for ToM refers to the general ability to understand that others have beliefs about the world that are different from your own, and a consequence of running your ToM is that you impute certain beliefs about the world to others. In this sense, a person builds a 'theory' (that is, not a direct physical observation) that other people possess minds and operate in roughly similar ways, though within a broad window of possibilities. The notion of ToM has gone through several revisions within psychology, however, beginning with a general attribution of mental states to others, then focusing only on the inferring of *belief* states in others (rather than imagining their perceptual or goal-driven volition, both of which have physical indices), and being used primarily to explain evolutionary divergence between humans and non-humans (see Belmonte 2008). In literary applications, however, the notion has been both particularised and extended.

> For the literary critic, ToM has been a vehicle for understanding the relations between characters in a text, between characters in a text and readers, and between narrator and reader. The psychological sense is thus driven to further differentiation and specification of ToM on the basis of interspecies, inter-individual, and inter-age comparisons, whereas the literary sense retains a general agency within a wide range of texts and settings. The modes of application differ, too: psychological ToM is an online, real-time process applied during the act of interpreting behavior, whereas literary ToM is an offline, temporally extended process applied during the act of reading.
>
> (Belmonte 2008: 192)

The most well-known application of ToM to literary reading is by Zunshine (2003, 2006), where it is most divergent from the psychological sense. Zunshine adapts psychological ToM into a model of metarepresentation, so that, for example, in a detective story, the status of the beliefs of others is always questionable, and that very uncertainty is also a generic feature of the fiction. She also extends the very collective sense of ToM in psychology into a sense that a reader can model characters' motivations, thoughts and perspective (including perceptual and volitional position) as well as their belief-systems. Furthermore, a reader has to keep track of the ToM of every character's ToM of every other character, including the filtering narrator's ToM about everyone else.

There are several problems in adapting the ToM notion in a cognitive poetic context, not least these different senses in which they are used. Part of the problem is that 'Theory of Mind' is not a 'theory' about minds but is a descriptive term aimed at accounting for human psychological distinctiveness; it is entirely possible that literary scholars have been distracted by the word 'theory'. An easy solution to this would be to talk about *mind-modelling* as an alternative and literary-specific term. This can then be generalised as Zunshine (2006) does, without irritating psychologists. Gallagher (2006) has argued that literary application does not need to import a ToM approach, since what is being described is simply intersubjective involvement (or 'identification').

> By representing one's own mind alongside others in an ongoing narrative, one becomes able to apply to these minds domain general mechanisms of reasoning (Herman 2003). In this view, ToM reduces to a special case of narrative processing, a model of intersubjectivity in which we read other people like a book, without explicitly simulating them into our own first-person experience like an actor (the so-called 'simulation theory' of ToM performance) and without explicitly theorizing them into third-person description like a critic (the so-called 'theory theory'), but rather by interacting with them in a second-person exchange (Gallagher 2006).
>
> (Belmonte 2008: 199)

Accounting for mind-modelling by readers and characters preserves the literary critical need for a systematic account of knowledge, beliefs and feelings of fictional entities. It does not bring with it the contentious baggage of ToM debates, where 'odd' literature such as that written by autistic authors or about autistic characters is made artificially prominent (Zunshine 2006; McDonagh 2008; Roth 2008).

The crucial difference between psychological accounts of ToM and literary ones is the fictionality boundary that intervenes in a literary account. An explanation of mind-modelling within a text world theory frame allows this difference to be accommodated. A text world account also allows mind-modelling to be extended to non-belief domains such as the imagined desires, wishes, physical needs (hunger, lust, thirst, sleepiness, and so on) of others. It can also include a consideration of the respective feelings of characters towards each other, filtered through narration or authorial voice, and in relation to the reader (as Miall 2005 advocates).

For an example, I will briefly discuss Rumer Godden's (1944) short story, 'You Needed to Go Upstairs'. (This was retitled for a 1968 anthology as 'You Need to Go Upstairs', a re-tensing that increases the anxiety, urgency and immediacy of the story.) The text is framed in the second-person, as a form of what Fludernik (1994: 290) calls 'the entirely nonrealistic case of a pure rendering of a second-person's consciousness'. (Her other two major types of second-person narrative are '*I* and *you* narratives (in which the narrator shares a fictional past with the narratee and can therefore be "in the know" about it' and 'the playful metafictional case of a deliberate manipulation of the irreality and ambiguity factors of the second-person pronoun'). Narratologists have been interested in texts such as this for their ontological puzzlement and their structural poetics; here I am mainly interested in what this sort of text feels like.

The story is told in the second person, which allows me to explore Gallagher's (2006) point above that this is a stylistic specification of the normal application of mind-modelling, though in literary fiction second-person narratives are not as common as first- and third-person texts. The story begins:

> And just when everything is comfortably settled you need to go upstairs.
>
> You are sitting in the garden for the first time this year, sitting on a cushion on the grass by Mother. The feel of the grass is good; when you press it down and lift your hand the blades spring up again at once as strong as ever; they will not be kept lying down.
>
> You sit with your legs straight in front of you; they have come out from their winter stockings and are very thin and knobbly, but the sun is beginning to warm them gently as if it were glad to see them again.
>
> Your back is against Mother's chair and occasionally she puts her finger between your collar and your skin, to feel if you are warm; you are warm and you pick up your knitting because you can knit; with your finger you follow the wool along the big wooden pins and you say, 'Knit one – knit another'; with the slow puffs of wind. The wind brings the garden scents and the sounds to you; sounds of birds and neighbours and the street.
>
> Rumer Godden (1944: 170)

A reader coming to this story without knowing anything about it in advance will immediately begin by creating a text world with the narrating character in it. As the story opens, this character initially is little more than a voice, though the second-person form here serves to claim an intimate relationship directly across the text world boundary with the reader. A curious aesthetic quality of second-person narratives is that the reader-character vector has the appearance of being direct and undeflected: in first- and third-person narratives, the authorial or narratorial mind is noticeable as a deflection of the R – C relationship; in second-person narratives, this feeling of authorial intervention is relatively diminished (though of course a reader who steps back from reading can still be conscious that this story is by Rumer Godden).

The directness of the reader's relationship with the character is also underlined by the opening 'And', which is a continuation technique that draws attention to the ongoing persona who seems to have a life prior to the intervention of the text. The mind of this speaker that is modelled by the reader seems, I think, to be a person who has a highly sensual and sensitive feeling, but is relatively inarticulate. The reference to 'Mother' might lead you to think this is a child-persona, and the inarticulacy of evaluative lexis like 'good', and the reference to 'winter stockings' and 'knobbly' legs, and the repetitive phrases might all support this model. The cohesive chains across the text are very closely co-referential: 'settled' > 'sitting in the garden' > 'sitting on a cushion on the grass' > 'feel of the grass' > 'press it down and lift your hand' > 'lying down' > 'sit with your legs', and then the echoic repetitions across clauses of 'sun . . . warm' > 'warm . . . knitting' > 'knit . . . wind' > 'wind . . . sounds' > 'sounds . . . street'. The effect of this onward close chaining is to establish the reader's vector very powerfully in the direction of the character, without his virtual gaze being averted anywhere in the discourse world. The strength of the vector is very strongly pointed at the text world character's mind.

The childish mind being built by the reader is also confirmed by the sense of simple reasoning that the tight cohesive chains also realise. The numerous semi-colons in the text point to a sense of close logical consequence in the mind that is being modelled, and often these connections are overly explicitly stated: 'to feel if you are warm; you are warm and you pick up your knitting because you can knit'. Coming from the mind of a child, this feels proud of the skill and anxious to claim the skill and point it out to be approved.

The tactile gestures in this opening (and further through the story) seem at this stage to point to an extraordinarily sensitive child, one who focuses her attention on sensual details such as the touch of the grass, the warmth of the sun, the feel of the knitting needles, the puffs of wind, garden scents and the sounds of the birds and scene around her. The absence of reference to visual sensation merely serves to foreground the other senses, and in fact the only object doing any 'seeing' is the sun on her legs 'as if it were glad to see them again'. Seeing is rendered as part of personification here, a switch to a metaphorical world initiated by 'as if', so seeing is distanced further along a vector on the other side of the child from the reader, embedded in a more distant world. In text world theory terms, all of the textual cues discussed so far are world-builders, but the world they are helping the reader to build is one with edges framing the quality of the character's belief world: in practice, they are primarily building a character-model in the reader's mind.

As the story progresses, it becomes clear that the girl is blind. This is not stated explicitly at any point, since the perception being focalised is the girl's not the reader's, and since she is already aware of her own blindness, it would be odd of her to state it explicitly. Instead, the reader's mind-model of the character is adjusted by the behaviour of a visitor, who speaks patronisingly and is introduced as 'a visitor; voices and footsteps'. This avoidance of physical description which would prototypically be expected with the introduction of a new character seems significant. Jarringly, in the context of the story's narrative technique, the visitor addresses a whispered third-person question to the girl's mother:

> 'What is her name?'
> 'Her name is Alice', says Mother loudly and clearly to blot out the whisper. 'We call her Ally. Ally, stand up and say how do you do'.
> Rumer Godden (1944: 170)

The foregrounding of address forms in these few lines is striking. The visitor's third-person address to the Mother about Alice is answered also in the third person. The mother then shifts to second-person plural to 'ally' herself and her daughter together and distance them from the viewpoint expressed by the visitor (the narrative intervention reporting the speech also makes a distinction between the victorious loudness of the mother's voice and the whisper of the visitor). The mother ends with a direct second-person address to the daughter in imperative form, that also draws attention to the politeness that is lacking in the visitor ('how do you do'), while drawing subtle attention to the technique ('how') of the second-person ('do you do').

The story goes on to describe the girl deciding to go to the toilet ('upstairs') by herself, a risky journey for her to negotiate around various half-remembered objects, but a decision made in defiance of the pity exhibited by the visitor. The close accessibility to her perceptual field of the route from the garden to the upstairs of the house is the basis for the reader's ongoing enrichment of the mind-model for Alice. The potential danger is understood by the reader in a series of hypothetical text worlds, vectored through Alice's mind, in which she takes a different route upstairs, or imagines falling from the landing like a dropped ball. The story ends with her arriving at the bathroom, expressing her triumphant achievement 'perfectly'.

The mind-modelling of Alice by the reader is the crucial thematic technique in the story. Without such a rich potential, the sense of achievement would not be as great, and the sympathetic feeling of the reader for the character would not be so powerful. The feeling is sympathetic rather than empathetic because the particular second-person form (Fludernik's (1994) second-person direct consciousness type) creates both intimacy and self-awareness of difference: the world-edge that the vector must cross is texturally foregrounded throughout.

> The story's present-tense second-person narration invites the reader to adopt the focalization of the blind girl not in order to align the reader with the protagonist, but to distance the reader from the protagonist by forcing us to see exactly what we are not.
>
> (DelConte 2003: 9)

A further quality of theme is achieved as the reader closes the story and steps back initially into the discourse world. The sensuality and potential danger within Alice's mind fill up the reader's view as the story is progressing. However, finishing the text allows you (the reader) to reflect on the resonance of the story. 'Alice', who starts her story sitting on a grassy bank and imagines falling, has obvious echoes of *Alice in Wonderland*, another story about shifting perspective and perception. While you are busy modelling Alice's mind as you read, the title itself, revised as 'You Need to Go Upstairs', is apparently a childish and euphemistic phrase for going to the toilet. It seems more metaphorical after the fact: where 'upstairs' is the view from Alice's head, and the injunction to sympathise with the viewpoints and lives of others becomes an ethical imperative.

Identity and modification

The process of mind-modelling can be a mechanism for self-modification, as Kuiken, Miall and Sikora (2004) demonstrate. In the case of the Rumer Godden short story, it is difficult to imagine a sense of reading that was not sympathetic – though of course it is at least possible. How can we account for situations where there are very disparate – and even antagonistic – responses and strong feelings in different readings of the same text? In this section, I consider this situation (in a development of Stockwell 2005a).

In 1995, the BBC programme *The Bookworm* held a vote in Britain to discover 'the nation's favourite poem' (a popular anthology was published as Jones 1996). The runaway winner, polling more than double the votes of the second placed poem, which was Tennyson's *The Lady of Shalott*, was this:

If

If you can keep your head when all about you
Are losing theirs and blaming it on you,
If you can trust yourself when all men doubt you,
But make allowance for their doubting too;
If you can wait and not be tired by waiting,

Or being lied about, don't deal in lies,
Or being hated, don't give way to hating,
And yet don't look too good, nor talk too wise:

If you can dream – and not make dreams your master,
If you can think – and not make thoughts your aim;
If you can meet with Triumph and Disaster
And treat those two impostors just the same;
If you can bear to hear the truth you've spoken
Twisted by knaves to make a trap for fools,
Or watch the things you gave your life to, broken,
And stoop and build 'em up with worn-out tools:

If you can make one heap of all your winnings
And risk it all on one turn of pitch-and-toss,
And lose, and start again at your beginnings
And never breathe a word about your loss;
If you can force your heart and nerve and sinew
To serve your turn long after they are gone,
And so hold on when there is nothing in you
Except the Will which says to them: 'Hold on!'

If you can talk with crowds and keep your virtue,
Or walk with kings – nor lose the common touch,
If neither foes nor loving friends can hurt you,
If all men count with you, but none too much;
If you can fill the unforgiving minute
With sixty seconds' worth of distance run,
Yours is the Earth and everything that's in it,
And – which is more – you'll be a Man, my son.

Rudyard Kipling (1909)

Published in the collection *Rewards and Fairies* in 1909, the poem is reputedly based on the British administrator in South Africa, Dr Leander Starr Jameson, who led a force of 600 men against the Boers in 1896 aiming to overthrow the government. Jameson was gaoled first by the Boer government and then sentenced in Britain to fifteen months in prison. The Jameson raid is largely credited as a major cause of the second Boer War, during which the British developed a range of atrocities including scorched earth tactics and the innovative use of 'concentration camps'.

From an academic and historiographical perspective, the poem is viewed as an expression of imperial, nationalistic Britishness, extremely jingoistic (the coinage of this term is contemporaneous with the poem), and with a patriarchal twist. Christopher Hitchens (2002), for example, notes: 'When he was alive many critics thought Kipling to be a bad writer, and also a bullying and jingoistic one, and many readers today agree'. Phillip Mallet (2003) quotes a contemporary view of Kipling as 'the voice of the hooligan':

> The poet most synonymous with, and if some were to be believed responsible for, the war was Rudyard Kipling. To his many detractors he was the Bard of Bloodshed, an apologist for aggressive Imperialism. They could point to 'If', inspired by Jameson and Rhodes, or the *Barrack Room Ballads'* hooliganism in the name of Queen and country.
>
> (Mallet 2003)

He adds a backhanded compliment: 'Kipling's talent lay in understanding public sentiments and expressing them in verse designed for the music hall'. The poem often appears in school-based anthologies and teachers' resources, but is largely seen in higher education as sentimental, corny and trite. Greeting the news that this was the nation's favourite poem, there was a broad academic sense of dismay and scorn in the letters pages of liberal British newspapers such as *The Guardian* and *The Times Higher Education Supplement* at the poverty of critical skills in the general populace.

However, this is obviously a poem that large numbers of non-academics regard fondly and would like to identify with in sympathetic terms. For example, Alan Chapman, a business guru with a consultancy company based in Leicester, UK, describes the poem as

> inspirational, motivational, and a set of rules for 'grown-up' living. Kipling's 'If' contains mottos and maxims for life, and the poem is also a blueprint for personal integrity, behaviour and self-development. 'If' is perhaps even more relevant today than when Kipling wrote it, as an ethos and a personal philosophy [. . .] The beauty and elegance of 'If' contrasts starkly with Rudyard Kipling's largely tragic and unhappy life.
>
> (Chapman 2004)

In a similar vein, the corporate team building specialists Progressive Resources Ltd quote the poem in full alongside a few lines by that other great imperialist, Theodore Roosevelt, neatly skewering the activities of critics:

> 'It's not the critic who counts, not the man who points out how the strong man stumbled, or when the doer of deeds could have done better. The credit belongs to the man who is actually in the arena; whose face is marred by dust and sweat and blood; who strives valiantly; who errs and comes short again and again; who knows the great enthusiasms, the great devotions and spends himself in a

worth cause; who at the best, knows in the end the triumph of high achievement; and who at the worst if he fails, at least fails while daring greatly, so that his place shall never be with those cold and timid souls who know neither victory or defeat.'

(Theodore Roosevelt).

The relevance of these words to team building: when trying to improve a situation at work people are often confronted by critics [. . .] These very powerful words [. . .] can be a comfort in these situations.

(Progressive Resources Ltd 2005)

Likewise, Sahar Huneidi (2004), writing in *Psychic and Spirit* magazine, directly challenges the prevailing academic view: 'Kipling is often seen as the archetype of Imperial poets, but he was no jingoist, but rather a man who could put complex ideas in a way that everyone could understand them, "If" is one of the best examples of this talent.' There are many similar positive comments. The Cancer Research UK website includes a testimonial from Paul Workman: 'While undergoing MRI scans I recite to myself "If" – by Rudyard Kipling. It gives a sense of purpose, and takes my mind off what is going on' (Cancer Research 2005). The poem is often quoted in various inspirational materials and greetings cards, and the two lines on 'Triumph and Disaster' appear over the players' entrance to the centre court at Wimbledon.

It is clear that there are two polarised responses to the poem: a largely academic one, which regards it as a hangover from late Victorian sentiment in the service of imperialism and a jingoistic precursor to the pre-World War period, and a larger response from natural readers who find it inspirational, aspirational and offered in order to modify one's behaviour and attitudes. In other words, there is a reading which is resistant to the perceived historicised message of the text, and a reading which adapts its history into a positive identification. Of course, each side is not completely isolated from the other. Some academic readers with whom I have discussed the poem appreciate its stirring and seductive message, while still distancing themselves from it, and students with whom I have discussed the poem often begin by ridiculing the sentiment of the poem, but then feel rather sheepish when presented with the testimony of cancer patients who find comfort in it. I have shared this awkwardness. On the other side, it is unlikely that those who have made their appreciation of the poem public in online fora as mentioned above would accept a tacit support for war atrocities and aggressive imperialism.

It is possible to sketch these two reading positions in text world theoretical terms (following Gavins 2007). The poem, again, is a second-person text, not so much a narrative (though there are narrativised elements within it) and more of the form of an '*I* and *you*' dialogue (in Fludernik's (1994: 290) terms). 'You' are a person in your discourse world being addressed by an author, to whom you might attach the description 'Kipling', and if you do, you will invoke all your own knowledge of Kipling-ness, whatever you think that is, into the common ground in which you will build the text world of the poem. World-switches in text world theory are generated by temporal alternations (such as flashbacks), spatial alternations, metaphors (which are literal in the sub-world but metaphorical in the text world), negatives (positive in the sub-world and negated in the text world), and modalised propositions (such as speculation, conditionals, imagined alternatives, obligation, desire and emotion). Clearly, 'If' is dominated by this final category. We can say that world-switches embedded in the text world create distance from 'you' in the discourse world (the $R \rightarrow C$ vector magnitude is large), but the dense switched-world conditionals of the poem also serve to create lots of opportunities for counterpart identification: there are a string of connected 'you's' across several world boundaries. 'If' consists almost entirely of modal switched worlds.

'If you can keep your head when all about you / Are losing theirs and blaming it on you'. As can be seen in Figure 5a, the poem begins by creating, very rapidly, a text-world consisting of an unknown speaker and an addressee 'you' – which is very naturally identified as a counterpart of the reader, actually you, in the discourse world (let's say you^{TW} is established as a counterpart of you^{DW}, with apologies for the oddities of the grammar here). This counterpart identification is natural in '*I* and *you*' second-person forms as in this poem. However, the poem leaves this text-world almost immediately, to enter a conditional modal switched-world, effected by the first 'If' in the text proper. In this WS1, you^{TW} 'can keep your head when all about you are losing theirs and blaming it on you.' In fact, if we want a closer analysis, there is even a further rapid double conceptual jump in this line where the modal auxiliary 'can' creates a further embedded world-switch to WS2 (arrow 1) and back (arrow 2), and then the comparator 'when' creates a parallel temporal world-switch to WS3 along arrow 3, returning again to WS1 along arrow 4. If we take this more delicate analysis, we can see that almost the whole poem consists of world-switch texturing of the form: 'If you^{TW} can [WS2] when/or [WS3]'. The first pair of lines then reads: 'If you^{TW} can keep your^{WS2} head when all about you^{WS3} / Are losing theirs and blaming it on you^{WS3}'.

On the basis of this first complex clause-structure, there are five main counterpart enactors of 'you' available for connection across world-edges (I am ignoring the fine granularity that would analyse a further world-switch in the metaphoricality of keeping and losing their heads):

you^{DW} you^{TW} you^{WS1} you^{WS2} you^{WS3}

However, there is a curiosity here, in that you^{WS1} is not actually realised in the first two lines. Clearly there is a counterpart 'you' in WS1, in order to complete the propositional meaning carried within the function-advancing sense of that world, but this conceptual entity is not textually realised. Instead, the

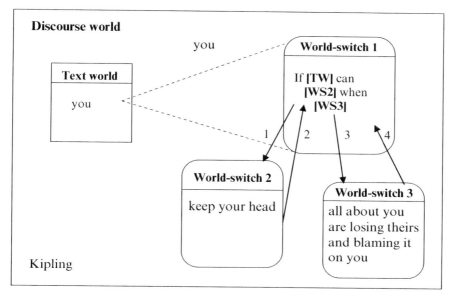

Figure 5a Text world diagram for Kipling's 'If'

implicit you[WS1] that receives the consequences of the further world-switches (to WS2 and WS3) deflects those acquired attributes onto you[TW]. It might even be a principle of text world theory dynamics if I suggest that attributes assigned to world-switched counterparts of a text world entity are always passed back up and out to the TW entity in order to enrich this higher level enactor. (You can see now why deictic shift theory terms of shifting 'in and out' can be regarded as viewing a text world structure edge-on, as proposed in Chapter 4). In other words, attributes attached to world-switched enactors are assigned in total to the overall sense of the composite character, and this character is best represented by the TW enactor.

It seems that all the subsequent lines perform this same manoeuvre; I count seventeen times, parsing the text by the structure defined by the text world loop as drawn in Figure 5a. The introductory 'If' in each one attaches to the you[TW] and instantly shifts by conditionality to another WS1, where 'you' as a complete character collect attributes from the further world-switches. The resolution of the conditional 'if' is resisted across these seventeen primary switched worlds, some of which contain additional secondary complications, consequences and elaborations. For example, the first stanza contains five primary world-switch conditionals: keeping your head, trusting yourself, waiting, being lied to, and being hated. Even within this density of situations, there are further embedded world-switch circumstances: a co-ordinate world when all men doubt you; a negated world in which you are tired by waiting; a metaphorical world in which you are a dealer of the cards or business of lies; and a co-ordinate and doubly negated final world in which you simultaneously don't look good and don't talk.

Other stanzas – such as the third – only contain two primary world-switches (the gambling loss and the forcing of your stamina), but have elaborated function-advancing propositions that develop your characterisation through mini-narratives: you make a heap of your winnings, then gamble it all away on one bet, then start again without complaining; and you work hard beyond the point of endurance, persisting only through the force of your will. This stanza in particular exploits the breathlessness of the additive syntax to force you to 'hold on' to your breath in order to be able to reach and hoarsely whisper out the final direct speech, 'Hold on!' A physical identification is being made between the material effort of your^{DW} reading with the grim mental determination of your$^{DW/TW}$ counterpart you$^{WS1/2}$ in the switched worlds.

The poem, then, sets out a series of seventeen enactors of you^{TW}. These are literally character-building, and the character that they build is a multifaceted and admirable you^{TW} addressee in the initial text world. Most of the attributes are likely to be approved by you^{DW}, I would imagine: such as courage, work, rationality, self-confidence, and so on. Other attributes that you^{DW} might not have approved, such as gambling away your gains on the chance flick of a coin, or what seems to be a propensity for pragmatism and compromise over conviction, are nevertheless presented in the same conceptual structure as the approving moves. It is quite difficult not to go along with these, buying into their ideology (in investment terms: see Chapter 3). This is the basis of the text's seduction of approval.

Your^{DW} readerly attention is focused on these qualities of the various enactors, of course, partly because the detail and conditional syntax holds your^{DW} attention, but also because the switched worlds are very much richer than the initial text world, which still only contains a vague speaker and you^{TW} the addressee. Throughout the poem, a composite you^{C}, consisting of all the enactor-attributes rolled into a character, are tested in the worlds of many different social and moral circumstances, involving both decisive material action and calm mental deliberation. In each case, other participants at the various world-switch levels are accumulating attributes diametrically opposite to yours^{C}, and are described as 'knaves', 'fools', and 'foes'; even your 'loving friends' are out to hurt you, and the poem repeatedly sets you^{C} up against 'all men'.

In the course of these switched world dependencies, the constant identification of you^{DW} and you^{C} is hard to resist. This is partly because the qualities being placed conditionally on all your^{C} enactors are either naturally attractive to you^{DW} or are rendered attractive by the conceptual structure, as I have suggested. Secondly, the dynamic I proposed – whereby enactor attributes in embedded switched worlds are passed on up the world levels towards the text world you^{TW} – creates an outward trajectory with some momentum. In other words, the attributions accumulated upwards continue to be passed on to you^{DW} in the discourse world. Of course, this momentum across the TW/DW edge is greatly assisted by the multiple possible referents of the stylistic 'you' in this poem. Any identification of you^{DW} with you^{TW} as a counterpart mapping is relatively easy because of this. Lastly, of course, as a reader you^{DW} are so anxious to resolve the conditional 'If . . . *then* . . .' that your^{DW} close analytical and potentially resistant attention to aspects of the embedded world-switches does not have time to work itself through before you are distracted with a further conditional. When the conditional resolution finally comes in the last two lines, it seems to me that there is a huge sense of completion:

Yours is the Earth and everything that's in it,
And – which is more – you'll be a Man, my son.

With 'Yours', your focus is returned to the text-world level, where it suddenly becomes apparent that the speaker is your^{TW} father-figure. Accepting (or at least, going along with) each of the seventeen WSs results in a very strong composite sense of the you^{TW} as the overall, richly delineated character (you^C). In contrast to 'all men' who are knaves and fools, you^C are now a 'Man', and the only other capitalised entities Triumph and Disaster are resolved and defeated by your^C 'Will'. As personification metaphors, 'Triumph' and 'Disaster' are now even more remote from you^{TW}, buried at several world levels deep from your current text world. The completion of the conditional ('Yours is the Earth') sets a true simple present tense against the modalised present of the seventeen switched worlds. The final clause takes advantage of the grammatical possibilities of conditionality to collapse what appears to be a future aspect ('you'll') with a reference to the present situation, as long as you^C have identified yourself^{DW} with all the testing circumstances of the conditional switched worlds.

Reading the poem, then, is both a test (of identification) and an ordeal (of syntax). In the course of reading, you^C is enriched by a series of attributes in conditional form. If you^{DW} map yourself^{DW} closely onto your^{DW} counterpart you^C through the accumulated text worlds, then these attributes become your^{DW} qualities too, and for all the reasons I have suggested above, this continuation of the mapping up and out of the text is very difficult to resist. It is the degree to which you^{DW} perform the trans-world mapping from text world to discourse world which determines how far you^{DW} identify with the sentiments of the poem or not. Those readers who hold the poem in high esteem clearly make a strong identification between themselves and the finally completed you^C of the text world level. For these readers, the acceptance of attributes and the identification of you^C and you^{DW} is full, rich and closely enacted.

By contrast, those (mainly academic) resistant readers who find the poem repellent or uncomfortable are making no such strong identification. For them, the you^C represented at the text world level is not closely mapped as a counterpart of you^{DW} the reader in the discourse-world. The identification is not performed, and the outward trajectory of enactor-attributes is halted at the text world edge. Indeed, we could model this reading as a further distancing, by which the text world level you^C remains a projected dramatic character, separate from you^{DW} in the discourse world. Even more complicatedly, a resistant reader trying to imagine the emotional impact of the text on an acceptant reader (such as I am trying to do here) must place a further projected text world between their discourse world and the 'you^{TW}-father-figure world – a text world which includes the acceptant reader as a participant in the father-figure's (and 'Kipling's') ideology. The resistant reader models the mind of a character as a disjunctive entity bounded by the text world, whereas complicit readers model a version of themselves as a continuation of the trajectory of the character.

Resistance and the nexus

The model of personality and personhood being set out in this chapter is a composite and configurable phenomenon. At the beginning of the chapter, I said that personality is adaptive to the conditions at hand, and it seems we are perfectly capable of *accommodating* our personality pattern (to borrow a sociolinguistic term) in order to engage with literary and fictional minds. We can configure our personae into less prototypical forms, when we encounter what we conceive of as less prototypical situations and characters. Accommodation usually refers to the modifications to accent patterns that most people exhibit when they have an extended conversation with someone with a different accent (see Auer, Hinskens and Kerswill 2005). Accommodation can consist of a move towards or away from the interlocutor, usually taken psychologically and often sub-consciously as an indication of solidarity or hostility, respectively (see Auer 2007). This is the fundamental adaptive capacity that we possess for dealing with new situations, but a consequence of it is that part of our personality is invested in the reconfiguration, and of course we are left with a resonant memory of the reconfiguration that we enacted. Similarly in literary reading and the relationships with characters, accommodation of personality can be configured towards or away from that fictional mind, as was sketched in the responses to the Kipling poem above.

   The social positioning and sensitivity of readers is not as deeply researched either in cognitive poetics or in literary scholarship at large, other than in very general or purely sociological and demographic terms. However, it seems clear that there is primarily often an actual social conversation conducted around readings (this takes the form of book group discussions, seminars or tutorials, or simply family or casual conversations), and also an anticipatory social adjustment made by a reader. What I mean by this latter suggestion is that readers tend not to make wild or eccentric responses to literary works (unless they are academics doing so wilfully); instead, we seem to operate a prior self-censorship policy of suppressing opinions that we think might be regarded as crazy or ridiculous. In fact, most readers' readings of given texts (apart from a few highly ambivalent works) are remarkably convergent (see Martindale 1988), as if in anticipation of a real conversation that in fact might never actually happen. Reading looks private and solipsistic but is in fact social and interactive.

This social accommodation is a function of the social network connections of the individual. A social network is a simple twofold measure of the inter-connectedness of a social group: firstly, people in the group might know only a few or a lot of other people, and secondly all these people might know each other only from one context (such as in their work) or in many different con-texts (their school, their street, their recreation). Social networks can thus be measured in terms of their multiplexity and density respectively (Milroy 1987). In sociolinguistic research, dense and multiplex social networks act as reinforcement mechanisms of linguistic innovation (spreading new accent patterns or new word coinages), and are the drivers of the diffusion of these features in the community. Bex (1996) extends the social network approach into the field of language and written discourse in order to discuss the prac-tices that generate meaning around literary and other types of texts. A similar *communities of practice* approach that superseded social networks in sociolin-guistics (Lave and Wenger 1991; Eckert and McConnell-Ginet 1992a, 1992b, 1995) has been most successful in the analysis of how identity is represented socially and individually. In this field, identity is regarded as a practice that is performed and constructed, rather than being given, essential or fixed (see Dyer 2007). Accommodation theory emphasises the agency of speakers in selecting their own identity and adapting towards their sense of it (Le Page and Tabouret-Keller 1985).

It should be clear how this brief sociolinguistic discussion has relevance for the things that readers do in relation to fictional characters, their virtual interlocutors in literary works. Just as speakers accommodate their speech towards each other in extended conversation, readers accommodate their personalities towards the fictional characters that they must engage with in the process of reading. The degree and awareness of this personality configu-ration is determined by our expectations of social convention. For an extreme and most obvious example, I recall several conversations with students who had just read Bret Easton Ellis' (1991) novel *American Psycho*, which features graphic accounts of the murders committed by a serial killer, investment banker Patrick Bateman. The largely first-person narrative engages a reader closely and vividly in the appalling descriptions of sexual violence coupled with emotional coldness. The students clearly expressed this conventional moral viewpoint on the character initially, but only in the extended course of the conversation did several of them admit that their attitude to the graphic descriptions was more ambivalent than their first articulations. The strong suggestion (though never authoritatively confirmed) that Bateman's narrative is in fact a delusional fantasy and the violence is all in his mind served for many as a justification for this ambivalence: it was alright to be lured in by the lyricism of the sadistic acts because they were not real. What was interesting about the discussion was the edginess and hedging as each person in the group attempted to gauge the others' feelings first before committing themselves to expressing this view. The final consensus on this occasion – that the murders were a fantasy and the novel therefore a satire rather than a horror story – was arrived at only after a process of accommodation of identity.

The psychological need that underlies this social accommodation is what Leahy (2005) calls *validation*. In the terms established by attachment theory (Bowlby 1968, 1973; Ainsworth et al. 1978), children seek validation from role-models such as parents, friends and teachers. In later life, we find validation in establishing intersubjective support for our perceptions, beliefs and interpretative decisions. Validation, according to Leahy (2005: 195), lies between empathy and sympathy. The process is not one of creating a belief and then going in search of support, though. Validation is more of a transforming process for our perceptions and beliefs in the first place. A tentative configuration is likely to be adapted in the social process of validation. This is what seems to be happening in the careful discussion around 'allowable' responses to *American Psycho*. The final, validated position of the students discussing the novel has hardened up from their initial timidity.

The cleverness of the novel's technique, of course, lies in the fact that the murders were only ever in the reader's mind as products of a work of fiction. The physical revulsion that many readers felt in reading especially nasty passages (involving a physical shuddering away from the page, squeamish narrowing of the eyes, tightening of the lips, and so on) is re-evaluated at the end of the novel as a sign of their moral position. Their physical resistance is taken as a sign of their ethical resistance, though of course these readers have already implicated themselves in the character of Bateman, regardless of their awareness of his fictionality. Resistance is also a form of validation.

It was clear to me in the course of the extended discussion (over ninety minutes) that the processes of accommodation towards and away from the character were in flux generally, in negotiation socially, and in question individually until near the end of the interactive process. The social network approach and the similar community of practice approach both involve relatively fixed notions, taking social group membership as a given and then applying research methodologies to it. The group is also bounded rather than frayed, in the sense that there might be some notion of the radiality of core and marginal members, but membership is categorical rather than prototypical (see Scollon 2001: 142). In literary reading, few readers (except fans and devotees) identify themselves as being solely 'a science fiction reader', or a 'romantic fiction reader', even if that is in fact what they exclusively read

– most people at least have a sense that they are adaptable as readers. They can successively be members of different, overlapping social groups as readers. As Scollon (2001: 145) points out, a potentially more useful notion is Swales' (1990) idea of the *discourse community*, in which membership is defined primarily by common use of language, discourse and register (stamp collectors, football supporters, readers of contemporary poetry, with their own jargon), regardless of whether these people have any physical or direct contact or even knowledge of each other. Unfortunately, Swales (1998) abandons the notion in favour of the identificatory power of *place*, but it seems to be legitimate to argue that the literal space and the conceptual space of connections between people are on a continuum in the embodied mind.

Ron Scollon's (2001; Scollon and Wong Scollon 2004) discourse analytical notion of the *nexus of practice* might help us here:

> The concept of the nexus of practice works more usefully than the concept of the community of practice which was the earlier framing (Scollon 1998) in that it is rather loosely structured as well as structured over time. That is, a nexus of practice, like practices themselves, is formed one mediated action at a time and is always unfinalized (and unfinalizable). The concept of the nexus of practice is unbounded (unlike the more problematic community of practice) and takes into account that at least most practices [. . .] can be linked variably to different practices in different sites of engagement and among different participants. [. . .] Mediated discourse analysis takes the position that it is the constellation of linked practices which makes for the uniqueness of the site of engagement and the identities thus produced, not necessarily the specific practices and actions themselves.
>
> (Scollon 2001: 5)

This understanding of social connections which render identification as a nexus corresponds much more closely with a sense of the common practices of a set of readings in prototypically radial terms. The nexus is psychologically and ideologically informed; this is the sense in which all actions (including readerly responses) are mediated. It is historically and culturally situated, and it can be regarded as more or less transient depending on how embedded the repeated engagements in the nexus become. In other words, readers who habitually read certain genres of texts become adept at that site of engagement, and those repeated readings in conjunction with other readers as a discourse community constitute a nexus of practice.

Habitual action is key to the creation and persistence of a nexus. The theory draws on Mauss' (1936) use of *habitus* as a set of practices in culture that derive from the physical nature of the body, including perceptions, tastes, physical needs, and so on. This has obvious correlations with recent cognitive science. Bourdieu (1972) extended the notion of *habitus* to include perceptions, dispositions, motives and beliefs, in order to mediate between social determinants and individual choice. Bourdieu emphasises the provisional and online nature of any given engagement with habitus. Habitus can be seen as the internalisation of culture. In all these terms, the nexus (singular) of reading activities around a particular literary work is constructed from prior similar experience as well as the new particular singularities of the text (Attridge 2004). The nexus (plural) across several literary works overlap and merge away from the prototypical centres.

To give an example, here is a poem by the poet Rupert Brooke, who most people associate with the First World War. Brooke died in 1915 from an infected mosquito bite on the way to Gallipoli, and so he never saw the battlefield. Nevertheless, my impression especially of non-specialist readers is that Brooke is aligned with other, more prototypically central examples of war poets such as Wilfrid Owen, Siegfried Sassoon and Isaac Rosenberg. A nexus of reading is immediately instantiated, then, by the name of the poet and the date in the title of the collection, *1914*:

I. Peace

Now, God be thanked Who has matched us with His hour,
   And caught our youth, and wakened us from sleeping,
With hand made sure, clear eye, and sharpened power,
   To turn, as swimmers into cleanness leaping,
Glad from a world grown old and cold and weary,
  Leave the sick hearts that honour could not move,
And half-men, and their dirty songs and dreary,
   And all the little emptiness of love!
Oh! we, who have known shame, we have found release there,
   Where there's no ill, no grief, but sleep has mending,
    Naught broken save this body, lost but breath;
Nothing to shake the laughing heart's long peace there
   But only agony, and that has ending;
    And the worst friend and enemy is but Death.

Rupert Brooke (1915: 111)

This is an enormously seductive poem. It evokes a romantic (and indeed Romantic) image of life and youthfulness, energy, honour, vigour and attractiveness that distracts the reader's attention from the fact that the poem is a celebration of the outbreak of the Great War. Its immediacy is captured by 'Now', in the first line, which is both conversational and exclamatory. There is a sense of relief in it, as if the speaker has been waiting for this opportunity for a long time. Brooke was not the only one agitating for war in the years before 1914. The poem can be seen as a continuation of Kipling's jingoism and the sense, popular in press editorials and public speeches, that an advanced nation's health could be tested only by military prowess against other nations. The romanticisation of war in this set of discursive practices does not omit the pain and grief of conflict, but it diminishes it and frames it as the worthwhile validation of the risk: life is enhanced by the risk, and close avoidance, of death.

The drawing in of a reader's persona to accommodate towards the mind-set of the speaker is achieved largely by the tailing syntax. Astonishingly, though 'God' is the subject of the entire first stanza, the passive forms 'be thanked', 'caught' and 'wakened' and the directionality of the transitive in 'who has matched us' serve firstly to put 'us' on a level with God and then in fact become greater than him. The rest of the stanza, though syntactically subordinate to this opening clause, consists of such a piling up of additive syntax that the focus of attention is very much on 'us' and not on God – to the extent that there is a syntactic slippage into an apparent imperative ('Leave the sick hearts'). The transition is the contracted prepositional phrase 'To turn' (meaning God did this 'in order to turn us') which turns its meaning in what follows into an apparent infinitive ('To turn [away] . . . from a world'). The infinitive occludes God as the subject, to focus on the poetic voice and our feelings and actions. At the same time as the focus turns to us, the poetic alliteration and internal rhyme which were not a feature of God's first two lines begin to be felt strongly ('Glad from a world grown old and cold and weary', and in all the other six lines).

It would be very difficult, of course, even for a poem at the heart of a cultural nexus featuring patriotic jingoism, for the pro-war sentiment to be advocated in a pure form. Along with stirring national feelings, bright uniforms, marching bands and regimental honours in distant campaigns, readers in 1914 would also have had a sense of the pain of war and its pity even before the Great War cast its long shadow over our history. A conventional war poem in this nexus (especially from our twenty-first-century vantage point) would align dirt and darkness with battle, and light and cleanness with peace. The poem reverses this cultural expectation, beginning with high action, motion, bright clarity and heightened awareness ('clear eye, and sharpened power') and following this with slowness ('old and cold and weary'), stasis ('could not move'), diminishment ('half-men', 'little emptiness'), dirt and darkness ('dirty songs and dreary'). The pivotal and most self-consciously striking image in the poem is the explicit metaphor of 'swimmers into cleanness leaping', with its sequential iconicity of action. This is the phrase most often quoted and recalled by readers. After 'we' have leapt into this bright and idealised 'world', and become 'Glad', the rest of the poem looks back 'from' this position at the tawdry physicality of our previous existence. The effect is to draw on a romantic ideal in the nexus, but also to assert the poem's transcendence over it. Even 'love!' – the central element in romantic poetry – is rendered ambivalently in 'And all the little emptiness of love!' This pulls in two directions: enlargement ('And all'), diminishment ('the little'), and a combination of these as the quality of being empty (a 'felt absence' lacuna of love: see Chapter 2). The exclamation mark signals the audacious rhetorical flourish of risking diminishing the romantic ideal in order even more power-fully to assert it.

The second, shorter stanza develops this pattern of lacunae, invoking the conventionalities from the cultural nexus of war while at the same time denying and diminishing them, setting them aside from the idealised and transcendent state in which 'we' now are. The technique places shame, illness, broken-ness and grief in the past and points towards their absence in the new circumstance. Compare the actual formulation 'Naught broken save this body' with its semantic equivalent 'This body is broken but nothing else'. The use of 'save' here is double-edged, literally meaning 'except' and used archai-cally alongside 'naught', but also generating a secondary, redemptive sense. 'Agony' is diminished ('only'), and adding 'and that has ending' belittles it even more. The possessing formulation (rather than 'and that ends') serves to make transience an existing quality of agony already.

It seems to me that it is the first stanza which most successfully achieves the accommodation of a reader's outlook towards the centre of the nexus embod-ied by this poem: the attractiveness of the message requires an accommoda-tion of persona into one who adopts the sentiments set out here as their own. The complicity of 'we' and 'us' is central to this, of course. This adapted persona is then fit to read the second stanza, and align itself with the poetic voice. 'Death' itself is diminished ('but Death') and placed at the end of the poem.

However, if a modern reader draws in the broader experiences of nexus relations around this text, there is much more likely to be a resistant reading. The scope of the relevance of these other experiences is a matter of readerly disposition, of course (Scollon and Wong Scollon's (2004: 10–11) term for this analytical scope-setting is *circumferencing*), but I find it difficult to imagine a reader who permanently occupies this persona-form and nexus position. Unfortunately, imagining such a principled enthusiast for war is not impossible. Nevertheless, my estimate would be that the legacy of the trenches, the brutality of the mass slaughter, and the stupidity of the com-manders' strategies would form strongly influential areas in the nexus that would shape the reading.

There are two possible forms that such readerly resistance to Brooke's sentiments might take. The first, and probably the most common, is to place Brooke within the nexus of poetry of the Great War in a position that is sepa-rate from the other 'soldier poets', as they were called at the time. This resist-ant reader places a discourse world Brooke[DW] on 'our' side of the text world boundary, and then the belief system embodied in the text world of the poem is vectored through this authorial entity. The poetic persona speaking in the poem (Brooke[TW]) then has a distance from the reader, and the world-edge that must be crossed has an ideological quality to it – an ideological edge that consciously belongs to Brooke^TW and not the reader. This sort of resistance frames the viewpoint as otherly, and the 'we' and 'us' in the poem are read non-inclusively, with reference only to others within the belief frame of the text world. The consequence of this sort of global resistance is that a reader can temporarily assign an avatar personality to vivify Brooke^TW, but there is always a conscious and textured disjunction between this entity and the reader's sense of his prototypical self. Brooke^DW, by close identification with Brooke^TW, stands then as a figure of ridicule, or pity, or historical oddity, or a person in a cautionary tale, and his ignominious death might be regarded as rather pathetic or even as an ironic poetic justice, by a reader of an unsympathetic disposition (like me).

A second possible form of resistance is to allow Brooke^DW some greater complexity, and retain some sympathy for the delusion that was, after all, shared by many young men at the outbreak of the war. Instead of an ideological hostility for the middle-class officers who led working-class troops to their deaths for the sake of king and country, a sympathetic human continuity might be accommodated between the reader and the poetic voice. Many of those who died in northern Europe in that war bear on their headstones Brooke's lines from later in the same collection: 'If I should die, think only this of me: / That there's some corner of a foreign field / That is for ever England' ('V. The Soldier', Brooke 1915: 115). Many readers – even perhaps those resistant to the poem 'Peace' – find these lines moving rather than sentimental, and their patriotism seems nostalgic rather than strident. A more sympathetic reader might yet resist the plain sentiment of 'Peace' by finding ambivalences in the text, and assigning those to the imagined poetic persona: this is accommodation of poetic and readerly personae towards each other. For example, the distracting technique of lacunae set out above can be read as an unflinching determination to face up to ordeal and transcend it. The complicity expressed in the poem is not sinister persuasion but an inclusive claim to our common humanity. And the immediacy and deictic closeness of grief, 'this body' and breath is a recognition that physical suffering in an ideal cause is admirable, and that the poetic sensibility placed around these fears is an attempt to come to terms with and face those anxieties bravely and honourably, however misguidedly. Such a relatively accommodating resistant reader might see ambivalence in the final line ('the worst friend and enemy is but Death'), parsing the phrase 'worst [friend and enemy]' as paradoxical rather than as a tautological synonymy '[worst friend] = [enemy]'.

The first, most resistant reader might regard the title, 'Peace', as uttered in a scornful voice by the poetic persona; the second, less resistant reader might read it as an ironically complex but desired consequence of war – the peace that satisfies those energetic for action, and the ultimate peace that death brings.

A major aspect of Scollon's (2001) nexus analysis is its interventionist agenda. The anthropological researcher intervenes in the nexus of practice in order to change it in ways that are ideologically motivated. Indeed, participation in the nexus, even by simply thinking about it, necessarily and unavoidably changes it. The same is true of my readerly adaptation of the theory within the reader's consciousness. The nexus that constitutes these readings, this poem, Rupert Brooke, war poetry, romantic poetry, poetry, and literature (in outward circumferencing of radiality) is experientially altered by the process of considering everything in this chapter. Since the person of the reader – even the temporary and provisional online configuration assembled to read the poem – is also part of that nexus, the reader too is changed by the experience. Resistance is not a firewall against this alteration, since even resistance, as I have tried to show, also involves the partial reconfiguration of persona in the encounter with the literary.

The ethics of worlds

In crude terms, ethics is the difference between what is and what should be; in cognitive linguistic terms, this makes ethics a matter of modalisation; and modalisation is a matter of world-switching. Ethical positioning and evaluation in literature, then, is best explored using text world theory. Readers position themselves in different places relative to the minds they are modelling in the text world, and these ethical positions correlate with the degree of support, acquiescence or resistance in the reading. The switched world presents for ethical comparison an alternative state of affairs. In some literary works, the reader and his discourse world are left as the other side of the comparison; in other works, parallel versions of readers are embedded in the text world structure within the work itself, with the reader[DW] as an omniscient observer.

An example of the latter situation is Thomas More's (1910) *Utopia,* written around 1515–16 (see Stockwell 2002a: 100). In this proto-novel, various counterparts of the reader are explicitly placed into and around the central description of the island of Utopia, an idealised land held up for unfavourable comparison with contemporary Europe. The text begins with a letter written by Thomas More, at that point the under-Sheriff of London, addressed to his friend Peter Giles, a clerk of the city of Antwerp. Both of these text world participants are real people in the discourse world: Giles was also the Renaissance equivalent of a copy-editor who helped More get the book published. However, the letter goes on to describe a tale told by a Portuguese explorer, the entirely fictional Raphael Hythloday (meaning 'teller of nonsense'). The main body of the novel then consists of his account of the corruption of present-day Europe, followed by a description of the island of Utopia.

There are thus several enactors of Thomas More within different world levels within the book: a More^{DW} as author located in 1515, a More^{TW} as addressee in 1515; then in the Europe-account there is a More^{WS1} who receives the story from the fictional Hythloday, also roughly in 1515; and there is a More^{WS2} who receives the description of Utopia, where it is 1760 by their reckoning. The reader^{DW} follows this narratological complexity but does not take part in it, especially a modern, twenty-first-century reader for whom even the European description is a historical curiosity rather than a matter of current affairs. The topography and geography of Utopia are impossible in our world: as a crescent 200 miles wide at its broadest and with its tips only eleven miles apart, it cannot possibly possess the 500-mile circumference that is claimed for it. Similarly, its fifty-four towns cannot possibly be equally twenty-four miles apart from each other, given the extent of the island. The reader of *Utopia* remains outside the embedded world structures in the novel; Utopia is inaccessible to them both narratologically and geographically.

It is clear from all of this that *Utopia* is a satire rather than a travelogue. As such, there is little ambivalence or free range of meaning in the novel. In fact, the reader has quite a job simply keeping track of all the different world-switches and embeddings of character and counterparts. The reader is triangulated along a series of vectors from all the different enactors of Thomas More, and thereby positioned very firmly in an ethical position. This ethical message must be recovered, in any reading which could be regarded as proto-typical. It would be perverse (though of course not impossible) for a reader to conclude *Utopia* by thinking that the island is a wretched place and actually the state of Europe in the early sixteenth century was the desirable place to be.

The only outlet of resistance that a reader has from *Utopia* is to step right back to the discourse world and take issue with the way that Europe has been portrayed. This seems to me the likely manoeuvre of the heads of state, government officials and church officers who are criticised in the novel – and the fear of the effects of such criticism is one reason why More couched the novel in deflected and thus deniable form. However, even this readerly resistance is not made easy by the embedded nature of the novel's narrative structure. It is not More^{DW} nor even More^{TW} who is portraying Europe as corrupt; he is only the trusted messenger mid-way along the vector between reader and Hythloday – and some of the trust seems to rub off qualitatively as the tale makes its way from teller to reader.

In any but the most wilfully eccentric reading of *Utopia*, then, an ethical reader is constructed in the course of reading the text. This reader is characterised as one who broadly agrees that the political economy and culture of Europe needs reform, and this agreement entails specific consensus on the details of agriculture, church organisation and politics as described throughout the book. The adoption of this ethical reading position, of course, like any performance of personality, is a configuration appropriate to the conditions at hand. Though there might be a resonant effect, and a permanent ethical revision of position as a result of reading the novel, no one permanently becomes stuck in a Thomas More personality for the rest of their lives.

The crucial point to be made here is that certain sorts of literary works provide an organisational framework that encourages a prototypical reading, rather than easily allowing a broad range of interpretation. There is a right way to read *Utopia*, and of course in saying this, there are a lot of wrong ways to read it. Furthermore, a major factor in the relative fixity of meaning in this literary work is its texture – the quality of textual organisation.

There are many texts like this where readings that stray very far from the prototypically-encouraged configuration can be regarded as highly eccentric. Imagine coming to the end of George Orwell's (1949) *Nineteen Eighty-Four* and thinking that the IngSoc state was a pretty good society and Winston Smith got all that he deserved; or reading John Fowles' (1963) *The Collector* and thinking that it would actually be quite good fun to trap and kill young women like butterfly specimens; or finishing Margaret Atwood's *The Handmaid's Tale* and thinking that the society of Gilead had all its priorities in the right order. I am not saying that such readings are impossible, nor even that some people might hold them or interpretations associated with them honestly. However, it seems to me that, in these cases, there is a prototypically ethical reading which is highly preferred in the novels' textures, and other readings that are far out along the radial structure.

There are also, of course, literary works in which the ethical positioning of the reader is altogether allowing of more ambivalence, or which create more potential places for a readerly configuration of personality to settle. This is the case in Audrey Niffenegger's (2004) *The Time Traveler's Wife*. The novel consists of a series of narratives, toggled between 'Clare' and 'Henry', often with each retelling from their own perspective the scene that has just been described. Henry suffers from a 'chrono-displacement' genetic disorder, which causes him to jump about in time around but not entirely within the boundaries of his life. The novel consists of the complex relationship he develops with Clare, whom he first met when she was six, and with whom he later has a child with the same condition. Henry arrives at each period of his life without any clothes or even dental fillings, and has developed skills to allow him to survive. This very odd, science fictional love story begins with the date – '*Saturday, October 26, 1991 (Henry is 28, Clare is 20)*' – told as Clare, the first-person narrator, goes into a library and asks the woman on the desk for help (I have added the underlining to the text below):

[. . .] she glances over my shoulder at someone passing behind me. 'Perhaps Mr. DeTamble can help you,' she says. I turn, prepared to start explaining again, and find myself face to face with Henry.

I am speechless. <u>Here is Henry, calm, clothed, younger than I have ever seen him. Henry is working at the Newberry Library, standing in front of me, in the present. Here and now.</u> I am jubilant. Henry is looking at me patiently, uncertain but polite.

'Is there something I can help you with?' he asks.

'Henry!' I can barely refrain from throwing my arms around him. <u>It is obvious that he has never seen me before in his life.</u>

'Have we met? I'm sorry, I don't . . .' Henry is glancing around us, worrying that readers, co-workers are noticing us, <u>searching his memory and realizing that some future self of his has met this radiantly happy girl standing in front of him. The last time I saw him he was sucking my toes in the Meadow.</u>

I try to explain. 'I'm Clare Abshire. <u>I knew you when I was a little girl . . .</u>' <u>I'm at a loss because I am in love with a man who is standing before me with no memories of me at all. Everything is in the future for him.</u> I want to laugh at the weirdness of the whole thing. I'm flooded with years of knowledge of Henry, while he's looking at me perplexed and fearful. Henry wearing my dad's old fishing trousers, patiently quizzing me on multiplication tables, French verbs, all the state capitals; <u>Henry laughing at some peculiar lunch my seven-year-old self has brought to the Meadow; Henry wearing a tuxedo, undoing the studs of his shirt with shaking hands on my eighteenth birthday. Here! Now!</u> 'Come and have coffee with me, dinner or something . . .' <u>Surely he has to say yes, this Henry who loves me in the past and the future must love me now in some bat-squeak echo of other time. To my immense relief he does say yes.</u> We plan to meet tonight at a nearby Thai restaurant, all the while under the amazed gaze of the woman behind the desk, and I leave, forgetting about Kelmscott and Chaucer and floating down the marble stairs, through the lobby and out into the October Chicago sun, running across the park scattering small dogs and squirrels, whooping and rejoicing.

Audrey Niffenegger (2004: 3–5, underlining added)

The same scene is retold in the next section of the novel from Henry's point of view, but this opening passage has already established its oddity. A reader might have framed this description as an ordinary experiential schema in which someone meets a former friend who does not recognise them, except for the underlined sections where this schema is disrupted. The first-person narration already cues a shift into the text world that circumscribes the beliefs, perceptions and mind-style of Clare, and it quickly becomes apparent that there are non-normative things going on in here.

The excerpts I have underlined draw attention to the text world edge that has been crossed. The first example occurs with the word 'clothed', which is odd because it is so schematic an expectation of meeting a stranger that its realisation in text as something to be commented on is marked. It clearly gestures towards a flashback world in which Henry was not clothed. Of course, this world-switch is a flashback world only for Clare (whose belief text world we are in at this moment), whereas for Henry it would be a flash-forward if he could realise it, and for the addressed reader it is simply an oddity. Similarly, the articulation of the temporal deictic ('in the present. Here and now') is significant because the present tense and locational description have already established these indices of the current text world, so repeating them is markedly redundant. The next underlined example ('It is obvious that he has never seen me before in his life') is similar in that it calls into question the world in which Henry *has* seen her before in his life. This time, the effect is generated by a triple world-switch firstly by epistemic modality based on perception ('It is obvious that'), secondly by negation ('he has never seen me') and finally by flashback ('before in his life').

These marked deictic, modal and negational shifters all point towards a richer back-story, but so far the detail of this context has not been revealed to the reader. It becomes more explicit in the next sequence I have underlined: 'searching his memory and realizing that some future self of his has met this radiantly happy girl standing in front of him. The last time I saw him he was sucking my toes in the Meadow'. Here, there is an apparent clash between 'searching his memory' and 'some future self'. A reader who does not know the premise of the novel by this point is likely to be confused. In the course of the novel, this state of confusion is altered gradually so that the reader after only a few more pages becomes one who accepts that Henry is capable of time travel. Given this attribute in this text world, the usual general pastness that is a central part of the prototypical semantics of 'memory' is made specific only to Henry – so he can have a memory of the future that he has just come from. By contrast, Clare's memory includes the normal recall of a chronologically past event of him 'sucking my toes in the Meadow'. By this simple manoeuvre, Henry and Clare are placed in particular and different vectors in relation to the reader, who has to keep track not only of both their perceptions in their belief worlds, but also of their different ontological status. The underlined examples that follow in the passage above add more detail to these relationships.

Even in the course of this short opening, as a reader you have had to adjust your position relative to Clare, and then especially Henry, and then to Clare again as you realise that Henry's time-shifting is part of her belief world and she was not as ordinary as you originally thought. The next section in the novel retells the same scene above from Henry's perspective, and the novel proceeds in that way, with the reader constantly having to adjust perspective. Figure 5b summarises the general progression in text world terms, though in fact the looping and paradoxes overall are much more complex than this suggests.

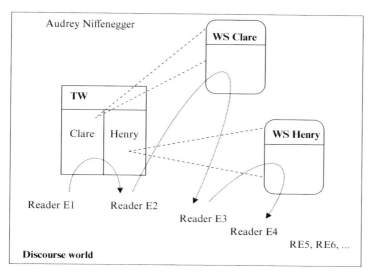

Figure 5b Text world diagram for Niffenegger's *The Time Traveler's Wife*

In the course of reading *The Time Traveler's Wife*, it would be very difficult for a reader to maintain a consistent configuration of personality with consistent beliefs between text world and discourse world throughout the novel. Certain positions which would be ethically at least questionable (an adult Henry meets his lover Clare when she is a six year-old girl) are rendered acceptable because of the framing beliefs that the reader has taken on at this point in the narrative.

There are so many adjustments that a reader has to make, simply in order to keep a basic track of what is going on in the novel, that it is necessary to talk of different *enactors* of the reader across the novel (the term also appears in the discussion of Kipling above). The notion of an enactor (from Emmott 1992, 1997) is usually applied to different text-world and world-switched versions of a single character, but since text world theory has a fractal principle of similar structure at every level, it seems reasonable to apply the notion to the role of the reader as well. So, in Figure 5b, the first enactor of the reader takes on first Clare's and then Henry's worldview, and in doing so is adjusted into a second enactor (E2) of the reader. Each subsequent toggling of the narrative viewpoint throughout the novel necessitates further readerly adjustments, so that further enactors (E3, E4, E5, and so on) are created.

These enactors of the reader constitute ethical positions because each varies in its beliefs in relation to the characters (and their enactors) in the novel. Each readerly enactor varies in relation to all the other readerly enactors too. And there are consequences for ethical judgements that are brought cumulatively to the overarching reading personality which is composed of all of these varied enactors. Older versions of Henry meet younger enactors of himself and so he teaches himself how to steal by pickpocketing, how to pick locks and break into houses, and how to fight successfully. In most other discourse world situations, these activities would be regarded by most people as morally questionable, but they are rendered ethically justified by the adjustments that the reader has had to make to get to these points in the story.

What this brief example illustrates is that a reader is a series of psychotextual traces, each of which is configured according to the requirements of the text world in hand. In the course of reading, these traces become assimilated by processes of modification and accommodation into a final, fairly consistent reading position that comes to consciousness as the reader's sense of his own interpretation. Though the process is spread out for inspection in *The Time Traveler's Wife*, I argue that this scheme applies to all literary fiction, and in fact to all discourse scenarios in which a text world boundary is crossed.

I began this section of the chapter with the logical reasoning that ethics is a matter of modalisation (the world as it should be, compared with how it is). It is apparent, under analysis, that the ethical dimension is not in the modalisation as such but in the experiential fabric of the transition across the world-switch, of which the modalisation is merely the grammaticalised consequence.

In ancient rhetoric, Aristotle (2005) divided the 'appeals' of rhetorical style into three aspects: logos, pathos and ethos. In various forms and shifting terms, these continue to represent the three main aspects of language in use. *Logos* (the 'word') relates to the informational structure and content of the text, whether spoken or written. Logos has been the main focus of stylistic analysis thus far. *Pathos* (originally meaning 'experience', though with a sense of 'trial' or 'suffering') can be taken as the emotional, affective, aesthetic dimension of language. This is the central concern of the present book. *Ethos* (originally 'character') refers to the ethical appeal, the authority or authenticity of the speaker or writer, the plausibility or accessibility of their belief worlds. Cognitive linguistics recasts these three dimensions into an integrated whole. It is impossible to separate linguistic form from experiential value, creating meaning; and it is impossible to separate meaning-making from the aesthetic and ethical dimensions of language.

If readers have dispositions (see Chapter 2), then texts can be regarded as having *impositions*, in terms of the degree to which they seem to close in on a singular message, or open out into a range of possible readings. In this chapter, I have concluded with a sense of a reader as a *positioned reader*, where the imposition offered by certain types of literary work is strongly narrowed onto a highly preferred reading. It is important to remember, though, that all literary works possess the qualities of informativity, affectivity and interactive value, even if different reading experiences seem to lean more heavily towards one or the other of these as a result of the interface between disposition and imposition. This interface is texture, of course, so we can close here by acknowledging the centrality of texture in our encounters with literature.

Reading

The text worlds model, which has been dealt with in greater detail in this chapter, receives its major theoretical statement in Werth (1999) and Gavins (2007), and is applied by Bridgeman (1998, 2001), Emmott (1994, 1995, 1997, 1998, 2002, 2003a, 2003b, 2003c), Gavins (2000, 2003, 2005a, 2005b), Hidalgo Downing (2000a, 2000b, 2000c, 2002, 2003), Lahey (2003, 2004), and Werth (1994, 1995a, 1995b, 1997a, 1997b). Text world theory has some of its origins in possible worlds theory; see, for example, Allen (1989), Bradley and Swartz (1979), Maitre (1983), Ronen (1994), Ryan (1998) and Semino (1997, 2003). Note that Gavins (2007: 83–7) draws a different analysis of second-person narratives from those presented in this chapter.

The importance of aesthetic arrangements and emotion in ethical considerations is the concern of Phelan (1989, 1996, 2005, 2007) from a cognitive narratological and literary perspective, and of Goldie (2003, 2004, 2006, 2007) from a philosophical perspective. There has been a revival of interest in ethics in literary criticism over the past few years, though it is mainly concerned with the ethical content of literature and its status in society, rather than with providing an account of ethical affect, and of course there is little textual engagement: see, for example, Adamson, Freadman and Parker (1998), Eaglestone (2004), Eskin (2004) and Arizti and Martinez-Falquina (2007). Cockcroft (2002) offers a cognitively informed analysis of rhetoric and literature.

6 Texture and Meaning

Throughout all of the preceding chapters, I have tried to stay close to the textuality of the text. Even where matters of global interpretation or general reading have been involved, I have at all times attempted to provide either a close, stylistically informed analysis or an indication that my general arguments arise directly from the interaction of textuality and readerliness that constitutes texture. There are places in the foregoing analyses where I have anticipated this chapter by using terms from cognitive grammar, though I have also relied on traditional grammatical descriptions and the terms usually associated with systemic functional linguistics (Halliday 1985; Halliday and Matthiessen 2003).

The use of systemic-functional terms in stylistics has become virtually paradigmatic over the last two decades. Early stylistic analyses attempted to adapt some aspects of transformational and generative grammar to literary texts (see, for example, Ohmann 1964; Traugott and Pratt 1977), or use the speech act theories and pragmatic approaches of language philosophers such as Austin (1976, 1979), Grice (1975) and Searle (1969) in literary analysis (see also Pratt 1977). Advances in the pragmatics of discourse in the 1970s allowed stylisticians to explore textuality above the level of the clause, with further adaptations of speech act theory, conversation analysis, and sociolinguistic matters such as dialectal shifting and code-choice. However, where close clausal analyses were required, it has been the Hallidayan framework which has been most widespread. There are two broad reasons for this. Firstly, the centre of stylistics through the last two decades of the twentieth century has been northern European and specifically British, and this 'home-grown' grammar was a natural tool for stylisticians. Systemic-functional grammar tended to be used in most forms of applied linguistics, leaving various generative and associated grammars to dominate pure and theoretical linguistics. Furthermore, generative grammars are primarily interested in competence rather than performance, so literary linguistic analysis was excluded as a matter of principle. Secondly, stylistics as a discipline gradually moved away from its origins in formalist and structuralist analysis towards a concern for the social effect and impact of textual organisation. Given this preoccupation, it is not surprising that a preference for a functional model of language emerged, with an equal emphasis on ideational and interpersonal dimensions alongside the textual dimension. Systemic-functional linguistics offers a principled connection between the smallest units of morphology and lexis and the largest units of text and discourse. Crucially for many stylisticians, it claims a validity in providing a semiotic linguistic coding of the world, and so it seems to incorporate the psychological sense of well-formedness as well as the social sense of language used in its ideological setting.

In this chapter, however, I present some literary analyses which draw explicitly on cognitive grammar, focusing on the work of Langacker (1987, 1990, 1991, 1999, 2008). Like systemic-functional grammar, cognitive grammar claims to offer a description of linguistic form that is motivated by real-world correlations. Rather than the grammar existing on an idealised and entirely abstract plane, cognitive grammar asserts continuities between linguistic forms and the perceptual and psychological mechanics that are their necessary mediating processes. I have observed elsewhere that systemic-functional grammar and cognitive grammar have points of contact (Stockwell 2002a: 70–2), and Langacker (2008: 492n.) has noted specifically that the 'functional description of subject is quite consistent with its conceptual characterization in CG as primary focal participant (trajector)'. This correspondence should not be too surprising, since it is plausible to suppose that the functions that seem to exist in the world are consequences of the ways we perceive them. Indeed, correlations and crossovers between the two approaches to grammar can even be seen as a form of validation for each of these approaches: they both seem independently to represent the world in similar linguistic ways.

Construal as a manner of making meaning

The fundamental principle underlying cognitive grammar is that linguistic forms are based on extensions of embodied perceptions and physical experience with roots in our human condition and early infant development. For example, a simple and basic phenomenon that we begin to learn even before we are born is the fact that if we push an object, it moves in relation to a background; it describes a certain path in relation to that background; and it might stop, break, merge with or pass through another object that it encounters at the end of its path. This very basic, pre-linguistic spatial schematic in infant minds persists into adult minds as an *image-schema*. It can be conventionally represented as in Figure 6a (note that the important keyword here is *schema* rather than *image* – an image-schema is a representation of a basic conceptual set of relations, not a mental picture).

Spatial prepositions are linguistic realisations of conceptual spatial movement. In Figure 6a, representing the notional abstraction of 'towards', a primary focus (an attentional figure) called the *trajector* moves in the direction

Figure 6a Basic image-schema for the preposition 'towards'

of a secondary (relatively backgrounded) object or field, called the *landmark*. It is simple to imagine how other prepositional relations can be understood as image-schemas in similar ways: for 'over', the trajector describes a path above and past the landmark; for 'in' and 'into', the trajector moves through the edge of the landmark; for 'through', the TR continues this path and emerges from the other side of the LM; for 'beside', the TR moves adjacent to the LM, and so on. It should be apparent that some of these trajectories are partial versions of others. For example, 'through' is a continuation of the path of the TR of 'in', and 'out' is the continuation of the path emerging from the other side. Other pairs of prepositional relations are closely related: the difference between 'over' and 'under' can be drawn as paths moving on different sides of the LM. There are also other cases – such as 'above' and 'below' – where the locations of the spatial relations are the same, but in the first the TR is in focus and is at the top, and in the second the TR in focus is at the bottom, relative to the LM. (See Lakoff 1987; Hampe 2005; Langacker 2008: 71.)

Image-schemas do not just apply to prepositions, but also to many basic forms of understanding. TR and LM relationships represented by an image-schema can be understood to form the bases of notions such as CONTAINER, FORCE, SOURCE-PATH-GOAL, and many others. Furthermore, the alignment of TR and LM can be regarded as the schema underlying clausal structures, in the form of an *action-chain*: clauses, with noun-phrase referents and predications, can be seen as transfers of energy along a trajectory of the focused TR relative to the LM. Almost all work in cognitive grammar restricts itself up to the clausal level, but moving further up the linguistic scale, it is possible to apply the notion of energy transfer along an action-chain across clauses and sentences in cohesive texts and discourse (as we will see later in this chapter).

In general, a hearer or reader performs an act of *construal* on all encountered language.

> [W]hat we actually see depends on how closely we examine it, what we choose to look at, which elements we pay most attention to, and where we view it from. The corresponding labels I will use, for broad classes of construal phenomena, are *specificity*, *focusing*, *prominence*, and *perspective*. They apply to conceptions in any domain.
>
> (Langacker 2008: 55)

Construal is the overall outcome of these four broad dimensions. Specificity refers to the degree of granularity in perception: in terms of literary reading,

I explored this as intensity and depth in Chapter 2. Focusing is the process of rendering figure and ground and appreciating their relationships: in literary reading, this underlies the discussion of attractors also in Chapter 2. Perspective refers to the viewing arrangement of the receiver relative to the elements in focus: these notions were adapted for the literary context in relation to viewpoint vectors and deixis in Chapter 4, and in relation to modes of scanning later in this chapter. Prominence is a matter of profiling, which I will also exemplify below.

Altogether, cognitive grammar offers these several new ways of understanding *construal* as a combined notion of the manner of meaningfulness. In other words, the propositional content of a piece of language is experienced in a variety of ways, depending on the manner in which it is presented and viewed. Grammatical construal, then, is not simply an issue of informational meaning but is also complicit in experiential value.

Profiling poetic texture

Even within the schematic relations of TR and LM, with the propositional focus on the trajector, a text can present itself in a stylistic configuration which disposes a reader to concentrate more on one particular part of the trajector-landmark relationship. A linguistic expression can *profile* either a thing or a relationship in the mind of the reader (Langacker 2008: 67). For example, in a 1980s parodic television advertisement for the beer Heineken, a character dressed as the poet William Wordsworth muses to himself and struggles to come up with his most famous line. First he tries out: 'I wandered about a bit'. In this sentence, the trajector 'I' is the attentional focus, with the verbal process 'wandered about a bit' serving very much a secondary role. The trajector is profiled, represented in Figure 6b as the bold of the line marking out the TR.

Figure 6b 'I wandered about a bit' profile

In the advert, 'Wordsworth' then takes a sip of the beer that 'reaches the parts other beers cannot reach', and utters his actual poetic lines, which begin one of the most famous and quoted verses in the whole of English literature. This poem is the canonical and prototypical nature poem, which ends with the Romantic focus on recollection, and invokes the poetic power of language used in roughly everyday diction to gesture towards the sublime:

Daffodils

I wander'd lonely as a cloud
   That floats on high o'er vales and hills,
When all at once I saw a crowd,
   A host, of golden daffodils;
Beside the lake, beneath the trees,
Fluttering and dancing in the breeze.

Continuous as the stars that shine
   And twinkle on the Milky Way,
They stretch'd in never-ending line
   Along the margin of a bay:
Ten thousand saw I at a glance,
Tossing their heads in sprightly dance.

The waves beside them danced; but they
   Out-did the sparkling waves in glee:
A poet could not but be gay,
   In such a jocund company:
I gazed—and gazed—but little thought
What wealth the show to me had brought:

For oft, when on my couch I lie
   In vacant or in pensive mood,
They flash upon that inward eye
   Which is the bliss of solitude;
And then my heart with pleasure fills,
And dances with the daffodils.

William Wordsworth (composed 1804,
published 1807, revised 1815)

Instead of a strong profiling of the trajector 'I', the phrasing of the poem instead presents a very strong profiling of the landmark material, as represented in Figure 6c.

Narrowly, all of the material after 'I' in the first two lines ('I wander'd lonely as a cloud / That floats on high o'er vales and hills') is profiled as the landmark, with further paths embedded of meandering motion ('wander'd'), floating motion, high motion and motion over other landmarks, in both the

Figure 6c 'I wander'd lonely as a cloud...' profile

cognitive linguistic and landscape senses ('o'er vales and hills'). More broadly, the entire first stanza after the 'I' can be regarded as a profiling of the tailing syntax. Even more broadly still, the start of the next stanza can be regarded as further tailing of the syntax, if we ignore the full-stop at the end of the first stanza, encouraged by the sense of 'Continuous' which begins the next.

Whichever of these options you take, the profiling pattern represented by Figure 6c also matches many further sequences in the poem:

I	wander'd lonely as a cloud . . .
I	saw a crowd . . .
(I	saw) ten thousand at a glance . . .
A poet	could not but . . .
I	gazed – and gazed . . .

It is noticeable across all of these that the trajector 'I' is in each case being diminished as an attractor. The reader is encouraged to profile the tailing material partly because the latter is textually longer, more voluminous, more active, and in fact more human (by personification of the daffodils) than the poet. The poetic voice is reduced to its smallest possible pronominal form 'I'; as a pronominal it is unmodifiable with any adjective that might enlarge it, and graphically, 'I' is the simplest and most 'narrow' grapheme that is available. This 'I' occurs twice in the list above, and is then further diminished by being embedded within the LM material ('Ten thousand saw I at a glance'), and also reversed so that the fleeting effect is of a rather ungrammatical-sounding but possible 'ten-thousand flowers saw [me] at a glance'. The next reference to the poetic voice renders him indefinite, generalised to third person and defined only by role – 'A poet' – and one who furthermore is modalised ('could'), grammatically negated ('not'), semantically negated ('but'), rendered into an existential essence ('be'), and then the 'poet' trajector finally loses his own distinctiveness as he is embedded 'in' the 'jocund company' of the daffodils. Even in the final example in the list above, the 'I' is re-established, but the directionality is towards the LM flowers ('gazed'), to the extent that the pronoun is omitted from the repetition ('– and [I] gazed'). Throughout, the poet is qualitatively passive ('wander'd', 'saw', 'could not but be', 'gazed and gazed'), and all of this serves to diminish the sense that he is in fact the active agent of the main verb.

At the same time as this deflection of profiling of the TR 'I' is occurring, the LM material is expanded in several ways. It extends across line-endings, including the line that ends 'never-ending line'. The daffodils do all the action: they 'dance' in every stanza, and their activity is predominantly grammatically 'Continuous' as well ('fluttering', 'dancing', 'tossing'). In attractor terms, they are also bright ('as the stars . . . on the Milky Way'), but their main focusing quality comes from their personification. As the poetic voice is diminished, the daffodils grow in human-ness: they are a 'crowd', a 'host', they dance in every stanza across all circumstances, they toss their heads, they are 'sprightly', they possess 'glee' and are 'jocund company'.

Overall, Figure 6c shows the situation in which the trajectory path, and not so much the trajector, is profiled as it is read online across the first three stanzas. This most likely profiling pattern, given this textual organisation, is rather odd. It focuses attention not on the speaking voice but on the object and the process. In Langacker's (2008: 111) term, the first three stanzas involve *sequential scanning*, where the path of the trajectory is followed step-by-step as it unfolds temporally across each line. The path is very precisely delineated in the locative spatial prepositional phrases: 'on high o'er vales', 'all at once', 'beside the lake, beneath the trees', 'in the breeze', 'on the Milky Way', 'in never-ending line', 'along the margin', and so on through 'of', 'at', 'in', 'beside', and 'in' twice more. The profiled landmark is being very precisely grounded through these locatives. The effect overall is a raised awareness of the viewing arrangement where the closely-grained texture of the daffodils is experienced as if online, where the degree of detail is exuberant, and the poetic textual organisation is arranged in such a way as to recapture the direct lived experience as closely as possible.

Of course, however canonically this may be thought of as the pre-eminent nature poem, its textuality can only ever mean that it is a representation of nature rather than the direct physical experience itself. Even a bunch of cut daffodils are more daffodilly than this poem, and the Cumbrian scene in which William and his sister Dorothy walked on 15 April 1802 will of course have been sensually richer than the 153 words of text. Langacker (2008: 536–8) also comments on the cognitive processes involved whenever experience of the world is not direct but is a *simulated* experience. He points out that all simulations (and here we must include all written literary texts that are disconnected from their immediate origins) are *attenuated* to a greater or lesser degree, compared with fully engaged experience. He goes on to say of simulation that, 'Because it is not driven by immediate perceptual input, or harnessed to actual motor activity, it lacks the intensity or "vividness" of such experience. (Given the choice between burning my hand and merely imagining the pain this involves, I would probably choose the latter)' (Langacker 2008: 536–7). However, attenuation varies considerably, depending on the literary texture – the skill of the writer's choices and the disposition of the reader in combination. In the Wordsworth poem, there is relatively little sensory attenuation compared, say, with a scientific report on the daffodil colony, or a developer's description of a prospective Lake District building site. The richness of the experience of the daffodils – though of course less than a direct physical experience – is nevertheless greater than what might be considered a written norm for simulations. (See also my discussion of the empathetic effects of emotional simulation at the end of Chapter 3).

The profiling of the trajectory and landmark across the first three stanzas of the poem entails a relative diminishment of awareness of the observing and speaking persona. If the act of perception were prominent, this would be *subjective construal* (Langacker 2008: 259). However, the emphasis in the poem at this point is on the object of viewing rather than the subject who views; it represents an *objective construal* (Langacker 2008: 260). This is the normal way in which elaborate and elaborated conceptual content (as in the close-grained detail of the daffodils) is processed. Objective construal is one dimension of attenuation (Langacker 2008: 537), in which the richly realised object is brought strongly almost to tactile prominence. This is the situation over the first three stanzas.

The final stanza effects a shift in the viewing arrangement. The transition is prefigured at the very end of the third stanza. The TR poetic voice has been diminished by this point, to the extent that the 'I' is ellipted in the sentence, '[I] little thought what wealth the show to me had brought'. However, even though this diminishment is maintained also in 'little thought' and further sustained in placing 'to me' in recipient position, the non-prototypical word-ordering of this line is at odds with the consistently rightwards trajectory of the syntax up to this point. The recursion of the phrases in the line points to the reflectivity that is the content of the final stanza, and which is anticipated by the colon at the end of the penultimate verse.

In the final stanza, the viewing position jumps outward to a later but continuous and repeated experience ('For oft, when on my couch I lie'). This, and the present tense, serve to make the past tense of the previous three stanzas noticeable – up until now, their past tense might simply have been taken as an unmarked and unnoticed normal narrative past. The carefully granulated sequential scanning and relative non-attenuation of the first three stanzas must now be zoomed out into a single experiential object: the daffodil scene becomes a unitary object, subject to *summary scanning* (Langacker 2008: 111) – that is, rather than being profiled step-by-step, it is taken in 'all at once' (this phrase sits in the third line as a precursor to the final retrospective view). By contrast, the final stanza is highly attenuated, with the immediacy of the daffodil scene relatively rarified from the online texture of reading the first three stanzas. This is *subjective construal* (Langacker 2008: 537), in which attention is focused back on the speaking 'I' trajector, the poetic voice, and the poetic text itself.

The first two lines of the final stanza represent a shift of the grounding to a position prior to the main clause ('For oft, when on my couch I lie in vacant or in pensive mood, they flash . . .'). This preparatory syntax is at odds with the tailing syntax of most of the preceding text. The only similar leftward syntax is in the first two lines of the second stanza: 'Continuous as the stars that shine and twinkle on the Milky Way, they stretch'd . . .'. Though there is a subtle resonant parallel here where the astronomical distancing quality of the first iteration echoes into the reflective distancing of the final iteration, the disjunction is also maintained. The first iteration is rendered 'Continuous' and over-rides the apparent closure of the full-stop in the preceding stanza – this overwhelming manoeuvre points to the breath-taking power of the daffodils. In the transition across the final stanza, however, the colon is literally misleading: it signals a disjunction in time rather than a further specification. The introductory phrase, 'For oft', with its apologetic and self-consciously awkward shortening of 'often', sets up the preparatory syntax of the first two lines of this stanza as a preparatory and overly defensive excuse for the poetic distancing that is about to be rendered, as we return our profiled focus to the speaking voice trajector (as in Figure 6b, in fact).

The effect of the last stanza attenuates the vibrancy of the daffodils, mediating them through summary scanning and subjective construal, so that the textual present of the speaking persona is returned to attention and heightened awareness. The daffodils are raised to a rarified essence or idealised object. The conventional reading of the poem as a practical demonstration of the Romantic rendering of nature into a sublime aesthetic is thus realised.

Placed at the point in Wordsworth's life in which he shifts from being a supporter of the French Revolution to being an old conservative, it is even possible to read the poem as a reflection on the revolution itself. The personification of the daffodils in this reading is specified as the crowds revolting on the streets, circumscribed between the heavens, the sea and the earth. 'Host', even at the turn of the eighteenth century, still had its original military sense as well as its religious connotation in the phrase 'host of heaven'. And Wordsworth's later revisionism can be detected in the negational and modal distancing that marks what he later regards as his reluctant support ('A poet could not but be . . .'). 'Flash' invokes both violence and brevity, and the older, reflective Wordsworth of the final stanza looks back on the revolutionary spirit and is taken back to it. 'Golden', rather than yellow, is a nostalgic rather than plainly descriptive choice; the daffodils are the glorious mob; and even 'ten thousand' is an oddly metrical and French calibration as adopted by the revolutionaries, rather than a more imperial English approximation of a large number. In the earlier 1807 three-stanza version, the second stanza has not yet been added, except for the 'Ten thousand' phrase, which originally appears where 'Fluttering and' is at the end of the first stanza, 'golden' was originally and repetitiously 'dancing', and 'jocund' was 'laughing'. The effect of the 1815 revision that I use above is to enhance the global significance and symbolism of the revolution, and strengthen the personification of the daffodils as people caught up in history (see Wordsworth 1807 and 1815).

Though Wordsworth revised both this poem and his own political ideas over the early years of the nineteenth century, there remains a sense of ambivalence available to a reader within the poem itself. Though the striking excitement of the daffodils is placed in the past, the reader too has shared in the revivified experience through art. The spatial prepositions across the first three stanzas are dominated by trajectories at the edge of the LM: 'on', 'beside', 'beneath', 'along', 'in' and so on. Only in the final stanza – once the viewpoint has come away from the LM – is there a merging of the TR and LM, quickly reiterated across the trajectory 'on', 'in', 'in', and 'upon'; the last of these profiles minutely the moment of alighting rather than the less granular 'on'. The merge is effected by the first use (twice in the final two lines) of the preposition 'with' (the moment of convergence of TR and LM is profiled). The moment is attracted by several aligned features: repetition of line-initial 'And', centrality of the figure in 'heart', enlargement of volume in 'fills', and alliteration 'dances with the daffodils'. The poetic self-consciousness in all this and in the shift to summary scanning and subjective construal serves to foreground the assignment of literariness, and the assignment of literariness in a reading serves to complicate Langacker's (2008: 536-8) comments on the poverty of attenuation in simulation. While it is true, as he suggests, that burning your hand hurts more than imagining the pain, and the emotional effect of lamentation is not the same as losing someone you love in reality, nevertheless there is a power in the necessary self-awareness that literariness conveys. In spite of the distancing, even real daffodils are enhanced by reading 'Daffodils'.

Discourse and dominion

By far the majority of work in cognitive grammar has been concerned with aspects of language up to the clausal level. Though some of this has been extended into discourse and text-level patterns (see Fillmore 1982, 1985; Talmy 1988, 2000a, 2000b), most discussion of cognitive principles has adapted Fauconnier's (1994, 1997, 1998) notion of *mental spaces* and its extensions in conceptual integration (*blending*: see Fauconnier and Sweetser 1996; Fauconnier and Turner 1996, 2002; Turner and Fauconnier 1995, 1999). Even Langacker (2008: 457–99) includes discourse only as one of the 'frontiers' of cognitive linguistics.

I find mental space theory and its developments in conceptual integration insufficiently text-driven, though it is interesting that Gavins (2007: 146–64) adapts blending into a text world theory approach. Compared with the achievements of systemic-functional linguistics' theorising of text and discourse, however, cognitive grammar is still in its infancy. Even so, there is no question that the principles on which cognitive linguistics is founded (such as continuities between embodied experience and grammaticalisation, conceptual correlates of sensory perception and focus, and so on) are highly amenable to understanding the processing of whole-text and whole-discourse events in language. This is one area in which I believe cognitive poetics can be of great usefulness, since literary applications necessarily involve considerations of textual and generic context and complexity, far beyond the more modest requirements of theoretical linguists for invented sub-sentence-level examples.

Rather than creating new theoretical templates to account for discourse, it is sensible to extend the existing cognitive grammar of clauses in ways which are sensitive to its complexity. Given my comments above, we can also orientate this extension with reference to systemic-functional linguistics as a useful comparator guide. This is what I will sketch out in this section. First, though, a text: an extract from *Bleak House*.

> The waters are out in Lincolnshire. An arch of the bridge in the park has been sapped and sopped away. The adjacent low-lying ground, for half a mile in breadth, is a stagnant river, with melancholy trees for islands in it, and a surface punctured all over, all day long, with falling rain. My Lady Dedlock's 'place' has been extremely dreary. The weather, for many a day and night, has been so wet that the trees seem wet through, and the soft loppings and prunings of the woodman's axe can make no crash or crackle as they fall. The deer, looking soaked, leave quagmires, where they pass. The shot of a rifle loses its sharpness in the moist air, and its smoke moves in a tardy little cloud towards the green rise, coppice-topped, that makes a background for the falling rain.
>
> Charles Dickens (1994: 7–8, published 1852)

Both Talmy (1988, 2000a, 2000b) and Langacker (1990, 1991: 13, 2008: 103, 355) describe the schematic content of predications in terms of *force dynamics*, simply understood as an archetypical 'billiard-ball model'. Objects (typically grammaticalised as noun-phrases) are imparted with kinetic energy either from the impact of other objects or because of their inherent properties; these motions result in transfers of energy to other objects, a process which is predication in conceptual terms and is typically grammaticalised in verb-phrases. The simplest version of this force dynamic is in an active sentence with two participants, the *agent* and the *patient*, where energy is transferred verbally from subject to object along an *action chain* (Evans and Green 2006: 42). In Figure 6d, an active version of a sentence from the Dickens passage (something like 'The waters sapped and sopped the arch away') would be drawn with the waters as agent, the arch as patient, and the verbs 'sapped and sopped' as the transfer of energy represented by the arrow. In such an active clause, the 'waters' are the *energy source* and 'the arch' is an *energy sink*, with the arrow showing the direction of energy transfer. In perspectival terms (as drawn in the discussion of Wordsworth above), the water is in primary focus as TR and the arch is a secondary focus as LM. In this invented sentence, the entire process is profiled, so all the elements in the action chain are represented in bold. Note too that in this example, the denotational, semantic meaning of 'sapped and sopped' involves the removal of structural integrity (a sort of loss of energy), but the energy transfer in the schematised concept is still positive because it is the predication that is being conceptualised.

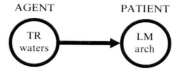

Figure 6d Profiling of an active verb in an action chain: 'The waters sapped and sopped the arch away'

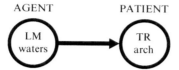

Figure 6e Profiling of a passive sentence with explicit agency: 'An arch of the bridge in the park has been sapped and sopped away by the waters'

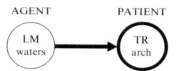

Figure 6f Profiling of the Dickens passive: 'An arch of the bridge in the park has been sapped and sopped away by the waters'

Of course, the actual sentence in the Dickens passage is cast in passive form: 'An arch of the bridge in the park has been sapped and sopped away'. Where the active situation drawn in Figure 6d is the prototypical form in natural language, a passive construction like this lies towards the opposite extreme of non-prototypicality. A mid-way form, cast in the passive but with the agent included, would be: 'An arch of the bridge in the park has been sapped and sopped away by the waters'. Here (as in Figure 6e) the arch now has attentional prominence (it is the TR), but the direction of the arrow remains the same since the waters are still the energy source of the predication. The waters remain in secondary focus in this 'mid-way' sentence, and so are the LM.

Of course, this sentence, in which the agency 'by the waters' appears, is not exactly the Dickens version. The authentic sentence deletes the agent from the passive altogether. This is shown in Figure 6f, which represents a passive construction, where the profiling (in bold) is only of the predication and patient, and the agent ('the waters') is implicit (unprofiled and thus unbolded). In this actual sentence, by contrast with the two alternatives set out above, there is a lingering sense of agency, though that agent is not profiled.

The agent, 'the waters', of course, is already in mind from the previous sentence, 'The waters are out in Lincolnshire'. In that sentence, 'The waters'

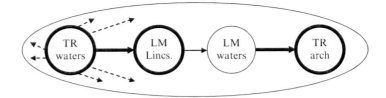

Figure 6g Dominion tracing of 'waters' in an extract from Dickens

is profiled as trajector, and placed in relation to the landmark ground, 'Lincolnshire' (see the left side of Figure 6g). In Langacker's (2008: 83) model, the first mention of an entity is the *reference point* (here, 'The waters' in the first sentence). Subsequent access to that reference point in working memory is a *target* of the referent. On first mention, 'A particular reference point affords potential access to many different targets. Collectively, this set of potential targets constitute the reference point's *dominion*' (Langacker 2008: 83–4). The dominion of an entity or relationship (it applies to predications as well) can be regarded as a network of all the possibilities that reference evokes from experiential memory. So 'the waters', in the passage from *Bleak House*, might bring forth images and memories of floodwaters, rivers in torrent, destructive deluges, as well as the aftermath of storms and floods. These (with specific memories in your experience) are likely to be prototypically central associations. Less central, but still available for evocation, might be waters as fountains, waterfalls, springs, or domestic water supply, or bottled water, or watering garden plants, or large-scale irrigation, and so on. Radiating outwards, this network of associations will have its own attachments to other networks (personal memories of domestic flooding, arable farms in Lincolnshire near where my mother-in-law lives, and so on). All of these possible mental paths associated with 'waters' constitute a sort of semantic and experiential cloud of possibilities (represented in Figure 6g by the dotted lines radiating out from the initial reference point of 'waters').

The text itself evokes this dominion as a set of associations, but it also goes on, as the discourse develops across sentences, to pick out the trace specification which then develops in the rest of the passage (represented by the oval shape in Figure 6g that delineates the action chain actually taken). The passive construction in the second sentence that was analysed above takes its implicit and unprofiled 'waters' agent from our recent memory of the first sentence TR. This initial TR 'waters' is specified across the entire passage as an expansive and all-pervasive wetness of flood-waters and misty, eastern English damp weather. The energy of this trace in the dominion is passed on across the action chains of each sentence in the excerpt, creating the textual cohesion in the passage which is felt as thematic coherence and a sustained lyricism.

The chain of co-reference across the passage is realised in a variety of ways. Central to the 'waters' dominion is the lexical cohesion between this word and 'river', 'rain', 'wet', 'soaked', and 'moist'. However, there is also a coherent association between these invoked targets and further objects, adjectival modifiers and the semantics of some of the verbs in the passage: 'bridge' is coherent in the dominion of water, and 'arch' is coherent in the further dominion of bridge; 'sapped and sopped' are watery verbs; 'low-lying ground' is experientially associated with waterlogging; 'islands' are defined by watery edges; 'stagnant' collocates prototypically with water (and only metaphorically with other words such as 'economy' or 'market'); 'dreary' and 'cloud' associate with wet weather, the 'soft loppings' of the axe recall wet wood; 'quagmires' are caused by water and mud; and even the 'green rise' is green because it is well watered. Note that the dominion network of associations allows a looser and more psychologically plausible sense than the restricted categories offered in a systemic-functional model (Halliday and Hasan 1976; Hoey 1991; Martin 1992). The passage is saturated with coherence (to borrow a metaphor suggested by the tone of the excerpt itself) in many richly different ways.

Figure 6g shows the dominion trace taken only across the first two sentences, but the force dynamics of the 'waters' trajector is sustained across most of the action chains in the excerpt as a whole. The path that this trajector takes across the discourse carries its connotational energy across the landscape in an identifiable and experientially plausible journey: flowing under the bridge, across the ground, around the melancholy islands; then becoming granulated as it is punctured by rain, which expands the direction of the energy upwards and outwards to the sky and the falling rain and the weather in general; in this permeating, vaporous form, it wets through the trees, deadens noise, softens human and animal work, saps the energy from possibly occluding distractions like the chop of the axe or the sharpness of a rifle-shot; and it ends falling on the hillside, finally becoming a landmark 'background'. The entire lyrical scene then forms the LM ground against which the next sentence begins a new action chain and dominion trace: 'The view from my Lady Dedlock's own windows is . . .' (Dickens 1994: 8).

The dominion of the reference points in the passage evokes schema knowledge, so 'the park' makes further objects such as the ground, the river, the trees, the deer, the woodman and his axe, and the coppice-topped green rise all available for the definite reference form in which they occur. The texture of this text is a matter not simply of this close reference chaining and the activation of already-poised schema knowledge, but its evocation from the cloud of untaken associations that are nevertheless potentially activated. This unrealised dominion is what creates the atmospheric set of connections and associations around the passage, a feeling that generates its tone and allows it to feel richer than the bare denotational values of the words might suggest.

This account of action chaining within a dominion of possibilities represents part of a cognitive discourse grammar. It has several advantages. It explains the connection between cohesion and coherence by denying the empirical difference between the two, since both are complicit in a sense of texture. It can account for atmosphere and tone. It allows for the sort of radial adjustment and experientiality that is not allowed by a categorical systemic-functional account. It offers a means of explaining how specific traces are taken through the generality of schema knowledge, by adopting the Werthian (1999) principle of text-drivenness: all of the textually-realised forms of energy transfer set out above constitute the consistent action chain through the dominions of the passage.

The terms I have been using here also constitute a cognitive typology of reference first introduced in Stockwell (2000: 148). Accommodated with Langacker (2008), we can summarise these processes as follows:

New evocation: a neologistic or proper noun reference point, directly placed by the current position in the text into working memory

Old evocation: a reference point from experiential memory, directly placed by the textual realisation into working memory

Renewing invocation: a target, maintained textually in working memory by cohesive devices and anti-shift devices

Recalling invocation: a target, revivified from recent, semi-active memory into active working memory (often from recent co-text)

Gradual revocation: the loss of a target from working memory by non-mention, or by occlusion of other, newer reference points and targets

Defeased revocation: the deletion by negation or verb-revocation of a target, and its subsequent non-reappearance.

The Dickens excerpt consists almost entirely of old evocation of familiar scenes and senses, and renewing invocation that sustains the tone through the passage. This conceptual content, in the broadest sense, is reinforced by the numerous rich patterns of alliteration, assonance and other sound-effects that permeate the text. In fact, the sentence which sets up the dominion and initiates the extended action chain – 'The waters are out in Lincolnshire' – contains all the elements that are responsible for the prominent sound-patterning in the rest of the passage: /w s t l k ʃ/. The echoic effects are particularly strong in the establishment of the first two sentences ('are', 'arch', 'park'), but further alliterative echoic phrases fill the text: 'sapped and sopped', 'soft loppings and prunings', 'axe . . . crash or crackle'. The /w s t l k ʃ/ flurry in the final sentence ('The shot of a rifle loses its sharpness in the moist air, and its smoke moves in a tardy little cloud towards the green rise, coppice-topped') shifts to the broadly softer, more affricated and approximant cluster /ð f l r n/, to iconically match 'the falling rain'. Perhaps it is a fanciful accident of terminology that it is only the liquids /w l/ that are consistent throughout the whole passage.

Narrative pace and action chaining

The two examples discussed so far (Wordsworth and Dickens) are lyrical in tone. Of course, extending the cognitive grammatical notion of force dynamics in action chains across whole sequences of text rather than limiting ourselves to clause-boundaries also allows us potentially to adapt the analysis for narrative passages. This is the concern of this final section.

In order to understand the path of predicate energy across an extended text, there are two dimensions of the force dynamic model that need to be revisited. Firstly, the nature of the participants in action chains needs to be clear, and secondly the quality of the energy transmission needs also to be specified further. These two factors are very closely interlinked. As I outlined in Chapter 3 (see Figure 3c there), Langacker (1991: 282–91, 2008: 365) sets out several available roles for participants: a default *zero* role of mere existence where no energy is transmitted; the energetic roles of *agent, patient, instrument, experiencer* and *mover*; an *absolute* role that resists the effects of energy transfer; and a *theme* role that summarises the action chain. Particular entities in an action chain can fill more than one of these roles at a time, even enacting multiple energetic roles at different points in the extended chain. Though action chains in cognitive linguistics are primarily described in relation to clauses, it is of course common that sequences of clauses in a text contain participants that are consistent from clause to clause. Texts that violate this are regarded as non-cohesive or fragmentary, illogical or obscure, absurdist or surrealistic, and so on.

An action chain with many participant roles realised might be thought of as being very densely populated with objects and entities relative to predications. Furthermore, we might think that some of the archetype roles suggested by Langacker are more or less likely to be sources of energy: agent, for example, seems the prototypically most likely source of energy for transmission to a patient, which is the least likely energy source. Patient, though, would be the most prototypical energy sink. The other roles can be placed across this radial structure, with instrument being a good conductor of energy, mover a good user and conductor of energy, and experiencer a good receiver of energy. Such a scale corresponds with work by Dowty (1991) who suggests that a *proto-agent* and a *proto-patient* are all that is required: these are prototypical energy-sources and energy-sinks (adapting cognitive grammatical terms), in relation to which all other possible participant roles are better or worse examples on a sliding scale. Though I believe this to be a more accurate account, for ease of analysis, Langacker's (1991, 2008) divisions can be taken as heuristic bands across the radial prototype structure.

Secondly, the quality of the energy transmission is a crucial factor in the discourse grammatical texture. Profiled predications within clauses are generally stronger in effect than co-referential links across clauses, which are usually more implicit in the form of lexical cohesion, common semantic domain, echoic phonoaesthetics, and so on. In Figure 6g above, the continuation of the energy transmission from the first sentence to the second, which allows the passivised sentence to omit the agency of the 'waters', has momentum to link the two sentences but is not as strongly felt as the predications within each clausal action chain on either side (in the diagram, the unbolded middle arrow compared with the two profiled and bolded predications).

Furthermore, taking a cue from the vector model drawn on in Chapter 4, the energy of an action chain is also a matter of its pace. The sense of pace might arise from verb-choices that denote speed, physical action and large transformations wrought on their participants. Close co-referential chaining across sentences and clauses should also increase the sense of pace, since this would mean that focus is being held and sustained rather than meandering around a scene.

So you might predict that a rattling action sequence has a density of predications, and that those predications would be constituted by powerful energy conductors (in their semantic meaning). Such a passage would also have a prominent sense of proto-agents that are very high energy sources, and proto-patient roles that are very receptive to the force transmission. Instruments, movers and experiencers would be correspondingly forceful or malleable as appropriate. You might expect clausal action chains to be short and direct, but with very close co-reference and highly normative dominion traces.

Having written that paragraph, I reach behind me in search of an action sequence and my hand falls on Tolkien's *The Lord of the Rings* and I think of the moment when the company of the ring confront their enemies underground in the Mines of Moria:

> Something was coming up behind them. What it was could not be seen: it was like a great shadow, in the middle of which was a dark form, of man-shape maybe, yet greater; and a power and terror seemed to be in it and to go before it.
>
> It came to the edge of the fire and the light faded as if a cloud had bent over it. Then with a rush it leaped across the fissure. The flames roared up to greet it, and wreathed about it; and a black smoke swirled

in the air. Its streaming mane kindled, and blazed behind it. In its right hand was a blade like a stabbing tongue of fire; in its left it held a whip of many thongs.

'Ai! ai!' wailed Legolas. 'A Balrog! A Balrog is come!' [. . .]

'A Balrog', muttered Gandalf. 'Now I understand.' He faltered and leaned heavily on his staff. 'What an evil fortune! And I am already weary'.

The dark figure streaming with fire raced towards them. The orcs yelled and poured over the stone gangways. Then Boromir raised his horn and blew. Loud the challenge rang and bellowed, like the shout of many throats under the cavernous roof. For a moment the orcs quailed and the fiery shadow halted. Then the echoes died as suddenly as a flame blown out by a dark wind, and the enemy advanced again.

'Over the bridge!' cried Gandalf, recalling his strength. 'Fly! This is a foe beyond any of you. I must hold the narrow way. Fly!' Aragorn and Boromir did not heed the command, but still held their ground, side by side, behind Gandalf at the far end of the bridge. The others halted just within the doorway at the hall's end, and turned, unable to leave their leader to face the enemy alone.

The Balrog reached the bridge. Gandalf stood in the middle of the span, leaning on the staff in his left hand, but in his other hand [his sword] Glamdring gleamed, cold and white. His enemy halted again, facing him, and the shadow about it reached out like two vast wings. It raised the whip, and the thongs whined and cracked. Fire came from its nostrils. But Gandalf stood firm.

You cannot pass', he said. The orcs stood still, and a dead silence fell. [. . .]

The Balrog made no answer. The fire in it seemed to die, but the darkness grew. It stepped forward slowly on to the bridge, and suddenly it drew itself up to a great height, and its wings were spread from wall to wall; but still Gandalf could be seen, glimmering in the gloom; he seemed small, and altogether alone: grey and bent, like a wizened tree before the onset of a storm.

From out of the shadow a red sword leaped flaming.

Glamdring glittered white in answer.

There was a ringing clash and a stab of white fire. The Balrog fell back and its sword flew up in molten fragments. The wizard swayed on the bridge, stepped back a pace, and then again stood still.

'You cannot pass!' he said.

With a bound the Balrog leaped full upon the bridge. Its whip whirled and hissed. [. . .]

At that moment Gandalf lifted his staff, and crying aloud he smote the bridge before him. The staff broke asunder and fell from his hand.

A blinding sheet of white flame sprang up. The bridge cracked. Right at the Balrog's feet it broke, and the stone upon which it stood crashed into the gulf, while the rest remained, poised, quivering like a tongue of rock thrust out into emptiness.

With a terrible cry the Balrog fell forward, and its shadow plunged down and vanished. But even as it fell it swung its whip, and the thongs lashed and curled about the wizard's knees, dragging him to the brink. He staggered and fell, grasped vainly at the stone, and slid into the abyss. 'Fly, you fools!' he cried, and was gone.

The fires went out, and blank darkness fell. The Company stood rooted with horror staring into the pit. Even as Aragorn and Boromir came flying back, the rest of the bridge cracked and fell.

J. R. R. Tolkien (1954: 313–14)

There is much to say about the texture of this extended passage, including the switch to mock-archaic register at the pivotal moment to create a sense of portent, the personification of the swords and the 'tongue of rock', the attractors of brightness and darkness that are aligned with moments of action, and the spatial deixis that places the narrative viewpoint with the observing company behind Gandalf who is facing the oncoming Balrog. However, all of these details must wait for another occasion. Here, I am mainly interested in the extended action chain and force dynamics across the passage.

This is a confrontation between good (the Company and our viewpoint) and evil (the orcs and the Balrog), a battle scene in which the balance of power shifts quickly from one side to the other until the resolution in which both evil and good prevail in different respects: Gandalf is apparently killed, but the Company are saved from the orcs by the chasm that is created. The passage begins with the energy on the side of evil. The agent in the first two paragraphs is largely the approaching monster. Seen from the experiencing viewpoint of the Company, it is not yet lexicalised other than as 'something' and 'it', but the co-referential chaining across the paragraph maintains a strong focus on the monster as agent. As the monster approaches, it increases in perspectival size, both through volume and zooming in of attention: 'a great shadow', 'in the middle', 'a dark form', 'man-shape', 'yet greater'. Where the normal schematic expectations of approaching motion and increasing volume might be an increase in clarity and light, an inversion of this expectation is placed here, as the monster brings darkness and removes the light. The energy level of the agent in the first paragraph is not as great as in the second. There is a steady momentum in the first paragraph, but the verbs deflect a sense of direct action: 'was coming up', 'was', 'could not be seen', 'was like', 'seemed to be', 'to go before'. These are either stative, perceptions, or where there is denoted motion it is rendered relatively weak by the verb-form: progressive 'coming' or infinitive 'to be' and 'to go'.

The restricted momentum is hugely increased in the second paragraph, to convey the rising panic in the experiencing Company. The action chain crosses the paragraph break as 'It came to the edge of the fire'. The text does not say explicitly that the monster paused at this point, but this sense is effected by the switch to a different agent. The 'fire', which was an LM in the last action chain, with its 'edge' profiled, becomes the TR agent in the next clause, co-lexicalised as 'light'. In accordance with the preceding inversion, the energy of the monster saps the power of the light ('and the light faded'), but the effect of this action chain with light as agent and a diminishing verb is to stall the onward motion of the monster, briefly. Its pause is only brief, though, and the text cleverly does not completely halt the momentum of the monster. The added phrase, 'as if a cloud had bent over it', co-refers 'it' ana-phorically to 'the light', with the monster implicitly as the agentive cloud in this sub-clause. However, 'it' has been so strongly identified with the monster so far that this could also be read fast as the monster coiled up ready to spring. The monster returns after this preparatory hiatus even more strongly: 'Then with a rush it leaped across the fissure'. The energy-source of the agent 'it' is charged up with the thematic role of 'with a rush' that encapsulates the entire action chain. The verb-choice 'leaped' is full of semantic energy that amplifies the action chain, especially considered against the static, absolute 'fissure' that is crossed.

So far there has been a switching back and forth between the monster and the light as TR and LM, but this apparent occasional weakness of the monster as the most powerful agent is transformed in this second paragraph. The TR switches apparently back to the light, with 'The flames' becoming the new agent of a powerful and energetic action chain ('roared up'). However, rather than falling into a patient role, the monster begins as an LM absolute being greeted by the flames, and then is transformed into a blended fire-monster: 'Its streaming mane kindled, and blazed behind it'. The earlier apparent toggling between monster and fire as separate participants is here combined into a more powerful agent, and the profiled verb-forms reinforce this. Even its instrument (the 'blade' in its right hand) conducts the energy embodied in its motion, personification and light: 'like a stabbing tongue of fire'. The adversary is thus presented with a strong and powerful impact, contrasted with the weak energy in the action chains associated with the Company: 'wailed', 'muttered', 'faltered' and 'leaned heavily'.

There is no question across the whole passage that there is a high density of predications, and many are realised by high-energy verbs: 'raced', 'yelled and poured', 'advanced', 'cracked', 'leaped', 'whirled and hissed', 'smote', 'broke', 'sprang up', 'crashed', 'plunged', 'lashed' and 'slid'. These provide smooth conductive material that amplifies the momentum of high-energy agents: 'dark figure streaming with fire', 'the enemy', 'the whip', 'a red sword', 'crying aloud he', 'blinding sheet of white flame', and so on. However, an entire passage of high-energy agents and amplifying action chains would be unre-mitting and lose its sustained force, so Tolkien periodically slows the pace with less energetic agents, more focus on the proto-patient roles, and verb-choices that dampen down the force transmission. Predications include 'quailed', 'halted' (several iterations), 'died', 'blown out', 'held their ground', 'leave', 'stood', 'said', and so on. Low-energy agents include 'a cloud', 'the others', and 'Gandalf' across the first two-thirds of the passage. There are also moments of calm where the experiencer role is prominent, through action chains realised with verbs of perception like 'seemed', and usually accompanied by explicitly denoted slowing: 'It stepped forward slowly . . . its wings were spread . . . but still Gandalf could be seen . . . he seemed small'. These serve to enhance contrastively the moments of rapid action in between. There is a small thematic emblem of this alternation of quiet and violence just before the fatal fall at the end, 'while the rest [an absolute] remained, poised, quivering'.

Where Gandalf is an obstacle to the Balrog across the first two-thirds of the passage, he is also an obstruction in the action chains in which he appears at these points. He is an experiencer of his own direct speech several times throughout the scene, as he stands still, defying the Balrog, and is simultane-ously an unmovable absolute. At other times, he is an experiencer while 'recalling his strength'. And he is often the patient LM to an action chain in which the TR is an experiencer ('seemed'), or there is a more energetic TR agent in the text close by ('leaning on the staff in his left hand, but in his other hand Glamdring gleamed'), or he is a simple LM patient ('behind Gandalf'), or he is even the unprofiled LM in an action chain that focuses agency on what would otherwise be his instrument: 'Glamdring glittered white in answer'.

At the crucial moment of the clash between Gandalf and the Balrog, the wizard becomes a high-energy agent. While still an experiencer of direct speech, the ground LM of his speech negates the action chain of the monster: '"You cannot pass!"' Nevertheless, the Balrog responds with a high-energy action chain. It combines its agency with a thematic role, 'With a bound the Balrog', and the action chain moves powerfully and expansively ('leaped full') to a position of superiority over its patient ('upon the bridge'). Then, prepared by a zero role for full contrast ('At that moment'), Gandalf becomes the agent in a flurry of amplifying predications, all with highly receptive patients to further emphasise his force: 'Gandalf lifted his staff . . . he smote the bridge'. From this point on, though, Gandalf becomes unprofiled. Though he remains as TR, his role as the source of the action is left implicit, as attention is focused on the environmental effects of his sudden and precipi-tous action: 'The staff broke asunder', 'The bridge cracked', 'it broke', 'the stone . . . crashed into the gulf'. Following this, the Balrog becomes an extremely strongly profiled agent in a highly forceful action chain, with 'the wizard's knees' as its patient. Gandalf's fate is sealed by the brevity of his role as a source of energy, even though his moment of action was decisive.

Where several of the predications act as good conductors of agentive energy, sometimes even amplifying their force, the pace of the passage is also conveyed in the conductive effect of smooth conjunctions such as 'and'. There are many of these, allowing the energy easy access across clausal action chains in order to be sustained over discoursal stretches: multiple examples include 'the flames roared up . . ., and wreathed about it, and a black smoke swirled', 'It stepped forward . . ., and suddenly it drew itself up . . ., and its wings were spread', but there are also several single 'and' conjunctions that transmit the energy efficiently and pacily across clauses. Just as some predications are amplifying, there are also conjunctions and clause connectors that act as accelerants: 'then', 'at that moment', 'suddenly', 'with a bound', and the semi-colons. Contrarily, there are some blocking conjunctions and (dis) connectors that disrupt the smooth transmission of the action chain: 'but' and 'yet' are the most used examples of these, tending to occur where the balance of power shifts from Gandalf to the Balrog and back again.

For the most part, the syntax of the passage is dominated by simple clauses. There are rather few complex sentences, in the sense of subordination and apposition rather than the simple additive and adversative conjunctions I have just described. This means that there are very many direct, dual participant action chains relative to the overall length of the passage. At the moment of clash, several paragraphs consist only of single sentences or single clauses. However, there is very close co-reference at these points, maintaining the force transmission across the sentence boundaries. In spite of the fantastical entities being described, the dominions that are created across the passage are familiar experiential schemas of confrontation and battle, accumulated most likely from other textual accounts. By this point in the novel (p. 313), the reader has built up quite a richly impersonated characterisation of Gandalf, his motivations, protector-status, stability, wisdom and bravery. The Balrog is newly encountered, but matches the familiar schema of faceless and monstrous evil from the prior text and countless other cautionary narratives and folk-tales. Both behave exactly as you might predict in this encounter, and throughout the passage this sense is closely and subtly reinforced by the dominion traces that are actually taken being the most prototypically normative and expected. For example, the action chain realised as 'Boromir raised his horn and blew' is followed exactly as you would unremarkably expect by 'Loud the challenge rang and bellowed'. The dominion of the sound of a loud hunting horn is compared in simile as being 'like the shout of many throats', an unremarkable and not particularly striking metaphor. Following the pattern of this and similar normative expectations being realised across the encounter on the bridge, Gandalf's tactical mistake and death is all the more a shock. The possible traces of a battle scenario certainly include losing, but for this dominion trace to be manifest after so much normative discourse is a surprise.

At the moment of this unsuspected trace being given momentum, the participant Gandalf reverses his roles up to this point in the passage, in quick succession. From being the LM patient to the Balrog's agency, after the monster falls into the abyss, Gandalf becomes an agent again, but a relatively weak one ('staggered and fell'), still essentially the unwilling recipient of the fallen Balrog's previous agency. Then he increases in wilfulness, but his renewed energy in agency is played out not against a patient role but against two unmoving absolutes, as he 'grasped vainly at the stone, and slid into the abyss'. In this latter action chain, it is even arguable that gravity (or his fate) has become the unprofiled agent and he ends at last in a helpless mover role.

Texture

The extension of cognitive grammar into the analysis of text and discourse immediately above is tentative, at this stage. However, it is clear that any advances within cognitive linguistics that can be made in this direction must at least meet the standard set by systemic-functional linguistics, as I suggested at the beginning of the chapter. The notion of texture has, in fact, a minor place within the SFL tradition. Mentioned by Halliday and Hasan (1976: 2) in their book on cohesion, and then developed by Hasan (1985), it is virtually synonymous with the notion of coherence. Eggins (2004: 24) defines it as follows: 'Texture is the property that distinguishes text from non-text. Texture is what holds the clauses of a text together to give them unity.' In this approach, texture remains an abstract and undeveloped notion, somewhat circularly defined as the unifying property of text, while a text is a text if it possesses texture. In the Hallidayan tradition, textuality is the more important concept. In spite of the functionalist emphasis on meaningfulness and process, *texture* in this perspective tends to be treated as an emergent property of the structure of texts – as textuality free of human intervention, as it were. Where textuality is the abstract feature of text, texture is the subjective characteristic of textuality. This is a distinction that vaguely touches on the sense I have developed across this book, though I suggest that any usage that lies outside cognitivist principles is doomed to a failure in application. Closer to usefulness is de Beaugrande's (1980; de Beaugrande and Dressler 1981) formulation, which treats textuality in terms of features that define sets of clauses as a text, and then distinguishes textuality from texture – the latter is defined as resulting from the process of a subjectivity engaging with a text. This formula is closer to a cognitive poetic sense, though it still lacks precision or an analytical framework such as I have developed across this book.

Systemic-functional linguistics also has a strong focus on spoken language, including interpersonal aspects. Together with its capacity for exploring text and discourse, this has made it attractive for ideological and social research, as in critical discourse analysis. Though I have briefly commented on the textural power of the spoken word at various points in this book, cognitive poetics has a long way to go to match the achievements of the systemic-functional analysis of conversation and dialogue. Though one or two dramatic works have been mentioned in this book, for the most part I have focused on written poetry and prose. Cognitive poetics still feels like a discipline newly stretching its limbs. Amongst my friends and colleagues around the world, I sense the same sort of excitement that is apparent in the pages of the new stylistic applications of systemic-functional grammar forty years ago (see the early papers in Carter and Stockwell 2008).

Nevertheless, texture as the experienced quality of textuality is fundamentally and exclusively a cognitive poetic notion, which also binds cognitive poetics up in stylistic analysis. Much of the work that generally falls under the umbrella term of cognitive approaches to literature remains at the interpretative, general and thematic level. Without a stylistic grounding, such work risks being regarded as simply yet another abstract critical theory. It is my hope that cognitive poetics has more longevity than that, not only because of its evident and demonstrable validity, nor because of its aspiration to discipline and rigour, but partly because it represents a progressive field of inquiry that is based on the oldest traditions of literary analysis. In twenty years of teaching I have seen students drawn to stylistics as to a light of revelation, and for me cognitive poetics is the natural development of that discipline.

Cognitive poetics enhances stylistics in a variety of ways. It makes explicit the interpretative aspect of texts which is often implicit in descriptions linking textual organisation and significance. It makes a direct claim to psychological validity, where the claim previously in stylistics has been indirect or an appeal for agreement on the basis of transparency and clarity. It increases the range of tools available to the stylistician. It might be objected that similar arguments as I have made could have been produced either with older stylistic terms or with traditional literary critical accounts. Where this might be the case in one or two details, I think the overall project invalidates this objection. Placing detailed arguments, which might accord with other ways of doing things, into a consistent overarching framework has several advantages. It lends the argument a validating context from within the frame itself; it draws external validity from other forms of evidence associated with the general approach; it retains a consistency of purpose and method; and the fact that there are points of contact with other forms of analysis suggests a commonality between them that points to precision.

In this book, I have tried to define texture not simply as a glossed definition, but by repeated and varied examples. The texture of this book as a whole exemplifies what texture is. It allows us to explore the depth of emotional responses to literary works created by other humans and featuring representations of other people. It offers a means of accounting for the evident power and persistence of some literary encounters. It allows us to understand better the nature of the relationship between text and characterisation. Texture involves a rich sense of the world of a literary experience. It includes a consideration of the ethical positioning of authors and readers. It requires aesthetics to be socially situated and properly, rigorously, systematically explored.

Throughout the book, I have been particularly scathing of the institution of literary scholarship as it currently stands. I insist this is largely institutionally deserved, though there is of course a great deal of value and variety in the broad enterprise of literary academicism. It will be a poorer, even more arid landscape if the whole field settles into general cultural history, valuable though that is in its own right. A recognition of the need to return to textuality, a reconnection with natural readers, and a further reconsideration of the intricacies, complexities and depths of texture together represent another way, one capable of establishing some necessary diversity in this landscape. Texture seems to me to be central to the future development of cognitive poetics. This book has been a work of literary criticism; literature is defined by its texture.

Reading

In this final chapter I have focused on Langacker's (2008) cognitive grammar for its consistency of principle across several levels, its apparent usefulness in connecting image-schemas to the force dynamics in clauses, its claim to psychological plausibility and its close correlation with functional accounts which seem to offer both coincidental verification and potential for extensions into discourse. There are, however, several other accounts of grammar based on cognitivist principles, principally the various other forms of construction grammar. See, for example, Traugott and Heine (1991), Goldberg (1995, 1996), Heine (1997), Croft (2001), Traugott and Dasher (2002), Bergen and Chang (2005), and the collection edited by Östman and Fried (2005). See Evans and Green (2006) for an overview.

Incursions of cognitive linguistics into critical discourse analysis offer promising advances for the discoursal developments of analytical tools. See, for example, Lakoff (1992, 2002, 2006) Kövecses (1994), Chilton and Lakoff (1995), Stockwell (2000b), O'Halloran (2003, 2007a, 2007b), Hart (2005), and the collection in Hart and Lukeš (2007).

References

Ackroyd, Peter (2001) *London: The Biography*. London: Vintage.

Adamson, Jane, Freadman, Richard and Parker, David (eds) (1998) *Renegotiating Ethics in Literature, Philosophy, and Theory*. Cambridge: Cambridge University Press.

Ainsworth, M. S., Blehar, M. C., Waters, E. and Wall, S. (1978) *Pattern of Attachment: A Psychological Study of the Strange Situation*. Mahwah: Lawrence Erlbaum.

Allen, S. (ed.) (1989) *Possible Worlds in Humanities, Arts and Sciences*. Berlin: de Gruyter.

Anderson, Joseph (1996) *The Reality of Illusion: An Ecological Approach to Cognitive Film Theory*. Carbondale: Southern Illinois University Press.

Andringa, Els (2004) 'The interface between fiction and life: patterns of identification in reading autobiographies', *Poetics Today* 25: 205–40.

Aristotle (2005) *The Art of Rhetoric* (trans. Hugh Lawson-Tancred). Harmondsworth: Penguin [original c.335–22 BC].

Arizti, Bárbara and Martinez-Falquina, Silvia (eds) (2007) *On the Turn: The Ethics of Fiction in Contemporary Narrative in English*. Newcastle: Cambridge Scholars Publishing.

Attridge, Derek (2004) *The Singularity of Literature*. London: Routledge.

Atwood, Margaret (1985) *The Handmaid's Tale*. Toronto: McClelland and Stewart.

Auer, Peter (2007) 'Mobility, contact and accommodation', in Carmen Llamas, Louise Mullany and Peter Stockwell (eds) *The Routledge Companion to Sociolinguistics*. London: Routledge, pp. 109–15.

Auer, Peter, Hinskens, Frans and Kerswill, Paul (eds) (2005) *Dialect Change*. Cambridge: Cambridge University Press.

Auster, Paul (1999) *Timbuktu*. London: Faber and Faber.

Austin, J. L. (1976) *How to Do Things with Words* (2nd edn). Oxford: Oxford University Press.

Austin, J. L. (1979) *Philosophical Papers* (3rd edn). Oxford: Clarendon Press.

Awh, E., Serences, J., Laurey, P., Dhaliwal, H, van der Jaght, T. and Dassonville, P. (2004) 'Evidence against a central bottleneck during the attentional blink: multiple channels for configural and featural processing', *Cognitive Psychology* 48: 95–126.

Bakhtin, Mikhail (1941) *Rabelais and His World* (trans. Hélène Iswolsky). Bloomington: Indiana University Press.

Bakhtin, Mikhail (1984) *Problems of Dostoevsky's Poetics* (trans. Caryl Emerson). Minneapolis: University of Minnesota Press.

Bal, Mieke (1985) *Narratology: Introduction to the Theory of Narrative*. Toronto: University of Toronto Press.

Barthelme, Donald (1981) *Sixty Stories*. Harmondsworth: Penguin.

Belmonte, Matthew K. (2008) 'Does the experimental scientist have a "Theory of Mind"?' *Review of General Psychology* 12 (2): 192–204.

Ben-Zeev, Aaron (1984) 'The passivity assumption of the sensation-perception distinction', *British Journal for the Philosophy of Science* 35: 327–43.

Benzon, William L. (2003) '"Kubla Khan" and the embodied mind', *PsyArt: A Hyperlink Journal for the Psychological Study of the Arts*, Article no. 030915 <http://www.clas.ufl.edu/ipsa/journal/2003_benzon02.shtml>

Bergen, Benjamin and Chang, Nancy (2005) 'Embodied construction grammar in simulation-based language understanding', in J.-O. Östman and M. Fried (eds) *Construction Grammars: Cognitive Grounding and Theoretical Extensions*. Amsterdam: John Benjamins, pp. 147–90.

Bex, Tony (1996) *Variety in Written English: Texts in Society; Societies in Text*. London: Routledge.

Booth, Martin (1985) *British Poetry 1964 to 1984: Driving Through the Barricades*. London: Routledge.

Booth, Wayne C. (1961) *A Rhetoric of Fiction*. Chicago: University of Chicago Press.

Bortolussi, Marisa and Dixon, Peter (2003) *Psychonarratology: Foundations for the Empirical Study of Literary Response*. Cambridge: Cambridge University Press.

Bourdieu, Pierre (1972) *Outline of a Theory of Practice*. Cambridge: Cambridge University Press.

Bowlby, J. (1968) *Attachment and Loss: I. Attachment*. London: Hogarth.

Bowlby, J. (1973) *Attachment and Loss: II. Separation*. London: Hogarth.

Bradbury, Ray (1977) *The Martian Chronicles*, London: Granada [1951, as *The Silver Locusts*, Rupert Hart-Davis Ltd].

Bradley, R. and Swartz, N. (1979) *Possible Worlds: An Introduction to Logic and its Philosophy*. Indianapolis: Hackett Publishing.

Bray, Joe (2007) 'The effects of free indirect discourse: empathy revisited', in Marina Lambrou and Peter Stockwell (eds) *Contemporary Stylistics*. London: Continuum, pp. 56–67.

Bridgeman, Teresa (1998) *Negotiating the New in the French Novel: Building Contexts for Fictional Worlds*. London: Routledge.

Bridgeman, Teresa (2001) 'Making worlds move: re-ranking contextual parameters in Flaubert's *Madame Bovary* and Céline's *Voyage au bout de la nuit*', *Language and Literature* 10 (1): 41–59.

Brône, Geert and Vandaele, Jeroen (eds) (2009) *Cognitive Poetics: Goals, Gains and Gaps*. Berlin: Mouton de Gruyter.

Brooke, Rupert (1915) *The Collected Poems of Rupert Brooke* (ed. George Edward Woodberry). New York: Vale-Ballou Press.

Brown, Penelope and Levinson, Stephen (1987) *Politeness: Some Universals of Language Use*. Cambridge: Cambridge University Press.

Browning, Robert (1842) *Dramatic Lyrics*. London: Edward Moxon.

Bruder, Gail A. and Wiebe, Janyce M. (1995) 'Recognizing subjectivity and identifying subjective characters in third-person fictional narrative', in J. F. Duchan, G. A. Bruder and L. E. Hewitt (eds) *Deixis in Narrative: A Cognitive Science Perspective.* Hillsdale: Lawrence Erlbaum, pp. 341–56.

Brugman, Claudia (1989) *The Story of Over: Polysemy, Semantics, and the Structure of the Lexicon.* New York: Garland.

Bühler, Karl (1982) 'The deictic field of language and deictic worlds', in R. J. Jarvella and W. Klein (eds) *Speech, Place and Action: Studies in Deixis and Related Topics* [translated from *Sprachtheorie*, 1934]. Chichester: John Wiley, pp. 9–30.

Butler, Judith (1990) *Gender Trouble.* London: Routledge.

Butler, Judith (1993) *Bodies That Matter: On the Discursive Limits of 'Sex'.* London: Routledge.

Butler, Judith (1997) *Excitable Speech.* London: Routledge.

Cancer Research UK (2005) 'Cancer help website.' <http://www.cancerhelp.org>, accessed March 2005.

Carroll, Jonathan (2003) *White Apples.* London: Tor.

Carstensen, Kai-Uwe (2007) 'Spatio-temporal ontologies and attention', *Spatial Cognition and Computation* 7 (1): 13–32.

Carter, Ronald and Stockwell, Peter (eds) (2008) *The Language and Literature Reader.* London: Routledge.

Chapman, Alan (2004) 'Business Balls Website'. <http://www.businessballs.com>, accessed March 2005.

Chatman, Seymour (1978) *Story and Discourse.* Ithaca: Cornell University Press.

Chilton, Paul (2004) *Analysing Political Discourse: Theory and Practice.* London: Routledge.

Chilton, Paul and Lakoff, George (1995) 'Foreign policy by metaphor', in C. Schäffner and A. Wenden (eds) *Language and Peace.* Aldershot: Dartmouth, pp. 37–59.

Clark, George and Timmons, Daniel (eds) (2000) *J. R. R. Tolkien and His Literary Resonances: Views of Middle-Earth.* Westport: Greenwood Press.

Cluysenaar, Anne (1976) *Introduction to Literary Stylistics.* London: Batsford.

Cockcroft, Robert (2002) *Renaissance Rhetoric: Reconsidered Passion – The Interpretation of Affect in Early Modern Writing.* London: Palgrave.

Cohn, Dorrit (1989) 'Fictional *versus* historical lives: borderlines and borderline cases', *Journal of Narrative Technique* 19 (1): 3–30.

Coleridge, Samuel Taylor (1950) *The Portable Coleridge* (ed. I. A. Richards). New York: Viking.

Coleridge, Samuel Taylor (1983) *Biographia Literaria: Biographical Sketches of My Literary Life and Opinions.* Princeton: Princeton University Press [1817].

Commons, Michael Lamport and Wolfsont, Chester Arnold (2002) 'A complete theory of empathy must consider stage changes', *Behavioural and Brain Sciences* 25 (1): 30–1.

Cook, Guy (1994) *Discourse and Literature.* Oxford: Oxford University Press.

Coppola, Francis Ford (dir.) (1986) *Peggy Sue Got Married.* Los Angeles: Tristar Pictures / Columbia.

Corbetta, M., Meizen, F. M., Shulman, G. L. and Petersen, S. E. (1993) 'A PET study of visual spatial attention', *Journal of Neuroscience* 13: 1202–26.

Croft, William (2001) *Radical Construction Grammar: Syntactic Theory in Typological Perspective.* Oxford: Oxford University Press.

Croft, William and Cruse, David Alan (2004) *Cognitive Linguistics*. Cambridge: Cambridge University Press.

Culler, Jonathan (1975) *Structuralist Poetics*. London: Routledge and Kegan Paul.

Culpeper, Jonathan (2001) *Language and Characterisation*. London: Longman.

Culpeper, Jonathan and McIntyre, Dan (2009) 'Activity types and characterisation in dramatic discourse', in R. Schneider, F. Jannidis and J. Eder (eds) *Characters in Fictional Worlds: Interdisciplinary Perspectives*. Berlin: De Gruyter.

Currie, Greg (1995) *Image and Mind: Philosophy, Film and Cognitive Science*. New York: Cambridge University Press.

Currie, Greg (2004) *Arts and Minds*. Oxford: Oxford University Press.

Currie, Greg and Ravenscroft, Ian (2002) *Recreative Minds*. Oxford: Oxford University Press.

de Beaugrande, Robert (1980) *Text, Discourse and Process: Toward an Interdisciplinary Science of Texts*. Hillsdale: Lawrence Erlbaum Associates.

de Beaugrande, Robert and Dressler, Wolfgang (1981) *Introduction to Text Linguistics*. London: Longman.

de Bellis, Jack (ed.) (2005) *John Updike: The Critical Responses to the 'Rabbit' Saga*. Westport: Greenwood Press.

DelConte, Matt (2003) 'Why you can't speak: second-person narration, voice, and a new model for understanding narrative', *Style* 37 (2): 204–19.

Descartes, René (1641) 'Meditations on first philosophy', in *The Philosophical Works of Descartes* (trans. Elizabeth S. Haldane, 1911). Cambridge: Cambridge University Press.

Dickens, Charles (1994) *Bleak House*. Harmondsworth: Penguin [originally serialised 1852–3, publ. Bradbury and Evans].

Dirven, René (2000) *Cognitive Linguistics*. Essen: LAUD.

Dirven, René and Verspoor, Marjolijn (2004) *Cognitive Exploration of Language and Linguistics*. Amsterdam: Benjamins.

Donne, John (1985) *The Complete English Poems of John Donne* (ed. C. A. Patrides). London: Dent.

Dowty, David (1991) 'Thematic proto-roles and argument selection', *Language* 67: 574–619.

Duchan, J. F., Bruder, G. A. and Hewitt, L. E. (eds) (1995) *Deixis in Narrative: A Cognitive Science Perspective*. Hillsdale: Lawrence Erlbaum.

Durand, Jacques and Laks, Bernard (2002) *Phonetics, Phonology, and Cognition*. Oxford: Oxford University Press.

Dyer, Judy (2007) 'Language and identity', in Carmen Llamas, Louise Mullany and Peter Stockwell (eds) *The Routledge Companion to Sociolinguistics*. London: Routledge, pp. 101–8.

Eaglestone, Robert (2004) 'One and the same? Ethics, aesthetics, and truth', *Poetics Today* 25 (4): 595–608.

Eagleton, Terry (2008) 'A puritan at play', *The Guardian*, *Review* section, 15 March 2008.

Eckert, P. and McConnell-Ginet, S. (1992a) 'Communities of Practice: where language, gender and power all live', in K. Hall, M. Bucholtz and B. Moonwomon (eds) *Locating Power: Proceedings of the Second Berkeley Women and Language Conference*. Berkeley: Berkeley Women and Language Group, pp. 89–99.

Eckert, P. and McConnell-Ginet, S. (1992b) 'Think practically and look locally: language and gender as community-based practice', *Annual Review of Anthropology* 21: 461–90.

Eckert, P. and McConnell-Ginet, S. (1995) 'Constructing meaning, constructing selves', in K. Hall and M. Bucholtz (eds) *Gender Articulated: Language and the Socially-Constructed Self.* New York: Routledge, pp. 469–507.

Eco, Umberto (1990) *The Limits of Interpretation.* Bloomington: Indiana University Press.

Egan, Greg (1994) *Permutation City.* London: Millennium.

Egan, Greg (2008) *Incandescence.* London: Gollancz.

Eggins, Suzanne (2004) *An Introduction to Systemic Linguistics* (2nd edn). London: Continuum.

Egri, Lajos (1960) *The Art of Dramatic Writing.* New York: Simon and Schuster.

Eliot, T. S. (1917) 'Rhapsody on a windy night', in *Prufrock and Other Observations.* London: The Egoist, pp. 19–23 [originally published in *Blast*, July 1915].

Ellis, Bret Easton (1991) *American Psycho.* New York: Vintage.

Emmott, Catherine (1992) 'Splitting the referent: an introduction to narrative enactors', in M. Davies and L. Ravelli (eds) *Advances in Systemic Linguistics: Recent Theory and Practice.* London: Pinter, pp. 221–8.

Emmott, Catherine (1994) 'Frames of reference: contextual monitoring and narrative discourse', in R. M. Coulthard (ed.) *Advances in Written Text Analysis.* London: Routledge, pp. 157–66.

Emmott, Catherine (1995) 'Consciousness and context-building: narrative inferences and anaphoric theory', in Keith Green (ed.) *New Essays in Deixis.* Amsterdam: Rodopi, pp. 81–97.

Emmott, Catherine (1996) 'Real grammar in fictional contexts', *Glasgow Review* 4: 9–23.

Emmott, Catherine (1997) *Narrative Comprehension: A Discourse Perspective.* Oxford: Clarendon Press.

Emmott, C. (1998) '"Situated events" in fictional worlds: the reader's role in context construction', *European Journal of English Studies* 2 (2): 175–94.

Emmott, C. (2002) '"Split selves" in fiction and in medical "life stories": cognitive linguistic theory and narrative practice', in Elena Semino and Jonathan Culpeper (eds) *Cognitive Stylistics: Language and Cognition in Text Analysis.* Amsterdam: John Benjamins, pp. 153–81.

Emmott, Catherine (2003a) 'Towards a theory of reading in the age of cognitive science: cross-disciplinary perspectives on narrative from stylistics and psychology', *BELL: Belgian Journal of English Language and Literature* 1: 17–29.

Emmott, Catherine (2003b) 'Reading for pleasure: a cognitive poetic analysis of "twists in the tale" and other plot reversals in narrative texts', in Joanna Gavins and Gerard Steen (eds) *Cognitive Poetics in Practice.* London: Routledge, pp. 145–59.

Emmott, Catherine (2003c) 'Constructing social space: sociocognitive factors in the interpretation of character relations', in David Herman (ed.) *Narrative Theory and the Cognitive Sciences.* Stanford: Center for the Study of Language and Information, pp. 295–321.

Emmott, Catherine, Sanford, Anthony J. and Morrow, Lorna I. (2006) 'Capturing the attention of readers? Stylistic and psychological perspectives on the use and effect of text fragmentation in narratives', *Journal of Literary Semantics* 35 (1): 1–30.

Emmott, Catherine, Sanford, Anthony J. and Dawydiak, Eugene (2007) 'Stylistics meets cognitive science: style in fiction from an interdisciplinary perspective', *Style* 41 (2): 204–26.

Engler, Barbara (2006) *Personality Theories.* Houghton Mifflin.

Eskin, Michael (2004) 'On literature and ethics', *Poetics Today* 25 (4): 573–94.

Evans, Vyvyan (2003) *The Structure of Time.* Amsterdam: John Benjamins.

Evans, Vyvyan (2007) *A Glossary of Cognitive Linguistics.* Edinburgh: Edinburgh University Press.

Evans, Vyvyan and Green, Melanie (2006) *Cognitive Linguistics: An Introduction.* Edinburgh: Edinburgh University Press.

Fauconnier, Gilles (1994) *Mental Spaces.* Cambridge: Cambridge University Press [original in French as *Espaces Mentaux*, 1984, Paris: Editions de Minuit].

Fauconnier, Gilles (1997) *Mappings in Thought and Language.* Cambridge: Cambridge University Press.

Fauconnier, Gilles (1998) 'Conceptual integration networks', *Cognitive Science* 22 (2): 133–87.

Fauconnier, Gilles and Sweetser, Eve (eds) (1996) *Spaces, Worlds and Grammar.* Chicago: University of Chicago Press.

Fauconnier, Gilles and Turner, Mark (1996) 'Blending as a central process of grammar', in Adele Goldberg (ed.) *Conceptual Structure, Discourse, and Language.* Stanford: Center for the Study of Language and Information.

Fauconnier, Gilles and Turner, Mark (2002) *The Way We Think: Conceptual Blending and the Mind's Hidden Complexities.* New York: Basic Books.

Fillmore, Charles (1982) 'Frame semantics', in Linguistic Society of Korea (ed.) *Linguistics in the Morning Calm.* Seoul: Hanshin, pp. 111–37.

Fillmore, Charles (1985) 'Frames and the semantics of understanding', *Quaderni di Semantica* 6: 222–54.

Fish, Stanley (1970) 'Literature in the reader: affective stylistics', *New Literary History* 2: 123–62.

Fludernik, Monika (1994) 'Introduction: second person narrative and related issues', *Style* 28 (3): 281–311.

Fludernik, Monika (1996) *Towards a 'Natural' Narratology.* London: Routledge.

Fokkema, Aleid (1991) *Postmodern Characters: A Study of Characterization in British and American Postmodern Fiction.* Amsterdam: Rodopi.

Forster, E. M. (1927) *Aspects of the Novel.* London: Edward Arnold.

Fowler, Roger (1986) *Linguistic Criticism.* Oxford: Oxford University Press.

Fowles, John (1963) *The Collector.* London: Jonathan Cape.

Fredericks, Miriam Marietta (2008) *Lyrical Resonance.* Philadelphia: Xlibris.

Fricke, Harald (2008) 'Response: theses on literary theory', *Journal of Literary Theory* 1 (1): 192–3.

Gadamer, Hans-Georg (1989) *Truth and Method* (trans. Joel Weinsheimer and Donald G. Marshall, 2nd edn, from *Wahrheit und Methode,* 1960). New York: Crossroad Press.

Gallagher, S. (2006) 'The narrative alternative to theory of mind', in R. Menary (ed.)

Radical Enactivism: Intentionality, Phenomenology, and Narrative. Amsterdam: John Benjamins, pp. 223–9.

Galloway, David D. (1981) *The Absurd Hero in American Fiction: Updike, Styron, Bellow and Salinger.* Austin: University of Texas Press.

Gavins, Joanna (2000) 'Absurd tricks with bicycle frames in the text world of *The Third Policeman*', *Nottingham Linguistic Circular* 15: 17–33.

Gavins, Joanna (2003) 'Too much blague? An exploration of the text worlds of Donald Barthelme's *Snow White*', in Joanna Gavins and Gerard Steen (eds) *Cognitive Poetics in Practice.* London: Routledge, pp. 129–44.

Gavins, Joanna (2005a) '(Re)thinking modality: a text-world perspective', *Journal of Literary Semantics* 34 (2): 79–93.

Gavins, Joanna (2005b) 'Text World Theory in literary practice', in Bo Petterson, Merja Polvinen and Harri Veivo (eds) *Cognition in Literary Interpretation and Practice.* Helsinki: University of Helsinki Press, pp. 89–104.

Gavins, J. (2007) *Text World Theory.* Edinburgh: Edinburgh University Press.

Gavins, Joanna and Steen, Gerard (eds) (2003) *Cognitive Poetics in Practice.* London: Routledge.

Geeraerts, Dirk (ed.) (2007) *Cognitive Linguistics: Basic Readings.* Berlin: Mouton de Gruyter.

Gentner, D. (1982) 'Are scientific analogies metaphors?', in D. S. Miall (ed.) *Metaphor: Problems and Perspectives.* Brighton: Harvester, pp.106–32.

Geronimi, Clyde, Luske, Hamilton and Jackson, Wilfred (dirs.) (1950) *Cinderella.* Los Angeles: Walt Disney.

Gerrig, Richard (1993) *Experiencing Narrative Worlds: On the Psychological Activities of Reading.* New Haven: Yale University Press.

Gibbs, Ray (2002) 'Feeling moved by metaphor', in S. Csabi and J. Zerkowitz (eds) *Textual Secrets.* Budapest, ELTE, pp.13–28.

Glenberg, A. (1997) 'What memory is for,' *Behavioral and Brain Sciences* 20 (1): 1–55.

Godden, Rumer (1944) 'You needed to go upstairs', *Harper's Magazine*, July 1944: 170–2 [republished as 'You need to go upstairs', in Rumer Godden (1968) *Gone: A Thread of Stories*, New York: Viking, pp. 141–8].

Goffman, Erving (1967) *Interaction Ritual.* New York: Anchor Books.

Goffman, Erving (1981) *Forms of Talk.* Philadelphia: University of Pennsylvania Press.

Goldberg, Adele (1995) *Constructions: A Construction Grammar Approach to Argument Structure.* Chicago: University of Chicago Press.

Goldberg, Adele (ed.) (1996) *Conceptual Structure, Discourse, and Language.* Stanford: CSLI Publications.

Goldie, Peter (ed.) (2002) *Understanding Emotions: Mind and Morals.* Aldershot: Ashgate.

Goldie, Peter (2003) 'One's remembered past: narrative thinking, emotion, and the external perspective', *Philosophical Papers* 32: 301–19.

Goldie, Peter (2004) 'Emotion, feeling, and knowledge of the world?' in Robert Solomon (ed.) *Thinking about Feeling: Contemporary Philosophers on Emotions.* Oxford: Oxford University Press, pp. 91–106.

Goldie, Peter (2006) 'Charlie's world: narratives of aesthetic experiences?' in Matthew

Kieran and Dominic Lopes (eds) *Knowing Art: Essays in Aesthetics and Epistemology.* Dodrecht: Kluwer Academic Press.

Goldie, Peter (2007) 'There are reasons and reasons', in D. Hutto and M. J. Ratcliffe (eds) *Folk Psychology Reassessed.* Dordrecht: Kluwer Academic Press, pp. 103–14.

Goldstein, E. Bruce (2006) *Sensation and Perception.* Florence: Wadsworth.

Green, Keith (1992) 'Deixis and the poetic persona', *Language and Literature* 1 (2): 121–34.

Green, Keith (ed.) (1995) *New Essays in Deixis: Discourse, Narrative, Literature.* Amsterdam: Rodopi.

Greenblatt, Stephen (1990) 'Resonance and wonder', in *Learning to Curse: Essays in Early Modern Culture.* New York: Routledge, pp. 161–83.

Gregoriou, Christiana (2009) *English Literary Stylistics.* Houndmills: Palgrave Macmillan.

Grice, H. P. (1975) 'Logic and conversation', in P. Cole and J. L. Morgan (eds) *Syntax and Semantics 3: Speech Acts.* New York: Academic Press.

Halliday, M. A. K. (1985) *An Introduction to Functional Grammar.* London: Arnold.

Halliday, M. A. K. and Hasan, Ruqaiya (1976) *Cohesion in English.* London: Longman.

Halliday, M. A. K. and Matthiessen, Christian M. I. M. (2003) *An Introduction to Functional Grammar* (3rd edn). London: Edward Arnold.

Halligan, P. W. (2002) 'Phantom limbs: the body in mind', *Cognitive Neuropsychiatry* 7 (3): 251–68.

Hamilton, Craig (2003) 'A cognitive grammar of "Hospital Barge" by Wilfred Owen', in Joanna Gavins and Gerard Steen (eds) *Cognitive Poetics in Practice.* London: Routledge, pp. 55–65.

Hamilton, Craig (2007) 'The cognitive rhetoric of Arthur Miller's *The Crucible*', in Marina Lambrou and Peter Stockwell (eds) *Contemporary Stylistics.* London: Continuum, pp. 221–31.

Hampe, Beate (ed.) (2005) *From Perception to Meaning: Image Schemas in Cognitive Linguistics.* Berlin: Mouton de Gruyter.

Hardy, Thomas (1878) *The Return of the Native.* London: Smith, Elder and Co.

Harrison, Tony (1978) *From 'The School of Eloquence' and Other Poems.* London: Rex Collings.

Hart, Christopher (2005) 'Analysing political discourse: toward a cognitive approach', *Critical Discourse Studies* 2 (2): 189–94.

Hart, Christopher and Lukeš, Dominik (eds) (2007) *Cognitive Linguistics in Critical Discourse Studies.* Newcastle: Cambridge Scholars Press.

Hartley, Jenny and Turvey, Sarah (eds) (2003) *The Reading Groups Book.* Oxford: Oxford University Press.

Hasan, Ruqaiya (1985) 'The texture of a text', in M. A. K. Halliday and Ruqaiya Hasan (eds) *Language, Context, and Text: Aspects of Language in a Social-Semiotic Perspective.* Melbourne: Deakin University Press, pp. 70–96.

Heine, Bernd (1997) *Cognitive Foundations of Grammar.* Oxford: Oxford University Press.

Henryson, Robert (1978) *Poems and Fables.* Edinburgh: Mercat Press.

Herman, David (2003) 'Stories as a tool for thinking', in David Herman (ed.)

Narrative Theory and the Cognitive Sciences. Stanford: Center for the Study of Language and Information, pp. 163–92.

Herman, David (2004) *Story Logic: Problems and Possibilities of Narrative.* Lincoln: University of Nebraska Press.

Hidalgo Downing, Laura (2000a) *Negation, Text Worlds and Discourse: The Pragmatics of Fiction.* Stanford: Ablex.

Hidalgo Downing, Laura (2000b) 'Negation in discourse: a text-world approach to Joseph Heller's *Catch-22*', *Language and Literature* 9 (4): 215–40.

Hidalgo Downing, Laura (2000c) 'Alice in pragmaticland: reference, deixis and the delimitation of text worlds in Lewis Carroll's Alice books', *CLAC Circulo de lingüística aplicada a la comunicación* 2.

Hidalgo Downing, Laura (2002) 'Creating things that are not: the role of negation in the poetry of Wislawa Szymborska', *Journal of Literary Semantics* 30 (2): 113–32.

Hidalgo Downing, Laura (2003a) 'Negation as a stylistic feature in Joseph Heller's *Catch-22*: a corpus study', *Style* 37 (3): 318–41.

Hidalgo Downing, Laura (2003b) 'Text world creation in advertising discourse', *CLAC Circulo de lingüística aplicada a la comunicación* 13.

Hillis Miller, J. (1965) *Poets of Reality: Six Twentieth-Century Writers.* Cambridge: Harvard University Press.

Hitchens, Christopher (2002) 'A man of permanent contradictions', *Atlantic Review* 289 (6): June 2002.

Hoey, Michael (1991) *Patterns of Lexis in Text.* Oxford: Oxford University Press.

Hogan, Patrick Colm (2003a) *Cognitive Science, Literature and the Arts.* New York: Routledge.

Hogan, Patrick Colm (2003b) *The Mind and its Stories: Narrative Universals and Human Emotions.* Cambridge: Cambridge University Press.

Hollander, John (1985) *Vision and Resonance: Two Senses of Poetic Form* (2nd edn). Cambridge: Yale University Press.

Huneidi, Sahar (2004) 'Inspiration: poetry'. *Psychic and Spirit*, 24 January 2004, available at <http://www.ps-magazine.com>

Ingarden, Roman (1973a) *The Literary Work of Art: An Investigation on the Borderlines of Ontology, Logic, and Theory of Literature* (trans. George Grabowics, from the third edition of *Das literarische Kunstwerk*, 1965; after a Polish revised translation, 1960; from the original German, 1931). Evanston: Northwestern University Press.

Ingarden, Roman (1973b) *The Cognition of the Literary Work of Art* (trans. Ruth Ann Crowley and Kenneth Olson, from the German *Vom Erkennen des literarischen Kunstwerks*, 1968; original Polish *O poznawaniu dziela literackiego*, 1937). Evanston: Northwestern University Press.

Iser, Wolfgang (1974) *The Implied Reader: Patterns of Communication in Prose Fiction from Bunyan to Beckett.* Baltimore: Johns Hopkins University Press.

Iser, Wolfgang (1978) *The Act of Reading: A Theory of Aesthetic Response.* Baltimore: Johns Hopkins University Press.

Jauss, Hans Robert (1982a) *Aesthetic Experience and Literary Hermeneutics* (trans. Michael Shaw). Minneapolis: University of Minnesota Press.

Jauss, Hans Robert (1982b) *Toward an Aesthetic of Reception* (trans. Timothy Bahti). Minneapolis: University of Minnesota Press.

Jarvella, R. J. and Klein, W. (eds) (1982) *Speech, Place and Action: Studies in Deixis and Related Topics*, Chichester: John Wiley.

Johnson, Barbara (1980) *The Critical Difference: Essays in the Contemporary Rhetoric of Reading*. Baltimore: Johns Hopkins University Press.

Johnson, Mark (1987) *The Body in the Mind: The Bodily Basis of Meaning, Imagination, and Reason*. Chicago: University of Chicago Press.

Johnson, Mark (2007) *The Meaning of the Body: Aesthetics of Human Understanding*. Chicago: University of Chicago Press.

Jones, Griff Rhys (ed.) (1996) *The Nation's Favourite Poems*. London: BBC Books.

Jonson, Ben (1984) *Epigrams* and *The Forest* (ed. Richard Dutton). Manchester: Carcanet Press.

Joyce, James (1939) *Finnegans Wake*. London: Faber and Faber.

Jung, Carl G. (1967) *The Development of Personality*. London: Routledge and Kegan Paul.

Jung, Carl G. (1970) *Four Archetypes; Mother, Rebirth, Spirit, Trickster*. Princeton: Princeton University Press.

Kafka, John (dir.) (2002) *Cinderella II: Dreams Come True*. Los Angeles: Walt Disney.

Kanwisher, N. (1987) 'Repetition blindness: type recognition without token individuation', *Cognition* 27: 117–43.

Keen, Suzanne (2007) *Empathy and the Novel*. New York: Oxford University Press.

Kelleter, Frank (2008) 'A tale of two natures: worried reflections on the study of literature and culture in an age of neuroscience and neo-Darwinism', *Journal of Literary Theory* 1 (1): 153–89.

Kitazawa, S. (2002) 'Where conscious sensation takes place', *Consciousness and Cognition* 11: 474–7.

Klenburg, Jana Liba (1996) *Timeless Resonance: A Poetic Adventure to Higher Consciousness*. Edmonton: Lone Pine Press.

Koffka, Kurt (1935) *Principles of Gestalt Psychology*. New York: Harcourt, Brace.

Köhler, Wolfgang (1947) *Gestalt Psychology*. New York: New American Library.

Köhler, Wolfgang (1959) 'Gestalt psychology today', *American Psychologist* 14: 727–34.

Kövecses, Zoltán (1994) 'Tocqueville's passionate "beast": a linguistic analysis of the concept of American democracy', *Metaphor and Symbolic Activity* 9 (2): 113–33.

Krajco, Kathy (2008) *Lighthouse Writing Tips* website. http://lighthouse-writing-tips.blogspot.com/2008/01/literary-resonance-in-art-of-writing.html, accessed October 2008.

Kuiken, Don; Miall, David S. and Sikora, Shelley (2004) 'Forms of self-implication in literary reading', *Poetics Today* 25 (2): 171–203.

Labov, William (1972) 'The transformation of experience in narrative syntax', in *Language in the Inner City: Studies in Black English Vernacular*. Philadelphia: University of Pennsylvania Press, pp. 354–96.

Lahey, Ernestine (2003) 'Seeing the forest for the trees in Al Purdy's "Trees at the Arctic Circle"', *BELL: Belgian Journal of English Language and Literature* 1: 73–83.

Lahey, Ernestine (2004) 'All the world's a subworld: direct speech and subworld creation in "After" by Norman MacCaig', *Nottingham Linguistic Circular* 18: 21–8.

Lakoff, George (1987) *Women, Fire and Dangerous Things: What Categories Reveal about the Mind*. Chicago: University of Chicago Press.

Lakoff, George (1990) 'The invariance hypothesis: is abstract reason based on image-schemas?' *Cognitive Linguistics* 1 (1): 39–74.

Lakoff, George (1992) 'Metaphors and war: the metaphor system used to justify the Gulf War', in M. Pütz (ed) *Thirty Years of Linguistic Evolution. Studies in Honour of René Dirven on the Occasion of his Sixtieth Birthday*. Amsterdam: John Benjamins, pp. 463–81.

Lakoff, George (2002) *Moral Politics* (2nd edn). Chicago: Chicago University Press.

Lakoff, George (2006) *Don't Think of an Elephant: Know Your Values and Frame the Debate*. White River Junction: Chelsea Green Press.

Lakoff, George and Johnson, Mark (1999) *Philosophy in the Flesh: The Embodied Mind and Its Challenge to Western Thought*. New York: Basic Books.

Langacker, Ronald (1987) *Foundations of Cognitive Grammar, Vol I: Theoretical Prerequisites*. Stanford: Stanford University Press.

Langacker, Ronald (1990) *Concept, Image and Symbol: The Cognitive Basis of Grammar*. Berlin: Mouton de Gruyter.

Langacker, Ronald (1991) *Foundations of Cognitive Grammar, Vol. II: Descriptive Application*. Stanford: Stanford University Press.

Langacker, Ronald (1999) *Grammar and Conceptualization*. Berlin: Mouton de Gruyter.

Langacker, Ronald (2008) *Cognitive Grammar: A Basic Introduction*. Oxford: Oxford University Press.

Langendoen, D. (1969) *Essentials of English Grammar*. New York: Harcourt, Brace and Winston.

Lave, Jean and Wenger, Etienne (1991) *Situated Learning: Legitimate Peripheral Participation*. Cambridge: Cambridge University Press.

Leahy, Robert L. (2005) 'A social-cognitive model of validation', in Paul Gilbert (ed.) *Compassion: Conceptualisations, Research and Use in Psychotherapy*. London: Routledge, pp. 195–217.

Leavis, F. R. (1952) *The Common Pursuit*. London: Chatto and Windus.

LeDoux, Joseph (1998) *The Emotional Brain*. London: Phoenix.

Lee, Hermione (1990) 'The trouble with Harry', *The New Republic*, 24 December, pp. 34–7.

Leech, Geoffrey N. and Short, Mick H. (2007) *Style in Fiction: A Linguistic Introduction to English Fictional Prose* (2nd edn). London: Longman.

Le Page, R. B. and Tabouret-Keller, A. (1985) *Acts of Identity: Creole Based Approaches to Language and Ethnicity*. Cambridge: Cambridge University Press.

Lerner, R. M. (2002) *Concepts and Theories of Human Development*. Mahwah: Lawrence Erlbaum.

Levinson, Stephen C. (1983) *Pragmatics*. Cambridge: Cambridge University Press.

Llamas, Carmen, Mullany, Louise and Stockwell, Peter (eds) (2007) *The Routledge Companion to Sociolinguistics*. London: Routledge.

Logan, G. D. (1996) 'The CODE theory of visual attention: an integration of space-based and object-based attention', *Psychological Review* 103: 603–49.

Louwerse, Max and van Peer, Willie (2002) *Thematics: Interdisciplinary Studies*. Amsterdam: John Benjamins.

Louwerse, Max and van Peer, Willie (2009) 'How cognitive is cognitive poetics? Adding a symbolic approach to the embodied one', in Geert Brône and Jeroen Vandaele (eds) *Cognitive Poetics: Goals, Gains and Gaps*. Berlin: Mouton de Gruyter.

Lyons, John (1977) *Semantics, Vols I and II*. Cambridge: Cambridge University Press.

McDonagh, P. (2008) 'Autism and modernism: a genealogical exploration', in M. Osteen (ed.) *Autism and Representation*. New York: Routledge, pp. 99–116.

McHugh, Roland (1980) *Annotations to Finnegans Wake*. Baltimore: Johns Hopkins University Press.

McIntyre, Dan (2004) 'Point of view in drama: a socio-pragmatic analysis of Dennis Potter's *Brimstone and Treacle*', *Language and Literature* 13 (2): 139–60.

McIntyre, Dan (2005) 'Logic, reality and mind style in Alan Bennett's *The Lady in the Van*', *Journal of Literary Semantics* 34 (1): 21–40.

McIntyre, Dan (2006) *Point of View in Plays*. Amsterdam: John Benjamins.

McIntyre, Dan (2007) 'Deixis, cognition and the construction of viewpoint', in Marina Lambrou and Peter Stockwell (eds) *Contemporary Stylistics*. London: Continuum, pp. 118–30.

Maclean, M. (1988) *Narrative as Performance*. London: Routledge.

Magritte, René (1979) 'La poésie est une pipe', in *Ecrits Complets* (reprinted from *La Révolution Surréaliste*, 15 December, 1929, p. 53). Paris: Flammarion, p. 59.

Maitre, D. (1983) *Literature and Possible Worlds*. London: Middlesex University Press.

Mallet, Phillip (2003) *Rudyard Kipling: A Literary Life*. London: Palgrave.

Margolin, Uri (1996) 'Characters and their versions', in Calin-Andrei Mihailescu and Walid Hamarneh (eds) *Fiction Updated: Theories of Fictionality, Narratology and Poetics*. Toronto: University of Toronto Press, pp. 113–32.

Margolin, Uri (2007) '(Mis)perceiving to good readerly effect'. Paper presented to the *Current Trends in Narratology* conference, University of Freiburg, June 2007.

Martel, Yann (2002) *Life of Pi*. Edinburgh: Canongate.

Martel, Yann (2008) 'How I wrote *Life of Pi*', *Powell's Books* website. http://www.powells.com/fromtheauthor/martel.html, undated posting, accessed October 2008.

Martin, J. R. (1992) *English Text: System and Structure*. Amsterdam: Benjamins.

Martindale, Colin (ed.) (1988) *Psychological Approaches to the Study of Literary Narratives*. Hamburg: Buske.

Mauss, Marcel (1936) *Sociologie et Anthropologie*. Paris: Presses Universitaires de France.

Miall, David S. (2000) 'Book review: *Experiencing Narrative Worlds: On the Psychological Activities of Reading* by Richard Gerrig', *Journal of Pragmatics* 32 (3): 377–82.

Miall, David S. (2005) 'Beyond interpretation: the cognitive significance of reading', in Harri Veivo, Bo Pettersson and Merja Polvinen (eds) *Cognition and Literary Interpretation in Practice*. Helsinki: University of Helsinki Press, pp. 129–56.

Miall, David S. (2007) 'Foregrounding and the sublime: Shelley in Chamonix', *Language and Literature* 16 (2): 155–68.

Miall, David S. and Kuiken, Don (1994) 'Foregrounding, defamiliarization, and affect: response to literary stories', *Poetics* 22: 389–407.

Miall, David S. and Kuiken, Don (1999) 'What is literariness? Three components of literary reading', *Discourse Processes* 28: 37–58.

Miall, David S. and Kuiken, Don (2002) 'A feeling for fiction: becoming what we behold', *Poetics* 30: 221–41.

Milesi, Laurent (ed.) (2003) *James Joyce and the Difference of Language*. Cambridge: Cambridge University Press.

Milroy, Lesley (1987) *Language and Social Networks* (2nd edn). Oxford: Basil Blackwell.

Mischel, W., Shoda, Y. and Smith, R. E. (2004) *Introduction to Personality: Toward an Integration* (7th edn). New York: Wiley.

Montgomery, Martin (1993) 'Language, character and action: a linguistic approach to the analysis of character in a Hemingway short story', in J. M. Sinclair, M. Hoey and G. Fox (eds) *Spoken and Written Discourse*. London: Routledge, pp. 127–42.

Moore, Patrick (1986) 'William Carlos Williams and the Modernist attack on logical syntax', *ELH* 53 (4): 895–916.

More, (St) Thomas (1910) *Utopia*. London: Dent [1516, in Latin, trans. R. Robinson, 1561].

Muller, W. and Fischer, O. (eds) (2003) *From Sign to Signing: Iconicity in Language and Literature*. Amsterdam: Benjamins.

Nanny, Max and Fischer, Olga (eds) (1999) *Form Miming Meaning*. Amsterdam: Benjamins.

Niffenegger, Audrey (2004) *The Time Traveler's Wife*. London: Harvest.

Niedenthal, Paula M., Krauth-Gruber, Silvia and Ric, François (2006) *Psychology of Emotion: Interpersonal, Experiential, and Cognitive Approaches*. New York: Psychology Press.

Nowottny, Winifred (1972) *The Language Poets Use*. London: Athlone.

Oakley, Todd (2004) *Elements of Attention: A New Approach to Meaning Construction in the Human Sciences*. <http:// www.mind-consciousness-language.com> [originally entitled *A Grammar of Attention: A Treatise on the Problem of Meaning*. Adaptations to appear in Oakley, T. (2009) *From Attention to Meaning: Explorations in Semiotics, Linguistics, and Rhetoric*. Bern: Lang Verlag].

Oatley, Keith (1992) *Best Laid Schemes: The Psychology of Emotions*. Cambridge: Cambridge University Press.

Oatley, Keith (1994) 'A taxonomy of the emotions of literary response and a theory of identification in fictional narrative', *Poetics* 23: 53–74.

Oatley, Keith (2003) 'Writingandreading: the future of cognitive poetics', in Joanna Gavins and Gerard Steen (eds) *Cognitive Poetics in Practice*. London: Routledge, pp. 161–73.

Oatley, Keith (2004) *Emotions: A Brief History*. Oxford: Blackwell.

Oatley, Keith, Keltner, Dacher and Jenkins, Jennifer M. (2006) *Understanding Emotions* (2nd edn). Oxford: Blackwell.

O'Halloran, Kieran (2003) *Critical Discourse Analysis and Language Cognition*. Edinburgh: Edinburgh University Press.

O'Halloran, Kieran (2007a) 'Critical discourse analysis and the corpus-informed interpretation of metaphor at the register level', *Applied Linguistics* 28 (1): 1–24.

O'Halloran, Kieran (2007b) 'Casualness and commitment: the use in critical discourse analysis of Lakoff and Johnson's approach to metaphor', in Christopher Hart and

Dominik Lukeš (eds) *Cognitive Linguistics in Critical Discourse Studies*, Newcastle: Cambridge Scholars Press, pp. 159–79.

Ohmann, Richard (1964) 'Generative grammars and the concept of literary style', *Word* 20: 423–39.

Opdahl, Keith (2002) *Emotion as Meaning*. London: Associated University Press.

Orwell, George (1949) *Nineteen Eighty-Four*. London: Secker and Warburg.

Östman, J.-O. and Fried, M. (eds) (2005) *Construction Grammars: Cognitive Grounding and Theoretical Extensions*. Amsterdam: John Benjamins.

Palmer, Alan (2002) 'The construction of fictional minds', *Narrative* 10 (1): 28–46.

Palmer, Alan (2004) *Fictional Minds*. Lincoln: University of Nebraska Press.

Palmer, Alan (2005) 'Intermental thought in the novel: the Middlemarch mind', *Style* 39 (4): 427–39.

Palmer, Alan (2007) 'Intermental focalization in *Middlemarch*'. Paper presented at *Current Trends in Narratology* symposium, University of Freiburg, June 2007.

Parker, Andrew and Sedgwick, Eve Kosofsky (eds) (1995) *Performativity and Performance (Essays from the Institute)*. New York: Routledge.

Paulin, Tom (2008) *The Secret Life of Poems: A Poetry Primer*. London: Faber.

Peterson, Mary A. and Enns, James T. (2005) 'The edge complex: implicit memory for figure assignment in shape perception', *Perception and Psychophysics* 67 (4): 727–40.

Phelan, James (1989) *Reading People, Reading Plots: Character, Progression, and the Interpretation of Narrative*. Chicago: University of Chicago Press.

Phelan, James (1996) *Narrative as Rhetoric: Technique, Audiences, Ethics, Ideology*. Columbus: Ohio State University Press.

Phelan, James (2005) *Living To Tell About It: A Rhetoric and Ethics of Character Narration*. Ithaca: Cornell University Press.

Phelan, James (2007) *Experiencing Fiction: Judgments, Progressions, and the Rhetorical Theory of Narrative*. Columbus: Ohio State University Press.

Poe, Edgar Allan (1838) *The Narrative of Arthur Gordon Pym of Nantucket*. New York: Harper and Borthers.

Posner, M. I. (1993) 'Attention before and during the decade of the brain', in D. E. Meyer and S. M. Kornblum (eds) *Attention and Performance, XIV: Synergies in Experimental Psychology, Artificial Intelligence and Cognitive Neuroscience*. Cambridge: MIT Press.

Posner, M. I. (ed.) (2004) *Cognitive Neuroscience of Attention*. New York: Guilford Press.

Pratt, Mary Louise (1977) *Towards a Speech Act Theory of Literary Discourse*. Bloomington: Indiana University Press.

Prince, Gerald (1973) *A Grammar of Stories*. The Hague: Mouton.

Prince, Gerald (1982) *Narratology: The Form and Function of Narrative*. Amsterdam: Mouton.

Progressive Resources Ltd (2005) *Team Building Website*. <http://www.teambuilding.co.uk>, accessed March 2005.

Purves, Dale, Brannon, Elizabeth M., Cabeza, Roberto, Huettel, Scott A., LaBar, Kevin S., Platt, Michael L. and Woldorff, Marty G. (2008) *Principles of Cognitive Neuroscience*. Sunderland: Sinauer.

Quiller-Couch, Arthur (ed.) (1913) *The Oxford Book of Victorian Verse*. Oxford: Clarendon Press.

Ramachandran, V. S. and Blakeslee, S. (1998) *Phantoms in the Brain: Probing the Mysteries of the Human Mind*. New York: William Morrow and Co.

Ramachandran, V.S., Rogers-Ramachandran, D. and Cobb, S. (1995) 'Touching the phantom limb', *Nature* 377: 489–90.

Rauh, G. (ed.) (1983) *Essays on Deixis*. Tübingen: Gunter Narr Verlag.

Reynolds, Alastair (2002) *Diamond Dogs, Turquoise Days*. London: Gollancz.

Ricard, Marcelle and Kamberk-Kilicci, Mary (1995) 'Children's empathic responses to emotional complexity', *International Journal of Behavioral Development* 18 (2): 211–25.

Richards, I. A. (1924) *Principles of Literary Criticism*. London: Kegan Paul.

Riffaterre, M. (1966) 'Describing poetic structures: two approaches to Baudelaire's "Les Chats"', *Yale French Studies* 36/7: 200–42.

Robertson, I. H. and Manly, T. (1999) 'Sustained attention deficits in time and space', in G. W. Humphreys, J. Duncan and A. Triesman (eds) *Attention, Space and Action: Studies in Cognitive Neuroscience*. Oxford: Oxford University Press, pp. 297–310.

Ronen, Ruth (1994) *Possible Worlds in Literary Theory*. Cambridge: Cambridge University Press.

Rorty, Amélie Oksenberg (2000) 'Characters, persons, selves, individuals', in Michael McKeon (ed.) *Theory of the Novel: A Historical Approach*, Baltimore: Johns Hopkins University Press, pp. 537–53.

Roth, I. (2008) 'Imagination and the awareness of self in autistic spectrum poets', in M. Osteen (ed.) *Autism and Representation*. New York: Routledge, pp. 145–65.

Russell, Bertrand (1921) *The Analysis of Mind*. London: George Allen and Unwin.

Ryan, M. L. (1991) *Possible Worlds: Artificial Intelligence and Narrative Theory*. Bloomington and Indianapolis: Indiana University Press.

Ryan, M. L. (1998) 'The text as world versus the text as game: possible worlds semantics and postmodern theory', *Journal of Literary Semantics* 27 (3): 137–63.

Ryckman, Richard M. (2008) *Theories of Personality* (9th edn). Belmont: Wadsworth.

Sanford, Anthony J., Sanford, Alison J. S., Molle, Jo and Emmott, Catherine (2006) 'Shallow processing and attention capture in written and spoken discourse', *Discourse Processes* 42 (2): 109–30.

Scarry, Elaine (2001) *Dreaming by the Book*. Princeton: Princeton University Press.

Schank, R. C. and Abelson, R. (1977) *Scripts, Plans, Goals and Understanding*. Hillsdale: Lawrence Erlbaum Associates.

Scollon, Ron (1998) *Mediated Discourse as Social Interaction: A Study of News Discourse*. New York: Longman.

Scollon, Ron (2001) *Mediated Discourse: The Nexus of Practice*. London: Routledge.

Scollon, Ron and Wong Scollon, Suzie (2004) *Nexus Analysis: Discourse and the Emerging Internet*. London: Routledge.

Searle, J. R. (1969) *Speech Acts: An Essay in the Philosophy of Language*. Cambridge: Cambridge University Press.

Segal, E. M (1995a) 'Narrative comprehension and the role of deictic shift theory', in

J. F. Duchan, G. A. Bruder and L. E. Hewitt (eds) *Deixis in Narrative: A Cognitive Science Perspective.* Hillsdale: Lawrence Erlbaum, pp. 3–17.

Segal, E. M. (1995b) 'A cognitive-phenomenological theory of fictional narrative', in J. F. Duchan, G. A. Bruder and L. E. Hewitt (eds) *Deixis in Narrative: A Cognitive Science Perspective.* Hillsdale: Lawrence Erlbaum, pp. 61–78.

Semino, Elena (1997) *Language and World Creation in Poems and Other Texts.* London: Longman.

Semino, Elena (2002) 'A cognitive stylistic approach to mind-style in narrative fiction', in Elena Semino and Jonathan Culpeper (eds) *Cognitive Stylistics.* Amsterdam: Benjamins, pp. 95–122.

Semino, Elena (2003) 'Possible worlds and mental spaces in Hemingway's "A Very Short Story"', in Joanna Gavins and Gerard Steen (eds) *Cognitive Poetics in Practice*, London: Routledge, pp. 83–98.

Semino, Elena and Culpeper, Jonathan (eds) (2002) *Cognitive Stylistics.* Amsterdam: Benjamins.

Semino, Elena and Swindlehurst, Kate (1996) 'Metaphor and mind-style in Ken Kesey's *One Flew Over the Cuckoo's Nest*', *Style* 30 (1): 143–66.

Sharon, T. and Woolley, J. D. (2004) 'Do monsters dream? Young children's understanding of the fantasy/reality distinction', *British Journal of Developmental Psychology* 22: 293–310.

Shelley, Percy Bysshe (1970) *Poetical Works* (ed. Thomas Hutchinson, 2nd edn ed. G. M. Matthews). Oxford: Oxford University Press.

Shen, Yeshayahu and Cohen, Michal (1998) 'How come silence is sweet but sweetness is not silent: a cognitive account of directionality in poetic synaesthesia', *Language and Literature* 7 (2): 123–40.

Shen, Yeshayahu and Cohen, Michal (2008) 'Heard melodies are sweet but those unheard are sweeter: synaesthetic metaphors and cognition', *Language and Literature* 17 (2): 107–21.

Silkin, Jon (1954) *The Peaceable Kingdom.* London: Chatto and Windus.

Simpson, Paul (1993) *Language, Ideology and Point of View.* London: Routledge.

Simpson, Paul (2004) *Stylistics: A Resource Book for Students.* London: Routledge.

Smith, Carter W., Johnson, Scott P. and Spelke, Elizabeth S. (2003) 'Motion and edge sensitivity in perception of object unity', *Cognitive Psychology* 46: 31–64.

Spelke, Elizabeth S. (1990) 'Principles of object perception', *Cognitive Science* 14: 29–56.

Stafford, Barbara Maria (2007) *Echo Objects: The Cognitive Work of Images.* Chicago: University of Chicago Press.

Stevenson, Robert Louis (1998) *Robert Louis Stevenson: Collected Poems* (ed. Angus Calder). London: Penguin.

Stockwell, Peter (1992) 'The metaphorics of literary reading', *Liverpool Papers in Language and Discourse* 4: 52–80

Stockwell, Peter (1994) 'To be or not to be a phagocyte: procedures of reading metaphors', in Roger Sell and Peter Verdonk (eds) *Literature and the New Interdisciplinarity: Poetics, Linguistics, History.* Amsterdam: Rodopi, pp. 65–78.

Stockwell, Peter (2000a) *The Poetics of Science Fiction.* London: Longman.

Stockwell, Peter (2000b) 'Towards a critical cognitive linguistics?', in Annette

Combrink and Ina Biermann (eds) *Discourses of War and Conflict.* Potchefstroom: Potchefstroom University Press, pp. 510–28.

Stockwell, Peter (2002a) *Cognitive Poetics: An Introduction.* London: Routledge.

Stockwell, Peter (2002b) 'Miltonic texture and the feeling of reading', in Elena Semino and Jonathan Culpeper (eds) *Cognitive Stylistics.* Amsterdam: Benjamins, pp.73–94.

Stockwell, Peter (2003) 'Surreal figures', in Joanna Gavins and Gerard Steen (eds) *Cognitive Poetics in Practice.* London: Routledge, pp. 13–25.

Stockwell, Peter (2005a) 'Texture and identification', *European Journal of English Studies* 9 (2): 143–53.

Stockwell, Peter (2005b) 'Stylistics and cognitive poetics', in Harri Veivo, Bo Petterson and Merja Polvinen (eds) *Cognition and Literary Interpretation in Practice.* Helsinki: Helsinki University Press, pp. 267–82.

Stockwell, Peter (2006) 'On teaching literature itself', in Greg Watson and Sonia Zyngier (eds) *Literature and Stylistics for Language Learners: Theory and Practice.* London: Palgrave, pp. 15–24.

Stockwell, Peter (2008a) 'Cartographies of cognitive poetics', *Pragmatics and Cognition* 16 (3): 587–98.

Stockwell, Peter (2008b) 'Cognitive poetics and literary theory', *Journal of Literary Theory* 1 (1): 135–52.

Stockwell, Peter (2009) 'The cognitive poetics of literary resonance', *Language and Cognition* 1 (1).

Styles, Elizabeth (2005) *Attention Perception and Memory: An Integrated Introduction.* London: Routledge.

Styles, Elizabeth (2006) *The Psychology of Attention* (2nd edn). Hove: Psychology Press.

Suter, Ann (ed.) (2008) *Lament: Studies in the Ancient Mediterranean and Beyond.* New York: Oxford University Press.

Suvin, Darko (1988) 'Can people be (re)presented in fiction? Toward a theory of narrative agents and a materialist critique beyond technology or reductionism', in Lawrence Grossberg and Cary Nelson (eds) *Marxism and the Interpretation of Culture.* Urbana: University of Illinois Press, pp. 663–96.

Swales, John M. (1990) *Genre Analysis: English in Academic and Research Settings.* Cambridge: Cambridge University Press.

Swales, John M. (1998) *Other Floors, Other Voices: A Textography of a Small University Building.* Mahwah: Lawrence Erlbaum.

Talmy, Leonard (1988) 'Force dynamics in language and cognition', *Cognitive Science* 12: 49–100.

Talmy, Leonard (2000a) *Toward a Cognitive Semantics. Vol. I: Concept Structuring Systems.* Cambridge: MIT Press.

Talmy, Leonard (2000b) *Toward a Cognitive Semantics. Vol. II: Typology and Process in Concept Structuring.* Cambridge: MIT Press.

Tolkien, J. R. R. (1954) *The Lord of the Rings. 1: The Fellowship of the Ring.* London: George Allen and Unwin.

Toolan, Michael (2001) *Narrative: A Critical Linguistic Introduction* (2nd edn). London: Routledge.

Traugott, Elizabeth Closs and Dasher, Richard (2002) *Regularity in Semantic Change*. Cambridge: Cambridge University Press.

Traugott, Elizabeth Closs and Heine, Bernd (1991) *Approaches to Grammaticalization* (2 vols). Amsterdam: John Benjamins.

Traugott, Elizabeth Closs and Pratt, Mary Louise (1977) *Linguistics for Students of Literature*. New York: Harcourt Brace Jovanovich.

Tsur, Reuven (1987) *The Road to 'Kubla Khan': A Cognitive Approach*. Jerusalem: Israel Science Publishers.

Tsur, Reuven (1992) *Toward a Theory of Cognitive Poetics*. Amsterdam: North-Holland.

Tsur, Reuven (2006) *'Kubla Khan' – Poetic Structure, Hypnotic Quality, and Cognitive Style: A Study in Mental, Vocal, and Critical Performance*. Amsterdam: John Benjamins.

Tsur, Reuven (2008a) 'The poetic function and aesthetic qualities: Cognitive Poetics and the Jakobsonian model'. Paper presented at the *Linguistics and Poetics* conference of the Danish Society for Language and Literature, Carlsberg Academy, Copenhagen, 24–5 January, 2008.

Tsur, Reuven (2008b) 'Deixis in literature. What *isn't* Cognitive Poetics?' *Pragmatics and Cognition* 16 (1): 119–50.

Turner, Mark (1991) *Reading Minds: The Study of English in the Age of Cognitive Science*. Princeton: Princeton University Press.

Turner, Mark (1996) *The Literary Mind: The Origins of Thought and Language*. New York: Oxford University Press.

Turner, Mark (2006) *The Artful Mind: Cognitive Science and the Riddle of Human Creativity*. Oxford: Oxford University Press.

Turner, Mark and Fauconnier, Gilles (1995) 'Conceptual integration and formal expression', *Metaphor and Symbolic Activity* 10 (3): 183–203.

Turner, Mark and Fauconnier, Gilles (1999) 'A mechanism of creativity', *Poetics Today* 20 (3): 397–418.

Ukala, Sam (2001) 'Impersonation in some African ritual and festival performances', in Dubem Okafor (ed.) *Meditations on African Literature*. Westport: Greenwood Publishing, pp. 133–47.

Ungerer, Friedrich and Schmid, Hans-Jörg (2003) *An Introduction to Cognitive Linguistics* (2nd edn). London: Longman.

Updike, John (1964) *Rabbit, Run*. Harmondsworth: Penguin [original 1960].

Updike, John (1971) *Rabbit Redux*. New York: Alfred A. Knopf.

Updike, John (1981) *Rabbit is Rich*. New York: Alfred A. Knopf.

Updike, John (1990) *Rabbit at Rest*. New York: Alfred A. Knopf.

Updike, John (2001) 'Rabbit Remembered' in *Licks of Love: Short Stories and a Sequel, 'Rabbit Remembered'*. New York: Ballantine Books.

Välimaa-Blum, Riitta (2005) *Cognitive Phonology in Construction Grammar. Analytic Tools for Students of English*. Berlin: Mouton de Gruyter.

van Peer, Willie (1986) *Stylistics and Psychology: Investigations of Foregrounding*. London: Croom Helm.

van Peer, Willie, Hakemulder, Jèmeljan and Zyngier, Sonia (2007) 'Lines on feeling: foregrounding, aesthetics and meaning', *Language and Literature* 16 (2): 197–213.

Wales, Katie (1981) *The Language of James Joyce*. London: Palgrave Macmillan.

Werth, Paul (1994) 'Extended metaphor: a text world account', *Language and Literature* 3 (2): 79–103.

Werth, Paul (1995a) 'How to build a world (in a lot less than six days and using only what's in your head)', in Keith Green (ed.) *New Essays on Deixis: Discourse, Narrative, Literature*. Amsterdam: Rodopi, pp. 49–80.

Werth, Paul (1995b) '"World enough and time": deictic space and the interpretation of prose', in Peter Verdonk and Jean Jacques Weber (eds) *Twentieth Century Fiction: From Text to Context*. London: Routledge, pp. 181–205.

Werth, Paul (1997a) 'Conditionality as cognitive distance', in A. Athanasiadou and R. Dirven (eds) *On Conditionals Again*. Amsterdam: Benjamins, pp. 243–71.

Werth, Paul (1997b) 'Remote worlds: the conceptual representation of linguistic *would*', in J. Nuyts and E. Pederson (eds) *Language and Conceptualization*. Cambridge: Cambridge University Press, pp. 84–115.

Werth, Paul (1999) *Text Worlds: Representing Conceptual Space in Discourse*. Harlow: Longman.

Wertheimer, Max (1958) 'Principles of perceptual organization', in D. C. Beardslee and Max Wertheimer (eds) *Readings in Perception*. Princeton: Van Nostrand, pp. 115–35.

Widdowson, Henry G. (1975) *Stylistics and the Teaching of Literature*. London: Longman.

Willems, Klaas and De Cuypere, Ludovic (2009) *Naturalness and Iconicity in Language*. Amsterdam: John Benjamins.

Williams, William Carlos (1934) *Collected Poems, 1921–1931*. New York: Objectivist Press.

Wolfe, Jeremy M., Kluender, Keith R., Levi, Dennis M., Bartoshuk, Linda M., Herz, Rachel S., Klatzky, Roberta L. and Lederman, Susan J. (2006) *Sensation and Perception*. Sunderland: Sinauer.

Woolley, J. D. and Cox, V. (2007) 'Development of beliefs about storybook reality', *Developmental Science* 10: 681–93.

Wordsworth, William (1807) [Untitled, first line: 'I wandered lonely as a cloud'], in *Poems in Two Volumes. Vol. II*. London: Longman, Hurst, Rees, and Orme, pp. 49–50.

Wordsworth, William (1815) *Poems* (2 vols), London: Longman, Hurst, Rees, Orme, and Brown.

Yamamoto, S. and Kitazawa, S. (2001) 'Sensation at the tips of invisible tools', *Nature Neuroscience* 4: 979–80.

Yang, Joseph Chih-Chiao (2005) *'Shall I compare thee to a summer's day?': Intralocution and the Teaching of Renaissance Poetry in Taiwan*. University of Nottingham: unpublished PhD thesis.

Young, K. G. (1987) *Taleworlds and Storyrealms: The Phenomenology of Narrative*. Higham: Kluwer.

Zillmann, Dolf (1994) 'Mechanisms of emotional involvement with drama', *Poetics* 23: 33–51.

Zunshine, Lisa (2003) 'Theory of mind and experimental representations of fictional consciousness', *Narrative* 11: 270–91.

Zunshine, Lisa (2006) *Why We Read Fiction: Theory of Mind and the Novel*. Columbus: Ohio State University Press.

Index